Corpus Linguistics for World Englishes

Corpus Linguistics for World Englishes offers a detailed account of how to analyse the many fascinating varieties of English around the world using corpus-linguistic methods. Employing case studies for illustration of relevant concepts and methods throughout, this book:

- introduces the theory and practice of analysing World Englishes
- illustrates the basics of corpus-linguistic methods and presents the vast World Englishes corpora
- links World Englishes to Learner Englishes and English as a Lingua Franca
- offers practical, hands-on exercises and questions for discussion in each chapter
- provides helpful overviews and course syllabi for students and instructors.

Corpus Linguistics for World Englishes is key reading for advanced students of English as a World Language and Corpus Linguistics, as well as anyone keen to understand variation in World Englishes with the help of corpus linguistics.

Claudia Lange, Technische Universität Dresden, Germany.

Sven Leuckert, Technische Universität Dresden, Germany.

Routledge Corpus Linguistics Guides

Series consultant: Michael McCarthy

Michael McCarthy is Emeritus Professor of Applied Linguistics at the University of Nottingham, UK, Adjunct Professor of Applied Linguistics at the University of Limerick, Ireland and Visiting Professor in Applied Linguistics at Newcastle University, UK. He is co-editor of the Routledge Handbook of Corpus Linguistics, editor of the Routledge Domains of Discourse series and co-editor of the Routledge Applied Corpus Linguistics series.

Series consultant: Anne O'Keeffe

Anne O'Keeffe is Senior Lecturer in Applied Linguistics and Director of the Inter-Varietal Applied Corpus Studies (IVACS) Research Centre at Mary Immaculate College, University of Limerick, Ireland. She is co-editor of the Routledge Handbook of Corpus Linguistics and co-editor of the Routledge Applied Corpus Linguistics series.

Series co-founder: Ronald Carter

Ronald Carter (1947–2018) was Research Professor of Modern English Language in the School of English at the University of Nottingham, UK. He was also the co-editor of the Routledge Applied Corpus Linguistics series, Routledge Introductions to Applied Linguistics series and Routledge English Language Introductions series.

Routledge Corpus Linguistics Guides provide accessible and practical introductions to using corpus linguistic methods in key sub-fields within linguistics. Corpus linguistics is one of the most dynamic and rapidly developing areas in the field of language studies, and use of corpora is an important part of modern linguistic research. Books in this series provide the ideal guide for students and researchers using corpus data for research and study in a variety of subject areas.

Other titles in this series

Corpus Linguistics for Online Communication
Luke Curtis Collins

Corpus Linguistics for World Englishes
Claudia Lange and Sven Leuckert

More information about this series can be found at www.routledge.com/series/ RCLG

Corpus Linguistics for World Englishes

A Guide for Research

Claudia Lange and Sven Leuckert

LONDON AND NEW YORK

First published 2020
by Routledge
2 Park Square, Milton Park, Abingdon, Oxon OX14 4RN

and by Routledge
52 Vanderbilt Avenue, New York, NY 10017

Routledge is an imprint of the Taylor & Francis Group, an informa business

© 2020 Claudia Lange and Sven Leuckert

The right of Claudia Lange and Sven Leuckert to be identified as authors of this work has been asserted by them in accordance with sections 77 and 78 of the Copyright, Designs and Patents Act 1988.

All rights reserved. No part of this book may be reprinted or reproduced or utilised in any form or by any electronic, mechanical, or other means, now known or hereafter invented, including photocopying and recording, or in any information storage or retrieval system, without permission in writing from the publishers.

Trademark notice: Product or corporate names may be trademarks or registered trademarks, and are used only for identification and explanation without intent to infringe.

British Library Cataloguing-in-Publication Data
A catalogue record for this book is available from the British Library

Library of Congress Cataloging-in-Publication Data
Names: Lange, Claudia, author. | Leuckert, Sven, 1989- author.
Title: Corpus linguistics for World Englishes : a guide for research / Claudia Lange and Sven Leuckert.
Description: New York : Taylor and Francis, 2020. |
Series: Routledge corpus linguistics guides | Includes bibliographical references and index.
Identifiers: LCCN 2019032148 (print) | LCCN 2019032149 (ebook)
Subjects: LCSH: English language–Globalization. | English language–Variation–English-speaking countries. | English language–Variation–Foreign countries. | Corpora (Linguistics)
Classification: LCC PE1073 .L358 2020 (print) | LCC PE1073 (ebook) | DDC 420.1/88–dc23
LC record available at https://lccn.loc.gov/20190321483
LC ebook record available at https://lccn.loc.gov/2019032149

ISBN: 978-1-138-59341-1 (hbk)
ISBN: 978-1-138-59345-9 (pbk)
ISBN: 978-0-429-48943-3 (ebk)

Typeset in Baskerville
by Swales & Willis, Exeter, Devon, UK

Visit the eResources: www.routledge.com/9781138593459

 Printed in the United Kingdom by Henry Ling Limited

Contents

List of figures	ix
List of tables	xi
List of abbreviations	xiii
Acknowledgements	xv

1 Introduction   1

    1.1   What is corpus linguistics? 1
    1.2   What are World Englishes? 3
    1.3   Who this book is for 3
    1.4   How to use this book 4
    1.5   Structure of the book 6

2 World Englishes   8

    2.1   Introduction 8
    2.2   How English became a world language 9
    2.3   Conceptualising World Englishes 21
    2.4   Making sense of variation 29
    2.5   Summary 36
    2.6   Exercises 36
    2.7   Recommended reading 37
    References 39

3 Corpus-linguistic approaches to language   41

    3.1   Introduction 41
    3.2   Getting started: the basics 42
    3.3   Basic corpus design features 47
    3.4   Accessing a corpus: concordances 55
    3.5   Handling frequencies 57

vi Contents

3.6 Collocations 63
3.7 Regular expressions 64
3.8 Statistics and significance testing 66
3.9 Summary 69
3.10 Exercises 69
3.11 Recommended reading 70
References 72

4 Corpora and World Englishes 74

4.1 Introduction: does size matter? 74
4.2 The 'Brown family' of corpora 76
4.3 The International Corpus of English (ICE) 81
4.4 GloWbE and large (web-based) corpora 95
4.5 Creating your own corpus 98
4.6 Summary 103
4.7 Exercises 104
4.8 Recommended reading 105
List of corpora 106
References 107

5 Tracing variation and change in World Englishes 109

5.1 Introduction 109
5.2 From variation to language change 110
5.3 Variation, mistake, innovation 115
5.4 Contact and the feature pool 121
5.5 Spoken and written language 128
5.6 Summary 131
5.7 Exercises 132
5.8 Recommended reading 132
References 133

6 Interpreting variation and change in World Englishes 135

6.1 Introduction 135
6.2 Researching the verb phrase 136
6.3 Researching the noun phrase 142
6.4 Researching sentence structure 148
6.5 Researching the lexicon 155
6.6 Researching pragmatics 160
6.7 Summary 164
References 165

Contents   vii

7   World Englishes, Learner Englishes, and English as a Lingua
    Franca   168

   7.1   *Introduction: World Englishes, Learner Englishes, and ELF 168*
   7.2   *Learner corpus design and learner corpora 170*
   7.3   *Comparing World Englishes, Learner Englishes, and ENL 176*
   7.4   *Corpus linguistics and English as a Lingua Franca (ELF) 181*
   7.5   *ELF corpora 182*
   7.6   *Multilingual conversations: code-switching in ELF 187*
   7.7   *Summary 190*
   7.8   *Exercises 190*
   7.9   *Recommended reading 191*
   List of corpora 192
   References 192

8   The state of the art and the way ahead   194

   8.1   *New Englishes 194*
   8.2   *New corpora 195*
   8.3   *New models 197*
   8.4   *New tools 198*
   8.5   *More statistics 198*
   8.6   *Limitations 199*
   8.7   *Summary 201*
   References 201

   Appendix
   Appendix A: Answer key   203
   Appendix B: Varieties of English and corpora   208
   Appendix C: Suggestions for course uses   210

   Index   217

Figures

2.1	Anglo-Saxon England and its dialect areas (Irvine 2006: 36; reprinted by permission from Oxford University Press)	11
2.2	The spread of English (speakers) around the world (Schneider 2011: 49; reprinted by permission from Cambridge University Press)	15
2.3	Kachru's 'Three Circles' of English (Crystal 2003: 61; reprinted by permission from Cambridge University Press)	23
2.4	The levels of language and linguistic analysis	30
3.1	Screenshot of the *AntConc* interface	45
3.2	Screenshot of the *WordSmith* interface	45
3.3	Components in a register analysis (Biber & Conrad 2009: 6; reprinted by permission from Cambridge University Press)	50
3.4	Hiding tags in *AntConc*	52
3.5	Concordance lines for the word *help* in the conversation files of ICE-Hong Kong	56
3.6	Illustration of the *'Zap'* function in *WordSmith*	57
3.7	Frequency of hapax legomena in Herman Melville's *Moby Dick* (https://commons.wikimedia.org/wiki/File:Moby_Dick_Words.gif; public domain)	62
3.8	Example of a regular expression in *AntConc*	65
3.9	Creative word-formation in spoken and written first-language (L1) and second-language (L2) varieties (Biermeier 2014: 329; reprinted by permission from John Benjamins)	67
4.1	Functions of *Sketch Engine*	79
4.2	Some tokens of *yeah* produced by extra-corpus speakers in the direct conversations in ICE-Hong Kong	89
4.3	Search results for the word *furnitures* in GloWbE	96
5.1	Acquisition of English in multilingual Outer Circle contexts (based on Thomason 2001: 75)	118
5.2	Sources and processes leading to PCEs (Schneider 2007: 100; reprinted by permission from Cambridge University Press)	122

5.3	Realisation of the variable (r) first in casual and then in emphatic speech by shop assistants in *Saks* (S), *Macy's* (M), and *Klein* (K) (Labov 2006: 48; reprinted by permission from Cambridge University Press)	132
6.1	*Madam & Eve* (from https://twitter.com/madamevecartoon/status/426232112824328192; reprinted by permission from the creators)	155
7.1	Countries and regions included in ICNALE (map created with mapchart.net; CC Attribution-SA 4.0 International Licence)	175
7.2	Frequency comparison of PVs with *up* between NEs, LEs, and ENL (Gilquin 2015: 105; reprinted by permission from John Benjamins)	178
7.3	Frequency comparison of PVs with *up* in spoken and written NEs, LEs, and ENL (Gilquin 2015: 106; reprinted by permission from John Benjamins)	179
7.4	VOICE Online with POS-tagging (www.univie.ac.at/voice/images/help/10_lemma_popup.jpg)	183
7.5	ASEAN+3 countries in the Asian Corpus of English (ACE) (https://de.wikipedia.org/wiki/ASEAN_Plus_Three#/media/Datei:ASEAN_Plus_Three_members.png; CC BY-SA 3.0 Licence)	185
A.1	Parsing of 'Buffalo buffalo Buffalo buffalo buffalo buffalo Buffalo buffalo' (from https://commons.wikimedia.org/wiki/File:Buffalo_sentence_1_parse_tree.svg; public domain)	205

Tables

2.1	The productive inflectional endings of English	33
2.2	Classifying varieties of English	36
2.3	Postcolonial Englishes and their position in the Dynamic Model (Schneider 2007)	38
3.1	Annotation examples from the *International Corpus of English*	51
3.2	Frequency of *dicit* and *dixit* in the Gospel of Matthew and the Gospel of John (www.lancaster.ac.uk/fss/courses/ling/corpus/Corpus3/3SIG.HTM)	68
3.3	Data for adverbs formed with and without *-ly*	70
4.1	Overview of corpora included in the 'Brown family'	77
4.2	Text types included in the Brown corpus (adapted from www.helsinki.fi/varieng/CoRD/corpora/BROWN/basic.html)	78
4.3	Structure of the ICE corpora (adapted from www.ice-corpora.uzh.ch/en/design.html)	82
4.4	Available ICE components and ICE components currently being compiled (as of June 2019)	84
4.5	Mark-up symbols used in the spoken sections of the ICE corpora (adapted from the ICE manual available at www.ice-corpora.uzh.ch/en/manuals.html)	86
4.6	Additional mark-up symbols used in the written sections of the ICE corpora (adapted from the ICE manual available at www.ice-corpora.uzh.ch/en/manuals.html)	92
4.7	Countries included in GloWbE and abbreviation and word count for each country (adapted from Davies & Fuchs 2015: 6; Loureiro-Porto 2017: 450)	96
4.8	Major steps in corpus compilation and potential issues	99
6.1	Frequencies of PVs normalised to 1 million words and rounded (Schneider 2004: 236; reprinted by permission from Wiley)	139
6.2	Range of meanings of selected PVs (meaning types/tokens) (Schneider 2004: 236; reprinted by permission from Wiley)	140

xii Tables

6.3	Definite articles across all text types and corpora normalised per 1,000 words (adapted from Sand 2004: 287; reprinted by permission from Wiley)	146
6.4	Inversion in main clause interrogatives in ICE-India (Hilbert 2008: 273; reprinted by permission from John Benjamins)	151
6.5	Inversion in indirect questions with constituent interrogatives in ICE-India and ICE-Singapore, relative frequencies (in %) (Hilbert 2008: 276; reprinted by permission from John Benjamins)	151
6.6	Verb types in inverted embedded constituent interrogatives (Hilbert 2011: 133; reprinted by permission from John Benjamins)	153
6.7	Verb types in inverted embedded polar interrogatives (Hilbert 2011: 134; reprinted by permission from John Benjamins)	154
6.8	Varieties covered in Biermeier's (2014) study on prefixation and compounding in World Englishes	158
6.9	Corpora, word count, and corresponding circle of the included varieties in Aijmer (2018) (Aijmer 2018: 109; reprinted by permission from Brill Rodopi)	162
6.10	Frequencies of *very*, *really*, and *so* per one million words in AmE, BrE, NZE, and SinE (adapted from Aijmer 2018: 112)	163
7.1	Learner-related and task-related variables in learner corpus design (see Granger 2008: 264)	171
7.2	Learner and task variables included in ICLE and ICLEv2 (adapted from https://cdn.uclouvain.be/public/Exports%20reddot/cecl/documents/LEARNER_PROFILE.txt)	172
7.3	Structure of ICNALE (adapted from http://language.sakura.ne.jp/icnale/index.html#6)	174
7.4	Corpora used in Gilquin's (2015) study of phrasal verbs with *up* (adapted from Gilquin 2015: 104; reprinted by permission from John Benjamins)	177
7.5	Error annotation task	191
A.1	Classifying varieties of English (solutions)	204
A.2	Data for adverbs formed with and without *-ly*	205
A.3	Error annotation task with solutions	207
B.1	Availability of corpora for different World Englishes	208
C.1	Syllabus using *Corpus Linguistics for World Englishes*	211

Abbreviations

ACE	*Asian Corpus of English/Australian Corpus of English*
AdvP	adverb phrase
AmE	American English
ANC	African National Congress
AP	adjective phrase
ASEAN	*Association of Southeast Asian Nations*
AusE	Australian English
BNC	*British National Corpus*
BrE	British English
CECL	Centre for English Corpus Linguistics
CED	*Collins English Dictionary*
CEFR	*Common European Framework of Reference for Languages*
CMC	Computer-Mediated Communication
COCA	*Corpus of Contemporary American English*
COHA	*Corpus of Historical American English*
CoRD	*Corpus Resource Database*
EFL	English as a Foreign Language
EIC	East India Company
EIF	Extra- and Intraterritorial Forces model
ELF	English as a Lingua Franca
EModE	Early Modern English
ENL	English as a Native Language
ESL	English as a Second Language
eWAVE	*electronic World Atlas of Varieties of English*
F-LOB	*Freiburg-LOB Corpus of British English*
FROWN	*Freiburg-Brown Corpus of American English*
GA	General American English
GloWbE	*Corpus of Global Web-based English*
HiCE Ghana	*Historical Corpus of English in Ghana*
ICE	*International Corpus of English*
ICLE	*International Corpus of Learner English*
ICNALE	*International Corpus Network of Asian Learners of English*

IDG	indigenous strand
IndE	Indian English
IPA	International Phonetic Alphabet
IrE	Irish English
KWIC	Keyword in Context
L1	first language
L2	second language
LD	left-dislocation
LEs	Learner Englishes
LINDSEI	*Louvain International Database of Spoken English Interlanguage*
LOB	*Lancaster-Oslo/Bergen Corpus*
LOCNEC	*Louvain Corpus of Native English Conversation*
ME	Middle English
NEs	New Englishes
NP	noun phrase
NZE	New Zealand English
ODE	*Oxford Dictionary of English*
OE	Old English
OED	*Oxford English Dictionary*
PCE	Postcolonial English
PDE	Present-Day English
POS	parts-of-speech
PP	prepositional phrase
PV	particle verb/phrasal verb
RD	right-dislocation
RegEx	regular expression
RP	Received Pronunciation
SAfE	South African English
SAR	Special administrative region
SAVE	*South Asian Varieties of English Corpus*
SBCAE	*Santa Barbara Corpus of American English*
SinE	Singapore English
SLA	Second Language Acquisition
SLE	Sri Lankan English
STL	settler strand
TOEFL	*Test of English as a Foreign Language*
ViMELF	*Corpus of Video-Mediated English as a Lingua Franca Conversations*
VOICE	*Vienna-Oxford International Corpus of English*
VP	verb phrase
WWI	World War One
WWII	World War Two

Acknowledgements

Celebrating and investigating the diversity of World Englishes is always an inspiring endeavour for us, which is why we are particularly happy to be the authors of a book that does exactly that. Since no book is ever written and published without the help of others, we would like to thank everybody who has contributed to this book in one way or another.

In particular, we would like to thank Julia Kruse for reading some chapters in detail, and all of our students who commented on parts of this book. We also thank Marie-Louise Brunner, Stefan Diemer, Beke Hansen, and Louise Mycock for their contributions. Furthermore, we would like to express our gratitude to Anne O'Keeffe and Mike McCarthy for giving us the opportunity to contribute to the *Routledge Corpus Linguistics Guides* series. We also thank Lizzie Cox, Ruth Berry, Isabella Ritchie, and everybody at Routledge for assisting us in the creation of this book.

Thanks also go to our friends and families who gave us the time to write this book.

Finally, we would like to thank the following publishers and copyright holders for allowing us to reprint their material:

Figure from Irvine (2006), Chapter 2; reprinted by permission from Oxford University Press.

Figures from Schneider (2011), Chapter 2; Biber & Conrad (2009), Chapter 3; Labov (2006), Chapter 4; Schneider (2007), Chapter 5; all reprinted by permission from Cambridge University Press.

Figures and tables from Biermeier (2014), Chapter 3; Hilbert (2008) and Hilbert (2011), Chapter 6; Gilquin (2015), Chapter 7; all reprinted by permission from John Benjamins.

Tables from Sand (2004) and Schneider (2004), Chapter 6; reprinted by permission from Wiley.

Table from Aijmer (2018), Chapter 6; reprinted by permission from Brill Rodopi.

Cartoon "Madam & Eve", Chapter 6; reprinted by kind permission from the creators.

Map of countries included in ICNALE, Chapter 7, created with mapchart. net; reprinted under the Creative Commons Attribution-ShareAlike 4.0 International Licence – we thank the creator of this website for this great tool.

Chapter 1

Introduction

As a citizen of the 21st century, you are not only aware of the existence of computers and of the spread of English around the world, you probably take both for granted (for better or worse). Wherever we live and whatever our first language happens to be, a lot of our online interactions will happen in English – online shopping, gaming, social media, and so on. Yet English and the computer are more than mere tools for international communication: we can use the considerable processing power and storage capacity of an average personal computer to help us investigate global English. In other words, we can do corpus-linguistic research on World Englishes. This chapter offers a first glimpse at the topics covered in this book. It gives an insight into the different kinds of English, what it means to do corpus linguistics, and how we can study English using so-called 'corpora' – that is, collections of spoken and written texts. In addition, the chapter introduces you to the structure as well as to the key features of the book.

1.1 What is corpus linguistics?

You might be familiar with linguistics, the study of the forms and functions of language. Linguists are interested in the unity and diversity of language in general, or of a particular language. They typically do not pass value judgments: You know you have run into a linguist when you say something like, 'Ain't nobody home' or 'She home already', and their reaction is, 'Interesting, where are you from?' What might be considered 'slang', or 'bad English', is food for thought for the linguist because it represents *variation*: different ways of saying the same thing. We will have more to say about variation later, but even at this stage you are likely to agree that variation in language is very often not random, but shows specific patterns. A *biscuit* in the United Kingdom is a *cookie* in the United States, to take just one simple example of regional variation. Linguists are then interested in finding patterns, classifying them, and ideally also explaining them.

Let us stick with this example of lexical differences between British and American English, the two most prominent 'standard' varieties of English (more about standard languages in Chapter 5). You might wonder whether

2 Introduction

it is really true that the *Harry Potter* books were slightly edited for the American market to make life easier for readers who are familiar with *cookies*, but not necessarily with *crumpets*. How are you going to find out for yourself (rather than turning to the internet, where fans have already compiled lists)? You could take the printed books, place the British and American editions parallel on your desk, and start reading and taking notes of the differences. If you intend to do a thorough job and tackle all the books it will take you some time. If, however, you have the electronic editions of the books, you can make the computer do the work for you. You can use any editing program to create word lists, and with a dedicated 'concordance program' (more about that in Chapter 3.1) you have an astounding range of tools at your disposal to analyse your *Harry Potter* corpus. A corpus is basically a collection of texts stored in an electronic, machine-readable format. Chapter 4 tells you more about corpora in the field of World Englishes and deals specifically with issues of size and content. In our example, we are working with a relatively small, single-genre, purpose-built corpus designed to answer a specific research question. To be precise, we are working not only with a single-genre, but also a single-author corpus, quite unlike the corpus projects which are the topic of Chapter 4.

Notions like genre, text type, or register play a big role in corpus linguistics. Some scholars in the field use these terms more or less interchangeably, while others ascribe nuanced differences to them. Right now, we just need to be aware that the corpus-linguistic idea of a text differs from the everyday understanding of the term in that a text need not be something printed, or even written; it can also be a transcript of a conversation. A second point to note, which is related to the concept of text type, is that of the representativeness of corpora, a tricky issue for corpus compilers. If you want to move beyond your *Harry Potter* corpus and work with a corpus that represents your variety of English faithfully, what kind of text types should be included? Think about the kinds of texts that you actively produce, and those that you passively consume, over the course of a week or month. You probably have lots of conversations, but in different degrees of formality; you will write some e-mails, post some comments on social media, draft a term paper. You might listen to song lyrics and the news on TV, you might read a novel, read and sign a contract. Your friends' and your parents' production and reception of text types are probably quite different from your linguistic experience, which already indicates the difficulty in coming up with a representative corpus for, say, Australian English – and we have not even talked about how to lay our hands on all those text types. Still, linguists have found some fairly solid solutions to these problems, as we will see in Chapter 4.

You now have a working knowledge of what a corpus is and what it might contain. Corpus linguistics obviously has to start with corpora, but whether corpus linguistics is more like a toolbox or a separate discipline is already a matter of debate – perhaps you might want to return to this question once you have worked your way through this book.

Introduction 3

1.2 What are World Englishes?

In the beginning of this chapter, we alluded to the fact that English is today's most important global language. Billions of people interact with and in English on a daily basis, but to different degrees. You might have grown up with English as your only language or as one of the multiple languages spoken in your home; you might have acquired English as a second language at school in a country where it has an official status; you might have learnt English at school or later in life, but you only need it in international communication and largely with others for whom it is likewise a foreign language. Many people around the world also simply pick up English as they go, in order to function in specific contexts such as tourism.

The label 'World Englishes' applies to all of these contexts. Some varieties of English are older, more prestigious, more widespread, and more stable than others, but all display the high degree of creativity that goes into people's communicative interactions. A traditional and well-known subdivision is the one between English as a Native Language (ENL), English as a Second Language (ESL), and English as a Foreign Language (EFL). We will see how this three-fold distinction shows up in different ways of categorising Englishes around the world. It is also important to realise that monolingual native speakers of English are a minority within the English-speaking world – many former British colonies in Asia and Africa retained English as one of their official languages after independence. In these countries, English serves both an intranational and an international function. Speakers in these postcolonial countries are typically multilingual and may use English as a link language amongst themselves. While language is constantly developing, the interaction of English with the local languages has become a particularly interesting and dynamic field to study.

The influence of English as a global language does not stop there. English is the preferred foreign language for millions of people worldwide. International institutions and companies use it as their working language. The term 'English as a Foreign Language' (EFL) stresses the learner perspective. The label 'English as a Lingua Franca' (ELF) focuses on how people who do not share a mother tongue use English as a resource for effective communication. Both approaches are taken up again in Chapter 7.

1.3 Who this book is for

If you cherish variation in English and want to get to the bottom of it, this book is for you. It will help you gain access to a vibrant field in linguistics and will equip you with the basic knowledge and the tools to embark on your own projects. We believe this book can be used in many different ways. In this section, we focus on who this book is written for rather than who it is *not* written for and provide brief ideas for usage scenarios.

4 Introduction

Undergraduate and graduate students

If you are interested in how corpus linguistics can fruitfully be applied to World Englishes, this book is the right choice for you: we introduce all important terms and illustrate new concepts and methods using examples, figures, and exercises. The only things we suggest you bring along is an interest in the English language and its many forms as well as a computer with access to the internet. The theory and methods taught by the book can be applied to term papers and final theses, which means that undergraduate and graduate students alike can benefit from the book. Furthermore, this book can be used in conjunction with or in addition to other titles published in the *Routledge Corpus Linguistics Guides* series.

University instructors

This book is designed in such a way that the chapters can be read one after the other on a weekly basis; exercises follow right at the end of each chapter. Thus, individual sections or entire chapters can be read in class or as part of the students' homework. The same goes for the exercises, which can be set as tasks in the classroom or just discussed after they have been assigned as homework. As a special component of this book, we designed a course syllabus including a description of weekly activities on the basis of the chapters and exercises. A template of the syllabus is also available on the book's accompanying eResources and can easily be modified to fit different needs. The example syllabus can be found in Appendix C.

Researchers

For a researcher in linguistics or adjacent fields, this book can serve both as a reference guide to fill individual gaps in corpus linguistics and/or World Englishes or as an introduction if you are not familiar with either of the two fields. The book's chapters can easily be complemented and built upon by referring to the literature suggested in the 'Recommended reading' sections.

1.4 How to use this book

In this section, we shed light on some key components of this book: *Key terms; In-text exercises and questions; Chapter exercises; Open exercises and discussion questions; and Recommended reading*. Please note that not every chapter features each of these components. Chapter 6, for instance, contains many exercises spread across the text, which is why there are no additional exercises at the end.

Key terms

Each chapter from 2 to 7 begins with a list of key terms. These terms are not only of particular relevance for their respective chapter (and, in some cases, the rest of the book) but they also represent terms and concepts that you should know and understand if you want to succeed in your corpus-linguistic endeavours. In order to make finding these terms in the chapter easier, they are printed in bold in the running text either when they are first mentioned or when we provide a definition for them.

In-text exercises and questions

Throughout this book, we included in-text exercises and questions. You can recognise them by paying attention to the following symbols:

⇒ Symbol for an in-text exercise or question,
◊ Symbol for the corresponding answer or comment.

These sections give you an opportunity to actively try out what you just read and an opportunity to think about issues related to the chapter you are working on. Almost every in-text exercise or question is immediately followed by an answer or a comment, so that you can compare your thoughts and ideas to our suggested answer. We do not include an answer if the question merely serves to familiarise you with or to let you explore a topic or an idea. Most of the exercises in this format are relatively short and do not take up too much of your time; others are a bit more complex – how you want to approach them depends on how much time you are willing to invest.

Chapter exercises

More complex tasks are featured at the end of most chapters. They give you the opportunity to apply your knowledge and work on exercises that, at times, require several steps to be solved. An answer key with our comments on how to approach the exercises as well as a suggestion for a solution is given at the end of the book. Since not all exercises feature answers (see the next section on open exercises and discussion questions), those that do are marked with an asterisk. The following is an example of a chapter exercise with a corresponding comment at the end of the book:

*Use the *Google n-gram viewer* (available at https://books.google.com/ngrams) to trace word pairs that are associated with BrE and AmE respectively over time, such as

- *cookie – biscuit*
- *sidewalk – pavement*
- or a grammatical example: *have gotten – have got*

6 Introduction

Change the setting from English/general to BrE and AmE separately and take note of any spikes or overlaps in usage.

Open exercises and discussion questions

In addition to chapter exercises that come with answers at the end of the book, there are also some open exercises and questions. These are designed to let you explore topics discussed in a chapter but do not necessarily have a fixed answer, which is why you will not find any commentary in the appendix. These questions can also be used as a basis for discussion in a seminar context.

Recommended reading

The last section of each chapter contains 'Recommended reading'. Rather than giving you a list of titles, these sections provide you with essential reading related to the topic of the chapter as well as comments on the included titles. This should be helpful, for instance, to decide whether a book is the right fit for you, since some books are geared more towards beginners and others more towards advanced researchers. The readings reflect our personal choices, but also our experience in research and teaching from the undergraduate to the postgraduate level.

1.5 Structure of the book

Out of the many ways of researching World Englishes, this book focuses on corpus-linguistic approaches. One overwhelming advantage is that everyone with access to a computer can do it – with so much free software available and so many accessible corpora around, you have a world of resources at your fingertips. This book proceeds by first introducing World Englishes and corpus linguistics individually and then gradually joining the two fields.

Chapter 2 opens up the incredibly fascinating field of World Englishes by answering some important questions, such as: How did English become a, perhaps *the*, major global language? How can we meaningfully group different forms of English world-wide? And, finally, how can we make sense of and study variation in World Englishes? The chapter begins with a historical perspective and gradually moves into the present.

Chapter 3 introduces corpus linguistics. After an introduction to some technical basics of doing corpus-linguistic research, the important terms and concepts of the field are introduced. In addition, general concerns relevant to conducting linguistic research are addressed: we stress the importance of the research question and ask you to consider the quality of any data source. Throughout the chapter, hands-on exercises give you the opportunity to apply what you have just read.

Bringing together what you have learned in the previous two chapters, **Chapter 4** provides an overview of available corpora of World Englishes and the means of accessing them, the way they are structured, the kinds of text that went into them, and the additional information that might come with them. 'Knowing your corpus' is a basic prerequisite for evaluating your own and others' corpus findings. Since creating your own corpus without even leaving your screen is much easier than you might think, the chapter will also give you an idea of how to do it.

Once you have worked your way through Chapters 3 and 4, you are familiar with a wide range of corpora and know how to retrieve data from them. So how do you interpret your findings? **Chapter 5** tells you more about variation and change with special reference to World Englishes. Languages and language use change all the time, and linguists have come up with different approaches towards explaining how variation turns into change. We consider how variation in language can acquire social meaning, for example as a marker of identity. You will also learn more about the role of language contact in shaping the Englishes spoken in multilingual environments.

Chapter 6 offers descriptions of corpus-linguistic case studies and has two main purposes: It serves to introduce you to the manifold possibilities of researching World Englishes using corpus-linguistic methods and, in addition, invites you to consider how previous studies can be used as a basis for your own research projects.

Chapter 7 moves beyond traditional approaches to World Englishes by considering 'Learner Englishes' and 'English as a Lingua Franca'. English as produced by learners has long been treated as separate from World Englishes. Over the last decade, attempts at integrating and comparing these two types of English have experienced a revival. The chapter introduces you to important aspects of designing a learner corpus, provides an in-depth look at a case study, and also considers corpora and studies involving English as a Lingua Franca, that is, English used as a link language for people who do not share another language.

Chapter 8, the final chapter of the book, provides an overview of the state of the art in this field and the way ahead. In particular, the chapter offers a perspective on many exciting current developments: with the development of new corpora, new tools, new models, and the emergence of new Englishes, further research directions, and more complex statistics, corpus linguistics and World Englishes remain at the forefront of English linguistics.

We have thoroughly enjoyed sharing our experience of World Englishes as teachers and researchers with you, and we hope you will also enjoy your computer-assisted journey around the English-speaking world!

Chapter 2

World Englishes

Key terms:

History of English as a World Language:
analytic; codification; Early Modern English; East India Company; historical input variety; Middle English; Old English; pluricentric; standardisation; synthetic

Models of English:
accent; cline of bilingualism; colony types (exploitation colony, plantation colony, settlement colony, trade colony); Creole; dialect; Dynamic Model (foundation, exonormative stabilisation, nativisation, endonormative stabilisation, differentiation); mutual intelligibility; New Englishes; Pidgin; Postcolonial Englishes; Three Circles Model (Inner Circle, Outer Circle, Expanding Circle); variety; World Englishes

Variation in English:
complementation patterns (ditransitive, intransitive, transitive, subject complement); constituent structure; lexicon (content vs. function words, open-class vs. closed class); morpheme (lexical vs. grammatical, free vs. bound); morphology (inflectional vs. derivational, prefix & suffix, productivity, zero derivation); morphosyntax; phoneme; phonotactics; phrase structure (noun phrase, verb phrase, adjective phrase, adverb phrase, prepositional phrase); pragmatics (intercultural pragmatics, politeness); rhoticity; stress-timed; substitution test; syllable-timed; syntax

2.1 Introduction

English today is the most widely used language in international communication, spoken by hundreds of millions of people as a first or second language and used by many more as a lingua franca (see Chapter 7.4). Languages such as Mandarin Chinese or Hindi also have hundreds of millions of native speakers, but are more regionally confined and do not enjoy the same status as the very language of globalisation. How did it come to be this way? It is important to realise that English is so widespread not because it is 'better' or 'simpler' than any other language, but rather due to historical events in the past. Britain gradually became a colonial superpower from the 17th century onwards, acquiring colonies all over the world and transporting the English language to new surroundings. In the 20th century, the remaining former colonies gained independence, but most kept the language, while the US-American political and cultural influence became a global phenomenon and secured the position of English. Ironically, English itself started out as an invader's language in the British Isles. Section 2.2 will trace the development of English from an islander's language to a global means of communication. Section 2.3 will sketch ways of dealing with the multitude of Englishes around the world. Section 2.4 will briefly introduce you to the levels of language which can be studied with corpus-linguistic tools.

2.2 How English became a world language

British English (BrE) is (directly or indirectly) the ancestor or **historical input variety** for Englishes around the world. The story of English as a world language is a story of travel, trade, and conquest. In the course of this massive enterprise of colonial expansion, Scottish tea planters, German missionaries who learned English as a foreign language, soldiers from the English Midlands, convicts from London, and Irish immigrants all left their marks on English in new territories, a point we will return to in Chapter 5. As a result, many countries today deal with English as their colonial legacy in one way or the other. But if we go back in time, we find that English is not the native language of England either. We will briefly follow the story of English as it took root in England and then spread around the world. On this tour, we will take one tiny, black, round object with us – a peppercorn. Read on and find out why!

English in the British Isles

We start our tour in England in the 8th century in a monastery where one of the greatest scholars of his age lived and worked. We will frequently have to come back to monasteries if we want to study the early history of English. The Christianisation of England in the 6th century had brought along with it the skill of reading and writing – mostly in Latin, but also in the local language **Old English** (OE). Monasteries typically kept libraries and a scriptorium for the production of sacred texts. Only a tiny part of the population was able to read and write, and most of those who could were trained in monasteries. A lot of the texts that have survived from the Old English period are thus religious or philosophical in a wider sense; some texts are related to the running of the state or society in general (for example

10 World Englishes

laws, wills, chronicles); only few texts offer a glimpse of people's everyday language (for example riddles) and their native traditions (for example in poetry).

The scholar we mentioned is known as Bede or the Venerable Bede. His *Historia Ecclesiastica Gentis Anglorum* ('Church History of the English People') is one of our important sources for early English history. His story starts with the original Celtic population of the British Isles, then moves on to the invasion by Roman legions in the 1st century AD and their departure in the 5th century. Members of a Germanic tribe arrived in the same century exploiting that power vacuum. They were to give a new name to the realm: *Anglorum terra*, the land of the Angles or *Engla-land* in OE.

We have no witness reports describing the contact between the Germanic Anglo-Saxons and the Celts, but the indirect evidence points to a rather strained relation. The present-day spread of the Celtic languages – Welsh, Irish, and Scottish Gaelic – suggests that the Celts were driven to the fringes of the British Isles. Furthermore, the OE word *wealh* had two meanings – 'foreigner, Celt' as well as 'slave, servant'.

Bede himself did not live to see two further invasions. The Anglo-Saxons themselves came under pressure from foreign intruders from the 9th century onwards. Scandinavian Vikings first mounted hit-and-run attacks on coastal areas and then larger-scale invasions before they settled down in an area known as the *Danelaw*. These speakers of North Germanic languages blended in with the Anglo-Saxon population, leaving more traces of language contact than the Celts. Figure 2.1 depicts Anglo-Saxon England and its dialect areas.

Bede was already quite famous in his time; his disciple Cuthbert recorded his last days in a letter for posterity. Cuthbert describes in Latin how Bede made his will:

> A nona hora dixit mihi: 'quaedam preciosa in mea capsella habeo, id est **piperum**, oraria et incens' ('At the ninth hour [around three o'clock] he said to me: 'I have something precious in my small box, that is **pepper**, napkins, and incense'')
>
> (Plummer 1896: clxiii)

Pepper in Bede's time was evidently so precious that he took care to pass it on to his fellow monks. We will hear more about exotic spices and their relation to the spread of English around the world in the upcoming sections.

From Old English to Middle English

The Norman Conquest in 1066 can be taken as shorthand for the end of the OE period. When the Norman contestant for the English throne, William the Conqueror, won the battle of Hastings, Anglo-Saxon rule came to an end and with it the tradition of writing OE. The new rulers brought a new language, French or Anglo-Norman, which was then used alongside Latin. Few texts were still written in English, and when English re-emerged as a language of written record in the 14th and 15th century, it looked considerably different. Historians of English are

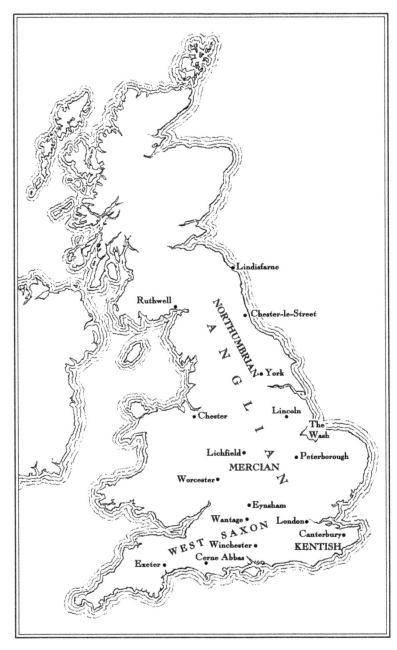

Figure 2.1 Anglo-Saxon England and its dialect areas (Irvine 2006: 36; reprinted by permission from Oxford University Press)

12   World Englishes

up against the fact that they have the least evidence for the period when the English language changed the most.

The **Middle English** (ME) period is generally characterised as a time of transition and great linguistic variation: "the ME period is, notoriously, the time when linguistic variation is fully reflected in the written mode" (Horobin & Smith 2002: 33). You can get a first impression about the extent of this variation by looking up the word 'she' in the online *Middle English Dictionary*. ME was on the move from a **synthetic** to an **analytic** language: Inflections for case and gender were lost, and word order became less flexible. The impact of French on the vocabulary of English was enormous and can be traced with the help of the online edition of the *Oxford English Dictionary* (OED), which lets you search for all words of Romance origin in English.

⇒ Consider the following example sentences from the OED entry on 'pepper'. The first one comes from an ancient manuscript known as *The Marvels of the East*, the second from *Mandeville's Travels*:

> (2.1) *On ðam londum byð piperes genihtsumnys* ('In those lands there is an abundance of pepper')
>
> (2.2) *In alle þe wide worlde noowhere Groweth noo peper but ooneli there* ('pepper grows nowhere else in the wide world but only there')
>
> You can explore a digitised version of one of the surviving manuscripts of the *Marvels of the East* here:
> http://www.bl.uk/manuscripts/FullDisplay.aspx?ref=cotton_ms_vitellius_a_xv
> You can access a version of *Mandeville's Travels* here:
> https://quod.lib.umich.edu/c/cme/aeh6691. Find out where the pepper grows!

–Takeaway Note–

Early English writing had some symbols unfamiliar to a modern reader. The letters 'ȝ' ('yogh') and 'ƿ' ('wynn') represent 'g' and 'w'; 'þ' ('thorn') and 'ð' ('eth') stand for the 'th'-sound and are still used in the *International Phonetic Alphabet* (IPA), as is the letter representing the vowel sound 'æ' ('ash').

Early Modern English

Scholars customarily date the **Early Modern English** (EModE) period from around 1500 to 1700, followed by **Late Modern English** (LModE) (until 1900). The printing press made texts of all kinds much easier to produce and therefore cheaper and more accessible. Literacy became slightly more widespread. The reading public slowly extended from a tiny upper class to the wealthy part of the population who had the leisure to read. Later in the period, reading and writing also became a necessity for those engaged in the growing trade beyond the British Isles. The cultural movement of the *Renaissance* brought a reconnection to the wealth of classical learning, and with it an increased influx of loanwords of Greek and Latin origin. The great variability of language that was the hallmark of Middle English slowly came to be more focused towards a norm. "Fixing English spelling in its present-day form was virtually completed in print by about 1650" (Nevalainen 2006: 32), but other levels of language lagged behind. The great age of **codification** of the English language was the 18th century, when numerous authors wrote grammars and other reference works which finally resulted in the **standardisation** of English.

–Takeaway Note–

The history of English is customarily divided into **Old English** (~ 700, the date of the oldest written records, to the 11th century), **Middle English** (1100–1500), **Early Modern English** (1500–1700), **Late Modern English** (1700–1900), and, finally, **Present-Day English**.

The spread of English

Mandeville's Travels remained a hugely popular book in the EModE period – despite the fact that its author had never travelled anywhere. But other European powers were already active in establishing and expanding their international network in the 15th and 16th century. The Venetian trader Marco Polo had already reached China at the end of the 13th century. The Portuguese sailor Vasco da Gama was commissioned by his king to open up the sea passage to India with his journey in 1498/99. Christopher Columbus, in the service of the Spanish Crown, famously had the same goal when he went westward to reach India, ending up in the Caribbean and the American continent instead. Reports of these and other voyages were quickly translated into English and circulated widely. Such descriptions of the marvels of the East stirred people's imagination as well the envy of politicians and traders. Some adventurous travellers even took the land route to South Asia, sneaking past the Portuguese-controlled sea routes. The trader Ralph Fitch travelled overland to South Asia at the end of the 16th century and spent eight years exploring the opportunities of the new continent. Towards the end of his report, he wrote again of – pepper:

> Here I thought good, before I make an end of this my booke, to declare some things which India and the countrey farther Eastward do bring forth.

14 World Englishes

The pepper groweth in many parts of India, especially about Cochin: and much of it doeth grow in the fields among the bushes without any labour: and when it is ripe they go and gather it. The shrubbe is like unto our ivy tree: and if it did not run about some tree or pole, it would fall downe and rot. When they first gather it, it is greene; and then they lay it in the Sun, and it becommeth blacke.

(quoted after Foster 1921: 48)

Queen Elizabeth I granted a Royal Charter for trade to a body of merchants called the **East India Company** (EIC), who set out to compete with the Portuguese, Spanish, Dutch, and French for new worlds and new riches (see Figure 2.2). Since all these explorations and exploits began as naval expeditions, we will sketch the spread of English around the world with a focus on three interconnected areas: the Atlantic, the Indian Ocean, and the Pacific.

⇒ Access the report about the first voyages of East India Company ships: *The Voyages of Sir James Lancaster, Kt., to the East Indies: With Abstracts of Journals of Voyages to the East Indies During the 17th Century, Preserved in the India Office: and the Voyage of Captain John Knight (1606), to Seek the North-west Passage*, republished in 1877 and available online: https://archive.org/details/voyagesofsirjame00mark rich/page/n8. Search for 'pepper' and 'peppercorn' in the text; note the contexts in which *pepper* is mentioned and trace the route of the ship *Peppercorn* on its voyage.

The Atlantic – North America

The Atlantic connects the West African coast with the Caribbean and the American continent. Two different sailing routes served two very different kinds of population movement. A straight route brought settlers from the British Isles to North America: the first successful settlements were in 1607 in Jamestown, Virginia and in New England in the 1620s. Some of these early settlers left England in search of religious freedom and self-determination; others were more attracted by the economic possibilities of the new world. One of the earliest British colonies was also the first to break its ties with the home country: thirteen colonies declared their independence in 1776 to become the Unites States of America. The westward expansion of the US territory continued throughout the 19th century, spurred by the gold rush in California and supported by the new railway. As one of the consequences of the American Civil War from 1861–65, slaves working on the plantations in the South were freed, but another century passed before the Civil Rights movement in the US took on the persistent racial segregation in the country. The United States in turn became a colonial power in 1898 after the Spanish-American War, when they took over the Philippines from the Spanish. American English (AmE) is thus the historical input variety to

Figure 2.2 The spread of English (speakers) around the world (Schneider 2011: 49; reprinted by permission from Cambridge University Press)

Philippine English, an exception to the dominance of BrE as ancestor of Postcolonial Englishes.

The settlement of Canadian territory proceeded from two directions, one from Europe via the Atlantic and the other from the neighbouring United States. The explorer John Cabot reached Newfoundland and claimed it for the British crown in 1497, thus preceding the great age of colonial expansion. However, most of the first settlers who came to stay were of French origin, and even though France lost its possessions in Canada to Britain after a war in the 18th century, Canada remains a bilingual English- and French-speaking country to this day. The settlers from England were joined by loyalist refugees, who fled the US in the wake of the Declaration of Independence in 1776. In

16   World Englishes

1867 Canada achieved autonomy by becoming a British Dominion, but fully fledged independence came as late as 1982. Canada has embraced immigration and shows an increasingly diverse cultural and linguistic profile: the 2016 census reports falling numbers of English and French mother tongue speakers (around 58% and 21% respectively), with the numbers of speakers of immigrant languages with around 22% on the rise.

The Atlantic – the Caribbean

Another shipping route formed a triangle between Britain, West Africa, and the Caribbean and America, devoted to the transport of slaves. The Portuguese had already established a trading post on the West African Gold Coast (now Ghana) at the end of the 15th century; the British founded their own outposts in the course of the 17th century which became centres for the trafficking in humans. Millions of people from different West African regions were enslaved and then sent to the Caribbean islands and the Americas to work on plantations. It was at the end of the 18th century that the first societies for the abolition of slavery were formed in Britain – more and more members of the public disapproved of treating human beings as a commodity and lobbied for an end to this disgraceful and racist practice. The British government finally stopped the involvement in the slave trade and made slavery in its empire illegal in 1834. By that time, '**Creoles**' were probably already established as the languages of the former slaves on Caribbean islands, who formed the majority of the population. European powers had competed intensely for possessions in the Caribbean throughout the 17th century; some islands changed hands several times. The islands of St. Kitts and Barbados were among the first to be occupied by English-speaking settlers, Jamaica was taken from the Spanish in 1655. Jamaica became independent in 1962, and today **Jamaican Creole** is known far beyond its homeland thanks to the many poets and musicians who use it as their medium of artistic expression.

–Takeaway Note–

The spread of English to North America has produced quite different varieties. US-American and Canadian English are fully standardised and are spoken by the vast majority of the population as their only language. Many people in the Caribbean grow up with Creole and learn standard English in school.

The Atlantic – Africa

European interest in Africa originally did not extend beyond the foundation of outposts for the slave trade. The countries which are today's Ghana, Nigeria, and Cameroon came under the influence of English missionaries in the first half of the 19th century. The so-called 'scramble for Africa' intensified the colonial activities of old and new imperial players. European powers held a conference in Berlin in 1884/85 and decided to help themselves to their piece of Africa – without any African involvement, of course. Germany, Italy, and Belgium joined the more established colonisers; Germany's colonies in West and East Africa (parts of today's Cameroon and Tanzania, respectively) were taken over as protectorates by the British following the end of WWI. Most African territories were thus formally turned into colonies at the end of the 19th or the beginning of the 20th century and all gained their independence in the decades after WWII. Tanzania is the only African country which does not grant an official role to the former coloniser's language any more, since the indigenous language Kiswahili has become the national language.

From the Atlantic towards the Indian Ocean

One important African country is still missing from our short history of European expansion. South Africa played a vital role for the ships going out to South Asia. Members of the Dutch East India Company first established a settlement at the Cape of Good Hope in the 17th century, the British conquered the Cape in the 18th century. The rivalry between Dutch and English settlers culminated in the so-called 'Boer Wars' at the end of the 19th century, which were won by the British. The language of the Boers, the descendants of the Dutch settlers, was called Afrikaans and co-existed with English when the different colonised territories were joined as the Union of South Africa in 1910. After the elections, which the Europeans held among themselves in 1948, the system of *apartheid* was established – a system of white supremacy and systematic degradation of the country's original population. The labels 'White', 'Black', or 'Coloured' in people's passports turned them into first- or second-class citizens. The liberation movement African National Congress (ANC) adopted English as their lingua franca; Afrikaans became more and more associated with the internationally stigmatised apartheid regime. In 1994, the apartheid system finally collapsed and Nelson Mandela became the first South African president in the first free general elections.

The Indian Ocean – India

Employees of the East India Company began trade with the Indian subcontinent in the 17th century. They founded warehouses (called 'factories') along the Indian coast, first on the west coast in Surat (today's Gujarat), later in Madras (today's Chennai), and in Calcutta (now Kolkata in West Bengal). The British managed to extend their grip on India by a very successful policy of divide-and-rule. They supported some local rulers against others in exchange for compliance, or they took over from them by brute force. Calcutta became the first administrative capital for the colonial administration; other regions were to

18   World Englishes

follow. In the aftermath of the 1857 rebellion against colonial dominance, command over India was transferred from the EIC to the British Crown, making India officially a British colony. But even before that date, matters of Indians' education were debated in the English parliament. *Orientalists* favoured Indian languages as medium of instruction in education, whereas *Anglicists*, who won, opted for English. Knowledge of English spread through the education system and became necessary for Indians who wanted to advance in the colonial administration or pursue higher education in the newly founded universities. Indian demands for self-determination became stronger in the 20th century and particularly vocal after Mahatma Gandhi joined the Indian National Congress. The independence of British India in 1947 went along with partition into India and Pakistan; Bangladesh broke away from Pakistan in 1971. English is India's associate official language alongside Hindi; its space within the Indian multilingual sphere is growing continuously and it is much more entrenched in society than in the neighbouring South Asian states. Today, Indian English (IndE) is one of the largest varieties of English in terms of numbers of speakers.

The Indian Ocean – Sri Lanka

Sri Lanka became a British Crown colony under the name Ceylon at the beginning of the 19th century. After independence in 1948, English was originally kept as official language, but then discarded in favour of the indigenous majority language Sinhala. Conflicts between the Sinhala-speaking population and the Tamil-speaking minority eventually erupted into a long and bitter civil war, which only came to an end in 2008. English has been officially designated the 'link language' in the constitution and is now being taught and used more extensively.

The Indian Ocean – Malaysia and Singapore

Malaysia and Singapore are situated at the Straits of Malacca, opposite the Indonesian island of Sumatra. The Straits connect the Indian Ocean with the Pacific and were thus the main shipping route for all traders venturing beyond South Asia. The Dutch East India Company was already well established in the region when British traders took the competition with them to Southeast Asia. Singapore, an island located at the tip of the Malayan peninsula, was founded in 1819 as a trading post with permission of the local rulers and quickly became a flourishing multinational port. Malaysia became a British colony in the 19th century. After independence in 1957, the role of English was restricted in favour of the national language Bahasa Malaysia. The British surrendered Singapore to the Japanese during WWII; the island joined Malaysia briefly in the postwar period before becoming an independent state in 1965. Multicultural Singapore today enjoys a lot of attention from linguists because of its local colloquial variety of

English – 'Singlish' – which displays a lot of influence from the surrounding languages Malay and varieties of Chinese, and seems to be developing into a first language for the younger generation.

Beyond the Indian Ocean – Hong Kong and China

China was quite successful in resisting European colonialism. Europeans' access to the trade in tea, silk, and porcelain (hence 'China') was restricted to the so-called treaty ports, originally only Kanton (today's Guangzhou). The British illegal import of opium from India was at the root of the Opium Wars, which forced the Chinese government to hand over Hong Kong Island to the British and to open up more ports for international trade. Hong Kong fell to the British for 100 years, until the handover in 1997, and is now a special administrative region (SAR) within the People's Republic of China. English is spoken and written mainly as a second language alongside Mandarin Chinese and the majority first language Cantonese.

–Takeaway Note–

The postcolonial countries in Africa, South Asia, and Southeast Asia are all multilingual. English as a Second Language is used in domains such as administration or higher education, and as a link language. The distinction between English as a First and Second Language is also becoming blurred in some countries where more and more people grow up with English as part of their multilingual repertoire.

The Pacific – Australia

British interest in the Pacific was originally scientific rather than profit-oriented; Captain James Cook, for instance, was commissioned to sail to the Pacific with a group of scientists on board. New Zealand, Australia, and several Polynesian islands in the Pacific came to the attention of Europeans for the first time in the course of three voyages in the second half of the 18th century. The so-called 'first fleet' arrived in Australia in 1788, bringing convicts, mainly from London and the south of England, to pass their sentence in the new land. They were joined later by settlers who came of their own free will and gradually extended the English-speaking population. Australia became a self-governing commonwealth in 1901, but kept close ties to the distant homeland. These ties started to weaken after WWI, and more so after WWII, and today the country orients itself more towards other nations in the Asia-Pacific region. The process of codifying Australian English (AusE) began in the 1980s against a lot of resistance, but now the *Macquarie Dictionary* is both an undisputed authority and a commercial success.

20 World Englishes

The Pacific – New Zealand

English whalers and sailors were the first Europeans to set foot on New Zealand in the early 19th century. Settlers arrived after the Treaty of Waitangi in 1840, when Maori leaders granted them access to their country in exchange for protection of their rights. The treaty did not prevent exploitation and seizure of the lands, which led to several wars between the new arrivals and the local population. New Zealand became a dominion in 1907 and independent in 1947 and, comparable to Australia, now focuses less on Britain and more on establishing a national identity which gives its Maori heritage its rightful place.

The Pacific islands

Trade and settlement in the Pacific has also given rise to several Creoles. *Pacific Creoles* developed later than the *Atlantic Creoles* and were not related to slavery; they came about as contact languages between Melanesian sailors, plantation workers, and Europeans. *Tok Pisin* (from 'talk Pidgin') has become the national language of Papua New Guinea, the only Creole to achieve this status.

–Takeaway Note–

The Pacific is home to the fully standardised varieties Australian and New Zealand English, as well as to Creoles, spoken on Pacific islands.

English in the 21st century

Two buzzwords of the 21st century are also linked to English as a world language: globalisation and transnationalism. The global spread of English does not necessarily proceed with physical settlement in specific territories, as it did in the past. Mass media and social media are produced and used in English, accessible everywhere. English is now a **pluricentric** language more than ever. There are several regional standards such as BrE, AmE, and AusE, and more are bound to be emerging in the future.

Before we move on to our next section, we conclude our historical tour of English with a reminder: English has always been a contact language (Mesthrie 2006), and when we start comparing Postcolonial Englishes with BrE as the input variety, we do well

> to keep in mind (1) that standard English of the period of exploration, trade, and colonization was slightly different from English in the twentieth and twenty-first centuries; and (2) that such standard English was not the only input in the formation of New Englishes.

> (Mesthrie 2006: 277)

2.3 Conceptualising World Englishes

Accent, dialect, variety, language?

The previous section has sketched the rise of English as the most prominent world language – but is it World *English* or World *Englishes*? Clearly, there are many different ways of writing – and especially speaking – English, and if you live in an English-speaking country, you do not have to travel far and wide to encounter different **accents** or **dialects** of English. Scholars traditionally use the label 'accent' when speakers of English only differ in their pronunciation – for example, you can speak Standard BrE with a Scottish accent. When we talk of 'dialects', the difference extends to vocabulary and grammar; a speaker who says 'Ah didnae ken' rather than 'I didn't know' is again very likely to come from Scotland.

The terms 'language' and 'variety' are not easily defined. A language has dialects, but not the other way round, and the border between languages is also not as clearly demarcated as one might think. One criterion for stating that we are dealing with different languages is **mutual intelligibility**: if we understand each other, we speak the same language or dialects of the same language. However, this criterion is not as clear-cut as you might like it to be once you review your experience. You might have encountered a speaker who was quite unintelligible to you, only to be very surprised to find out that she just spoke a dialect totally unfamiliar to you. The same kind of under-specification holds for **variety**. It would be very awkward if we called Canadian English a 'dialect' of AmE, since this also implies a hierarchy that speakers rightfully reject. 'Language', then, is partly a linguistic, but also partly a political term, while 'variety' emerges as a neutral term that does not imply any hierarchy or historical relation between Englishes. Furthermore, people may speak and write English as their first (and frequently only) language, as one of several languages they use on a daily basis, or as a foreign language for international communication. Scholars have come up with different models to conceptualise the multitude of Englishes out there, to which we will now turn.

English: who is a native speaker?

One extremely important scholar who played a decisive role in establishing the field of World Englishes is the late Braj Kachru (1932–2016). Kachru was born in Kashmir, India, studied in India and later Scotland, and completed his PhD on IndE in the 1960s, at a time when his object of study was considered by many as just being 'bad English'. As professor of linguistics at Illinois, he went on to challenge established notions of 'good' versus 'bad', 'native' versus 'non-native', and 'standard' versus 'non-standard' when it came to varieties of English. In a nutshell, many people were of the opinion that varieties such as 'Indian English' should not exist: what is 'Indian' about it is the influence of the local languages that speakers also have in their repertoire. From the perspective of Second Language Acquisition (SLA), recognisably 'Indian' features point to incomplete acquisition – speakers have not mastered the target language (BrE or AmE) fully, but still show signs of interference from their mother tongues. In that view, the English-speaking world is divided into native speakers such as British, American, Canadian, Australian or New Zealand speakers, and speakers of English in India, South Africa, Ghana, and many other countries where English is an official language – all of whom are considered non-native and should therefore follow the example of the established native varieties.

Kachru challenged what amounted to a monolingual bias lurking behind this line of thinking. First of all, he rejected the narrow view of what it means to be a 'native speaker'. Since many Western countries are monolingual, the notion that a 'native speaker' is someone who grew up with only one language as their mother tongue appeared natural. However, multilingualism is the norm worldwide, and monolingualism is the exception. Millions of speakers worldwide grow up with English as one of their mother tongues alongside others, or they learn English in school at a later age. Kachru introduced the terms 'genetic' and 'functional' nativeness to cover these scenarios: *Genetic nativeness* refers to having English as a mother tongue from childhood onwards, while *functional nativeness* covers everyone who is a proficient user of English, regardless of how and when they were exposed to the language. Kachru then claimed that the label 'non-native' does not really apply to countries like India, where there might be hardly any 'genetically native' but millions of 'functionally native' speakers of English. He further introduced the notion of a **cline of bilingualism**, acknowledging that proficiency in English might come in different degrees. Speakers who can claim to be functionally native often occupy white-collar positions for which English is the working language. Since most former British colonies in Asia and Africa have retained English as official language, areas such as administration, the judiciary, and higher education are still typically associated with English. At the lower end of the cline, we find speakers who have little or no access to education in English and acquire the language on an ad hoc-basis, giving rise to grassroots and *hybrid* Englishes.

The Three Circles Model

To round it all off, Kachru introduced his model, **Three Circles of English** (Figure 2.3). The **Inner Circle** comprises those countries where **English is a Native Language** (ENL), for example the UK, the US, or Australia. The **Outer Circle** covers countries where **English is a Second** (or official) **Language** (ESL), and the remaining **Expanding Circle** brings countries where **English is a Foreign Language** (EFL) into the picture. Even though Kachru acknowledged that Inner Circle countries are norm-providing for the rest of the world, he insisted that Outer Circle countries are norm-developing and fully capable of setting their own standards if they wished to do so. He also gleefully

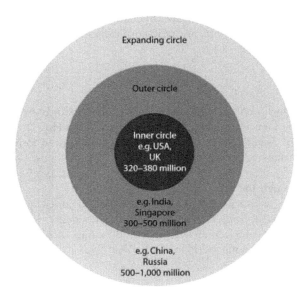

Figure 2.3 Kachru's 'Three Circles' of English (Crystal 2003: 61; reprinted by permission from Cambridge University Press)

pointed out that Inner Circle or native speakers of English are in a minority, compared to the Outer Circle – a pronouncement that is even truer today than it was in 1985 when he first made it.

The Expanding Circle covers the rest of the world to different degrees, wherever English is acquired as a foreign language. Countries such as South Korea are said to be under the spell of an 'English fever': parents go out of their way to treat their children to English-medium education, and are willing to pay substantial amounts for what they consider a competitive advantage in today's globalised world. The People's Republic of China, on the other hand, did not place the learning of English high on the agenda until the Beijing Olympics in 2008, when a program to increase the knowledge of English for the benefit of foreign visitors to the Olympics was initiated. In most countries of the European Union, English is taught as the first or second foreign language in schools, and the degree of proficiency is quite high in countries such as the Netherlands.

World Englishes

The label 'World Englishes' is thus the most inclusive of all the terms in this section, covering all the Three Circles. The scholarly journal of the same

24 World Englishes

name, co-founded by Kachru in 1985, testifies to this broad coverage; articles published range from English in the Shetland Islands to English in Brunei. Quite a lot of its contributions are now corpus-based, as we will see in Chapters 4 and 6.

New Englishes

Another label which also came up in the 1980s is **New Englishes**, originally the title of a book by John Platt, Heidi Weber, and Mian Lian Ho. Their focus was on those varieties of English which remained official languages in former British colonies. Their definition stressed that New Englishes

*   develop through the educational system
*   are used in a territory where English is not the majority language
*   fulfil intranational (rather than international) functions
*   have become localised/nativised; that is they have acquired features from the surrounding languages (Platt et al. 1984: 2–3).

The label **New Englishes** separates varieties of English in (largely) monolingual countries from those in multilingual countries. Neither American nor New Zealand English are New Englishes, even though both are also former British colonies, because English is the uncontested national and official language in both countries. Many of these Inner Circle countries do not even have any legislation concerning their national/official language, simply because it is too obvious to merit a clause in a constitution. The features these varieties have taken over from surrounding languages tend to be restricted to words for initially foreign flora and fauna or peoples and customs, such as *moose* and *racoon* in North America or *haka* and *hongi* in New Zealand. At the other end of the scale, we find South Africa whose constitution recognises 11 official languages, with English among them. According to the 2011 census, English is the home language of only 9.6% of the population, but it is also the language of the government, the higher education system, and it serves as a link language between speakers who otherwise do not share a mother tongue. New Englishes such as South African English (SAfE) are then all Outer Circle Englishes, and it is the lasting merit of Platt et al.'s book to offer numerous examples of what 'localised' or 'nativised' actually meant in linguistic terms. We will return to some of the features they found to be typical of New Englishes in Chapter 6.

Beyond the Three Circles Model

Kachru's insistence on treating Outer Circle Englishes as varieties in their own right proved to be a milestone for the emerging field of World Englishes. Slowly, a change in perspective gained ground. Non-native varieties were no longer framed in terms of *deviance*, but of *difference*, and these differences in turn harboured the potential of becoming unique markers for a new variety of English. But after a while, researchers pointed out that the Three Circles Model might be too static to capture the dynamics of English as a world language. The model assigns each country to a circle, regardless of its internal differentiation. Take the example of South Africa again: After the final collapse of the ruthless apartheid system in 1994, the divisions in society along ethnic lines obviously did not disappear overnight. Today we can still recognise White South African English, Black South African English, and South African Indian English as distinct varieties, and English is learnt as a foreign language by the large majority of the Black population. That is, English can be a first, second, or foreign language for citizens of South Africa, a scenario that holds for many multilingual postcolonial countries. The same internal variability also holds for Inner Circle countries. The UK alone hosts many traditional regional dialects as well as newly emerging varieties such as 'Multicultural London English', not to mention Welsh English or Scottish English. The Circles Model is not designed for new developments concerning the language policies and attitudes within a speech community. Singapore is a case in point: the small city state has received a lot of attention by linguists because it offers a quite unique example of English turning from a second to a native language almost within a generation. So despite its considerable merits, "the Three Circles concept is a nation-based model that draws on historical events which only partially correlate with current sociolinguistic data" (Bruthiaux 2003: 172).

The Dynamic Model

The World Englishes community was ripe for a new perspective when Edgar Schneider, from the University of Regensburg, Germany, published a first paper in 2003 on what came to be known as his **Dynamic Model** of the evolution of Postcolonial Englishes – the monograph *Postcolonial English* appeared in 2007. Schneider's model was quickly recognised as a major new paradigm which triggered a flurry of research, especially research combining World Englishes with a corpus-linguistic perspective. Schneider argued that there is no difference in principle between, for example, AmE and SAfE – both developed out of colonial beginnings, away from the historical input variety BrE. "The model assumes five developmental stages, and on each of them a unilateral implication of four social and linguistic sets of conditions:

- the political history of a country is reflected in
- the identity re-writings of the groups involved in these processes, which, in turn, determine
- the sociolinguistic conditions of language contact, linguistic usage and language attitudes; and these affect
- the linguistic developments and structural changes in the varieties evolving" (Schneider 2011: 33–35).

26 World Englishes

These 'identity rewritings' affecting the relationship between the settlers and the indigenous population (or the STL strand and the IDG strand in Schneider's terminology) are the driving force behind the five stages for the development of a postcolonial variety of English. The model does not predict that all varieties go through all stages, but it does postulate that the evolution of a variety proceeds with the stages in the same order.

Dynamic Model, stage 1: foundation

Colonial expansion brings English-speaking people to new lands. The initial contact with the indigenous population remains limited; some of the participants in these first contact situations may bother to acquire a smattering of the others' language for trade purposes. The new arrivals may borrow some indigenous expressions, typically for place names from the unfamiliar territory.

Dynamic Model, stage 2: exonormative stabilisation

'Stabilisation' refers to the successful continuation of the colonisation process (that is, successful from the British point of view). The English-speaking settlers have made inroads into the new lands and are clearly there to stay. Interaction with the local population becomes inevitable for both sides and thus also more extensive. 'Exonormative' means that the English inhabitants of the colony perceive themselves as primarily British and continue to follow the norms of the distant homeland, linguistic and otherwise. Still, with increased contact comes increased lexical borrowing from the surrounding languages, typically for unknown plants and animals, as well as first transfer effects in the areas of pronunciation and grammar.

Dynamic Model, stage 3: nativisation

"This is the most vibrant and interesting of all the phases" (Schneider 2017: 49) because of the ways the socio-cultural and the linguistic dynamics of the colonial contact situation interlock. The STL strand's ties with their homeland weakens after some generations of settlement in the new territory, and their identity constructions now include their expatriate experience: "it may be assumed that this emerging 'British-cum-local' identity carries a positive attitude, is construed as an enriching experience in the service of the less challenging, distant home country" (Schneider 2007: 37). Contact with the local population intensifies on a personal level and the more abstract level of running the colony. British colonial rule typically went along with the setting up of institutions such as the legal system based on English customs and the English language; administration and education sooner or later relied on English. Local elites embrace the English language as a means of advancement in the colonial state, but also as a path to modernity and advanced Western knowledge. The language of the colonisers also opens up new possibilities for the colonised – this two-faced dimension of English language use remains a matter of debate to this day in (now post-) colonial countries and drives "the schizophrenia about English" (Kachru 1994: 549). Linguistically, 'structural nativisation' happens on a larger scale: "this stage results in the heaviest effects on the restructuring of the English language itself; it is at the heart of the birth of a new, formally distinct PCE [=Postcolonial English]" (Schneider 2007: 44).

Dynamic Model, stage 4: endonormative stabilisation

WWII ushered in the end of European colonialism – the irony of fighting a war for freedom and democracy while at the same time being denied those rights was not lost on the millions of British colonial subjects, who demanded and won their independence. The process of nation-building, the forging of a new national identity typically involves language(s). What should be the new national or official language, what should be the role of English as the former colonial language in the new state? Postcolonial countries around the world have overwhelmingly opted for continuing their former European colonisers' languages. However, Schneider points out that independence is a necessary but not sufficient factor for reaching this stage: "not only political independence but also a step towards cultural self-reliance, loosening also mental ties and associations with one's roots" (Schneider 2017: 50). The case of Australia is a good example. The former colonial outposts in the southern hemisphere formed the Federation of the Commonwealth of Australia in 1901, thus becoming nominally independent but still keeping close cultural and economic ties to the mother country. However, during WWII the Australians learned the hard way that these ties were a rather one-sided affair, when Britain failed to extend its military protection after the Japanese army had conquered nearby Singapore in 1942. Such an experience counts as an 'Event X' in Schneider's terminology – initially a shock for the population, but in the long run a rallying point for a spirit of independence.

Local usages that have developed over time set the new varieties apart from their historical input variety and are now accepted as markers of a common identity. It is at this stage that linguists, as well as the general public, move from talking about 'English in X' to 'X English'. 'Endonormative' also means that the variety becomes codified – that is reference grammar books and dictionaries are produced. This is important for the inward and outward acceptance of new varieties of English, as the example of Noah Webster's efforts for the codification of US-AmE show. Webster's *The American Spelling Book* (1783), as well as his *Compendious Dictionary of the English Language* (1806), asserted the autonomy of AmE both politically and linguistically. In the preface to his *Dissertations on the English Language*, he wrote:

> Our political harmony is therefore concerned in a uniformity of language. As an independent nation, our honor requires us to have a system of our

28 World Englishes

own, in language as well as government. Great Britain, whose children we are, and whose language we speak, should no longer be our standard -, for the taste of her writers is already corrupted, and her language on the decline. But if it were not so, she is at too great a distance to be our model, and to instruct us in the principles of our own tongue.

(Webster 1789: 20–21)

The example of AmE illustrates nicely that the speech communities' 'identity rewritings' are ultimately more important than what is happening to the language. The actual differences between Standard American and Standard BrE are smaller than, say, the differences between Southeastern and Northern dialects of BrE. However, Webster was so adamant and so successful in promoting the idea of a new language for a new nation that his books became bestsellers and AmE the first truly autonomous standard variety alongside BrE.

Dynamic Model, stage 5: differentiation

Once a young nation has distinguished itself politically and linguistically, a somewhat paradoxical process might set in. In the initial stages of nation-building, the emphasis is on homogeneity and internal coherence, on a collective 'we' as distinct from neighbouring countries and the former coloniser. Once the national identity is secure and the national variety taken for granted, "new dialectal distinctions are born" (Schneider 2017: 50). Social and regional variation provide markers of group identity for speech communities below the level of the nation state. Chapter 5.1 tells you more about how variation in language tends to acquire social meaning.

Colonisation types

The original contact situation remains a crucial factor for the progress of a variety along the cycle, in particular the sheer numbers of new English-speaking arrivals in relation to the original population. **Trade colonies** were founded for the exchange of goods, the contact between Europeans and locals remained restricted to that purpose. Typically, neither party bothered to learn the other's language, so that communication had to rely on a simple makeshift language, a **Pidgin**. Such short-lived trade colonies could also develop into more permanent settlements when trade between equals more or less gradually turned into **exploitation colonies**. India is a classic case in point for this development from individual trading posts scattered along the coast of a vast subcontinent to full-fledged colonial rule, including a language policy that made English accessible to a minority of the indigenous population who were to act as go-betweens. In such a scenario, the English-speaking colonisers always remained in a minority, but the impact of colonial institutions (law, administration, higher education) on the countries' social fabric was so

World Englishes 29

momentous that they typically kept English among their national or official languages even after decolonisation and independence.

In **settlement colonies**, the new English-speaking arrivals came to stay, and in large numbers. A lot of people from the British Isles – and later from all over Europe and other parts of the world – tried to escape poverty, religious or other persecution and looked for new lands to start a new life. The steady stream of settlers deprived the original population of their lands and marginalised them, which frequently involved considerable violence. It is only now that the present-day governments of some former settlement colonies have begun to address this issue and to apologise to the remaining native peoples, such as in Canada and Australia. Settlement colonies were marked by dialect contact between the English-speaking immigrants rather than by language contact with the local population. Still another settlement type is the **plantation colony**; typical examples can be found in the Caribbean, where English-speaking settlers established large plantations for growing sugar cane, tobacco, or cotton and met their demand for labour through the institution of slavery. In the course of this industrial-scale crime against humanity, millions of people from West Africa were captured, transported to the Caribbean and the Americas and bought, sold, and abused at their white slaver masters' will. The linguistic outcome of such a gruesome contact situation typically is a Creole, a stabilised form of a Pidgin that has acquired native speakers among the enslaved population.

–Takeaway Note–

There are different terms for varieties of English around the world. *World Englishes* is the most inclusive and applies to all forms of English, including Englishes in the Expanding Circle. *New Englishes* is a label for second-language varieties of English which excludes Pidgins and Creoles. *Postcolonial English* applies to English as a first or second language around the world, with the exception of the historical input variety British English.

2.4 Making sense of variation

When you study your own or any other language, you typically do so in chunks – information about language is typically compartmentalised into pronunciation, vocabulary, and grammar (see Figure 2.4).

The sound(s) of language

You do not waste time in school with the pronunciation of your mother tongue, as this comes naturally to you. However, you do put a lot of effort into

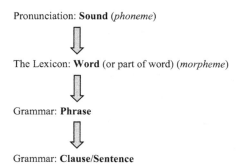

Figure 2.4 The levels of language and linguistic analysis

acquiring the sounds or rather the sound system of a foreign language, that is, not only the individual sounds, but also their specific combinations, stress patterns, etc. Pronunciation provides the most immediate and conspicuous indicator for different varieties, yet this level of language will not be covered by the remainder of this book. The reason is simple: spoken language in corpora is usually represented by transcripts, the original sound recordings from which those transcripts are derived are mostly not accessible. Still, we would like to encourage you to explore the richness of varieties of English worldwide by talking to their speakers, watching movies, and listening to radio stations from all over the English-speaking world. Some basic differences crop up time and again in descriptions of regional and national varieties; we will outline these briefly and provide references and exercises for more in-depth information at the end of this chapter. One of these differences concerns **rhoticity**. Speakers of AmE pronounce the r-sound, which is also visible in the spelling of words like *car* or *bird*, while speakers of BrE do not. At the time when settlers from England migrated to North America, their dialects were still **rhotic**; southern BrE only became **non-rhotic** in the 19th century. Another noteworthy feature goes beyond the pronunciation of individual words and is related to the way speakers assign stress or special emphasis to their utterances. A speaker of an Inner Circle variety of English who utters 'What do you mean?' is very likely to stress only the most important words and de-emphasise the function words, such that their utterance will rather sound like 'Waddya mean?' with the main stress on the last word, a content word. Varieties whose speakers use stress to foreground the more relevant parts of an utterance while backgrounding others are labelled **stress-timed**, and more or less all Inner Circle varieties fall into this category. By contrast, Outer Circle varieties are typically **syllable-timed**, which means that each syllable receives equal stress regardless of the information they carry. A further consequence of syllable-timing relates back to pronunciation, or, more generally, to the overall sound system of a variety – a technical term would be

phoneme inventory, where **phoneme** refers to each sound which realises a distinction in meaning, such as *big* vs. *pig*. The phoneme inventory of syllable-timed World Englishes, then, does not include the reduced, unstressed sound which goes by the name of **schwa** as frequently. Whereas a speaker of BrE would pronounce 'water' with a stress on the first syllable only and an unstressed e-sound for the second syllable, a speaker of Nigerian English is more likely to pronounce both syllables with equal stress and realise the vowel in the second syllable closer to an a-sound.

More variation can be found at the level of permissible sound combinations, or **phonotactics**. Speakers in multilingual environments frequently carry over constraints from their mother tongues into English. Many East Asian languages, for example, do not permit consonants at the end of a syllable, such that words like 'rice' or 'mouse' are difficult to pronounce. Speakers may resort to several strategies if they experience a clash between the phonotactic rules of their mother tongue and English, depending on their position on the cline of bilingualism. They may go for the Inner Circle English pronunciation straight away, without interference from the mother tongue; they may pronounce 'rice' without the final consonant; or they may break up the one-syllable word 'mouse' into two which are then compatible with their mother tongue: 'mou-su'.

The lexicon of a language

We now move on to the vocabulary or **lexicon** of a variety, the sum total of all its different words. An exact definition of 'word' is remarkably tricky. For computers, a 'word' is simply anything with a space to its left and right, and as corpus linguists we need to be aware that we might have a different idea of what constitutes a 'word' than our concordance programs (see the upcoming section). An important distinction to be made is the one between **content words** and **function words**, or **open-class** and **closed-class** lexical items. The logic behind this distinction will be immediately obvious to you once you sit back and consider some of the new words that have come up in recent years. Some examples from politics would be 'Brexit', or 'fake news'; examples from popular culture include 'doxing', or '(to) smurf'. New additions to the vocabulary of a language, short-lived or there to stay, are typically nouns and verbs, which make up the bulk of the content words or open-class items (besides adjectives and adverbs). Unlike the function words, they have a lexical meaning: Nouns typically refer to someone or something, verbs capture actions, adjectives describe qualities. Function words such as pronouns, prepositions, articles, or conjunctions have grammatical rather than lexical meaning, and it hardly ever happens that their closed ranks are joined by new forms. A word frequency list that you generate from any corpus of English will invariably have function words occupying the top 10 or even top 20 positions, with the content words following, and those content words that occur only once in a text bringing up the rear.

32 World Englishes

Words may have an altogether different meaning in another variety, e.g. *robot* ('traffic light' in South Africa), or they may be unique to a variety because they were borrowed from local languages, for example *ang moh* ('foreigner') in Singapore English. We will look more closely at research on the lexicon in World Englishes in Chapter 6.5.

Lexicogrammar

We have tackled pronunciation/phonetics and phonology as well as the lexicon first because differences at these levels of language are immediately apparent to speakers even without specialist expertise. Before we move on to larger linguistic structures, we need to consider the term 'lexicogrammar'. Schneider has urged the linguistic community to pay close attention to this level of language in our research on World Englishes, since:

> grammatical innovations, also in the process of structural nativization, typically start out where the regular meets the chaotic, i.e. at the intersection of grammar and lexis. Therefore, many of the characteristic innovations of PCEs [=Postcolonial Englishes] can be located at this boundary; they concern the co-occurrence potential of certain words with other words or specific structures.
>
> (Schneider 2007: 86)

The structure of words of a language

The next level of language to tackle is **morphology**, which comes in two branches: **word-formation** or **derivational morphology** and **inflectional morphology**. Unlike the phoneme which creates meaning by contrast, the **morpheme** has meaning in itself, either lexical or grammatical. Take the word 'newspaper', for example. You do not need linguistic training to recognise that this word consists of several elements, two of them words in their own right, namely 'news' and 'papers'. By adding 'news' to 'papers', a word with a new meaning was created and that is what **derivational morphology** is about: Describing the different strategies we have for combining forms to create new words. Such forms can be independent words, but need not be, as the next example shows. In 'uninstalled', the 'un-' clearly has a lexical meaning – in this case negative – and combines with 'installed' to form a new word, but 'un-' cannot stand on its own. It is a **bound lexical morpheme**, but not a word. Conversely, all words are also morphemes, more precisely **free lexical morphemes**. English has such bound morphemes either at the beginning of a word, as in 'uninstalled' or 'regroup', or at the end, as in 'shipment' or 'teacher' – **prefixes** and **suffixes**, respectively. You might have noticed that we have not said anything yet about the final '-s' in 'newspapers', nor about the '-ed' in

World Englishes   33

Table 2.1 The productive inflectional endings of English

Inflection	Occurrence
-s	with verbs: 3rd person singular (*she walks*) with nouns: plural (*feathers*)
-'s	with nouns: possessive (*her mother's voice*)
-ed	with verbs: past tense (*she walked*)
-ing	with verbs: progressive (*she is walking*)
-er	with adjectives: comparative (*faster*)
-est	with adjectives: superlative (*fastest*)

'uninstalled'. These are clearly also forms that cannot stand on their own, and they also carry meaning, but in a different way. The final '-s' in our first example indicates a plural noun, '-ed' in the next example marks the word as a past tense verb ('she uninstall<u>ed</u> the app'). That is, both carry grammatical rather than lexical meaning, and they are not used to create new words, but rather different grammatical forms of the same word. A dictionary of English will reflect this distinction between lexical and grammatical meaning in its entries. Products of word-formation processes are listed separately under one head word (or **lemma**); you will find both 'paper' and 'newspaper' in a dictionary, but not 'newspaper<u>s</u>'.

We will briefly come back to word-formation in Chapter 6.5, where we discuss research on the lexicon of World Englishes. However, much more attention has been given to inflectional morphology as part of grammar, or **morphosyntax**. Present-day English is very much unlike its OE predecessor in that it makes do with only a handful of inflections, captured in Table 2.1. These are the **productive** inflectional morphemes of English, that is only those that are currently in use; old plural forms such as *child – child**ren*** are not considered.

Again, we will return to these topics in Chapters 6 and 7, where we will review the morphosyntactic variability of World Englishes and Learner Englishes.

⇒ Consider the following sentences and decide whether the underlined forms belong to derivational or inflectional morphology:

*Kim receiv**ed** a text message.*
*Kim put down the receiv**er**.*
*Kim has been shop**ping**.*
*Kim has bought a small**er** cell phone.*

◊ The same form may do double duty as inflectional and derivational morpheme, for example '-er': It is derivational in 'receiver', creating a noun out of

34 World Englishes

the verb 'receive', but inflectional in 'smaller', indicating the comparative of the adjective. The morpheme '-ing' can be tricky. In our example, it is clearly the inflection for the progressive form of the verb, but in 'Kim carried the shopping home' or 'the food was disgusting' the words ending in '-ing' are not verbs. 'The shopping' is a noun derived from a verb without change of form by a word-formation process called **zero derivation**, and 'disgusting' is an adjective. The '-ed' in 'received' marks the past tense and is, therefore, inflectional.

The grammar of a language

We finally turn to the level of syntax, or grammar – the finer terminological distinctions need not concern us here. A sentence can be analysed at the level of form, or **phrase structure**, or at the level of function – that is referring to subjects, objects, adverbials, and so on. The understanding of **phrase structure** we follow here is the one also employed in reference grammars of English, which in turn mirror your intuitive understanding of the **constituent** structure of English. Let us look at a line from Lewis Carroll's famous nonsense poem *Jabberwocky* for a striking demonstration of your linguistic knowledge – a knowledge that comes simply by virtue of being a native speaker of your language, not from knowledge acquired in school. This is the line:

Beware the Jubjub bird, and shun / the frumious bandersnatch!

Whether you know the poem or not, you have no idea what 'bandersnatch' is supposed to mean. However, the word in its context gives you an important clue straight from your linguistic knowledge: consider 'the frumious bandersnatch'. You still have no idea what 'bandersnatch' refers to, but you know now that it is a noun because it occurs in a **noun phrase**. 'Bandersnatch' is preceded by the definite article 'the' and another nonsense word 'frumious'. Your linguistic knowledge will strongly suggest to you that 'frumious' is an adjective, drawing on two kinds of information: firstly, you probably remember other words in '-ous' (*jealous, humorous, outrageous* ...) which are all adjectives. The second clue comes from the word's position in the noun phrase. The slot between the article and the noun can only be taken up by a limited range of words, as a **substitution test** shows: 'Frumious' can be replaced by 'green' or 'big' (adjectives), or 'one' (numeral or quantifier), but that is about it. The noun phrase (NP) 'the frumious Bandersnatch' has the noun 'Bandersnatch' as its **head** – the element that gives the phrase its name – and further consists of two **pre-modifying** words. An NP may also only consist of a bare noun, or a pronoun (he/she/it), or it may be **post-modified**, as in 'the frumious Bandersnatch who scared the hell out of me'. We distinguish noun phrases, verb phrases (VP), adjective phrases (AP), adverb phrases (AdvP), and prepositional phrases (PP). Phrases combine to larger units such as clauses and sentences, which we can then analyse in terms of function. Our example sentence from above consists of two clauses joined by the conjunction 'and'. Both are

World Englishes   35

imperatives, which syntactically means that they have no overt subject. Both have the same structure: a verb (with 'you' as pronominal subject implied) followed by a direct object.

The sentence also illustrates the basic word order of English, which is subject-verb -object (SVO). Other languages with which English has been in contact past and present feature different basic word orders, for example Celtic languages with VSO, or Hindi with SOV. 'Basic word order' is a term from the linguistic sub-discipline of typology, which is concerned with cross-linguistic patterns; but saying that the basic word order of English is SVO obviously does not mean that all English sentences look that way. We will get to know more about variation in **complementation patterns** in Chapter 6, of which subject-verb-object is one example. The verb 'shun' takes the direct object 'the frumious Bandersnatch' and is therefore **transitive**. An **intransitive** verb does not require an object, as in 'the Bandersnatch burbled'. **Ditransitive** verbs are followed by two objects, for example 'the son gave the Bandersnatch the vorpal blade'. Another sentence pattern which is prone to variation in World Englishes occurs with **copula** or linking verbs, for example 'the Bandersnatch is dead'. 'Dead' is the **subject complement**, providing more information about the subject. Object complements similarly tell us more about the object, as in 'everybody considers the Bandersnatch a monster'.

What we say and what we mean

Everything said so far relates to the formal, structural properties of language. We can analyse word-formation patterns or phrase structure within a sentence without knowing the context in which it was uttered. However, the way we use language everyday goes far beyond coding and decoding information as faithfully as possible. When you think about your communicative interactions in a single day, you will be surprised about the huge gap between what you say and what you actually mean. You might say that someone is two sandwiches short of a picnic in order to indicate that they are dumb; you might ask 'Can you pass me the salt, please?' and expect to be handed the salt and not just get 'yes' or 'no' for a reply; you might answer 'I have an exam tomorrow' when someone asks you to join them for a movie in the evening. In all of these exchanges, you are using language not literally, but figuratively or indirectly, and you are relying on the listeners to recognise your **intentions**. While the desire to use language creatively, or indirectly out of **politeness**, is surely universal, the discipline of **intercultural pragmatics** has uncovered interesting differences in the communicative behaviour of people belonging to different cultures. We will discuss the specific corpus-linguistic perspective on pragmatics in World Englishes in Chapter 6.6, but we might as well acknowledge at this point that corpus linguistics may not be the best tool to tackle pragmatic variation in Englishes around the world. There are several reasons for this: As you will see in Chapter 3, it is relatively straightforward to add information about word-class membership to a corpus automatically, but it is infinitely more complex to encode the intentions that come with an utterance. That is, you will be able without much

36 World Englishes

hassle to find all past tense forms of a specific verb in a corpus, but so far there is no way to extract all ironic utterances, unless you decide to read through all corpus material. Furthermore, knowing what counts as a polite or impolite utterance in a variety requires a much deeper understanding of cultural contexts. The more culturally diverse the community of World Englishes scholars becomes, the better for our overall understanding of pragmatic aspects of English around the world.

2.5 Summary

Congratulations – you have tackled more than a thousand years of language history in this chapter! On top of that, you have gained an insight into the most important concepts in World Englishes research, plus a basic understanding of the levels of language. You are now more than ready to get physical and try your hands on corpora of varieties of English. Chapter 3 is ready when you are!

2.6 Exercises

Exercise 2.1

Tick the box in Table 2.2 if the term in the header of the column applies to the varieties of English in the left column. If you are unsure about the location and/ or status of a variety, we recommend the *electronic World Atlas of Varieties of English* (eWAVE), accessible at http://ewave-atlas.org/, as a quick reference guide.

Exercise 2.2

David Graddol wrote two reports on the future of English for the British Council, one in 1997 and another in 2006 and both available online:

- *The Future of English?* (1997): https://englishagenda.britishcouncil.org/sites/default/files/attachments/books-the-future-of-english.pdf
- *English Next* (2006): https://englishagenda.britishcouncil.org/sites/default/files/attachments/books-english-next.pdf

Table 2.2 Classifying varieties of English

Variety	New English	World English	Postcolonial English
Chinese English			
Jamaican Creole			
Newfoundland English			
Nigerian English			
Sri Lankan English			

World Englishes 37

Compare the figures for speakers of English worldwide: How did Graddol arrive at these figures? Which of his 1997 predictions have come true? How do you evaluate his 2006 predictions?

Exercise 2.3

This exercise requires access to the online version of the *Oxford English Dictionary* (available via many university libraries): use the *Timelines* function, click on the tab *'Origin'* and then on 'Indian subcontinent languages' to get an overview about vocabulary of Indian origin in English. Click on any column in the bar chart of first attestations and go into more detail about your search further by choosing a tab in the column *'Refine your search'*. This way, you can also search for the first Viking words to enter English, or the first Spanish or Chinese words.

Exercise 2.4

Table 2.3 lists all varieties of English that are described in Schneider's *Postcolonial English* (2007) in terms of his Dynamic Model. It will come in handy while working your way through this book and as reference for your own projects. We would like to encourage you to read the variety portraits in Schneider (2007). You can then use the information provided about these varieties in different ways:

- you can simply tick the appropriate box for the stage the variety has reached in the Dynamic Model;
- you can flesh out your table by adding more information about each stage (historical and/or linguistic);
- you can return to this table after having tackled Chapter 4 and add information whether there are corpora available for the varieties;
- you can expand the table by adding further varieties discussed by other authors.

The table is also available for download on the book's accompanying eResources.

2.7 Recommended reading

History of English

Horobin (2016) covers the whole history of English from its beginnings to the present day in an entertaining and non-technical way. *The Penguin Historical Atlas of the British Empire* (Dalziel 2006) provides a very concise overview of British colonial expansion, with a lot of illustrative maps and also an extensive timeline at the end. McArthur (2003) is a comprehensive, non-technical guide to varieties of English around the world; chapters include historical background for each variety as well as its most typical features. If you are interested in specific historical stages of English, we recommend the introductory

Table 2.3 Postcolonial Englishes and their position in the Dynamic Model (Schneider 2007)

Variety	Foundation	Exonormative Stabilization	Nativization	Endonormative Stabilization	Differentiation	Corpora
Australia						
Barbados						
Cameroon						
Canada						
Fiji						
Hong Kong						
India						
Jamaica						
Kenya & Tanzania						
Malaysia						
New Zealand						
Nigeria						
Philippines						
Singapore						
South Africa						
USA						

textbooks in the Edinburgh University Press series, which can be used without extensive prior knowledge of linguistics (Old English: Hogg (2002), Middle English: Horobin and Smith (2002), Early Modern English: Nevalainen (2006)).

Models of English and varieties of English

Galloway and Rose (2015) offer a broad perspective on varieties of English; the textbook includes exercises and also features a companion website with additional material. Schneider (2017) explains the assumptions between different models of World Englishes, including his own. Schneider (2011) is an accessible introduction to the Dynamic Model, but 'the real thing' is Schneider (2007). Both books outline the logic behind the Dynamic Model and proceed to apply it to selected varieties, that is, the development of these varieties is mapped onto the five stages of the model.

References

Bruthiaux, Paul (2003). "Squaring the circles: Issues in modeling English worldwide." *International Journal of Applied Linguistics* 13(2): 159–178. doi: 10.1111/1473-4192.00042.

Crystal, David (2003). *English as a Global Language.* Second edition. Cambridge: Cambridge University Press.

Dalziel, Nigel (2006). *The Penguin Historical Atlas of the British Empire.* London: Penguin.

Foster, William (1921). *Early Travels in India, 1583–1619.* Oxford: H. Milford, Oxford University Press. URL: https://archive.org/details/earlytravelsinin00fostuoft/page/n10. (Last access: 12 July 2019).

Galloway, Nicola & Heath Rose (2015). *Introducing Global Englishes.* London: Routledge. Companion URL: www.routledgetextbooks.com/textbooks/9780415835329/. (Last access: 9 July 2019).

Hogg, Richard (2002). *An Introduction to Old English.* Edinburgh: Edinburgh University Press.

Horobin, Simon (2016). *How English Became English: A Short History of a Global Language.* Oxford: Oxford University Press.

Horobin, Simon & Jeremy Smith (2002). *An Introduction to Middle English.* Edinburgh: Edinburgh University Press.

Irvine, Susan (2006). "Beginnings and transitions: Old English." In Mugglestone, Lynda (ed.), *The Oxford History of English.* Oxford: Oxford University Press, 36–60.

Kachru, Braj B. (1994). "English in South Asia." In Burchfield, Robert (ed.), *The Cambridge History of the English Language.* Vol. 5. *English in Britain and Overseas: Origins and Developments.* Cambridge: Cambridge University Press, 497–553. doi: 10.1017/CHOL97805 21264785.011.

McArthur, Tom (2003). *Oxford Guide to World English.* Oxford: Oxford University Press.

Mesthrie, Rajend (2006). "Contact linguistics and World Englishes." In Kachru, Braj B., Yamuna Kachru, & Cecil L. Nelson (eds.), *The Handbook of World Englishes.* Oxford: Wiley-Blackwell, 273–288. doi: 10.1002/9780470757598.ch16.

Middle English Dictionary. URL: https://quod.lib.umich.edu/m/middle-english-dictionary/dictionary. (Last access: 1 July 2019).

Nevalainen, Terttu (2006). *An Introduction to Early Modern English.* Edinburgh: Edinburgh University Press.

40 World Englishes

Platt, John, Heidi Weber, & Mian Lian Ho (1984). *The New Englishes*. London: Routledge & Kegan Paul.

Plummer, Charles (1896). *Venerabilis Baedae Historiam ecclesiasticam gentis anglorum, Historiam abbatum, Epistolam ad Ecgberctum una cum Historia abbatum auctore anonymo*. Oxford: Clarendon Press. URL: https://archive.org/details/venerabilisbaeda00bedeuoft/page/n11. (Last access: 9 July 2019).

Schneider, Edgar W. (2007). *Postcolonial English: Varieties around the World*. Cambridge: Cambridge University Press.

Schneider, Edgar W. (2011). *English around the World: An Introduction*. Cambridge: Cambridge University Press.

Schneider, Edgar W. (2017). "Models of English in the world." In Filppula, Markku, Juhani Klemola, & Devyani Sharma (eds.), *The Oxford Handbook of World Englishes*. Oxford: Oxford University Press, 35–62. doi: 10.1093/oxfordhb/9780199777716.013.00.

Webster, Noah (1789). *Dissertations On the English Language: With Notes, Historical and Critical*. Boston: Isaiah Thomas and Company.

Chapter 3

Corpus-linguistic approaches to language

Key terms:

Corpus design and types of corpora:
Corpus; annotation (annotated vs. unannotated); balanced corpora; language of immediacy vs. language of distance; metadata; parsing; parts-of-speech (POS) tagging; transcription; representativeness; text; variable

Concordance tools and their features:
AntConc; bigrams and n-grams; concordance lines; Keyword in Context (KWIC); regular expressions (RegEx); word list; *WordSmith Tools*

Digital corpus collections:
CQPweb

Analysing data:
Corpus-based vs. corpus-driven approaches; deductive and inductive approaches; dispersion; false positives; frequency (absolute, normalised, relative); hapax legomenon/legomena; Observer's Paradox; qualitative and quantitative approaches

Statistics:
Chi-squared test; descriptive and inferential statistics; *p*-value; population and sample

3.1 Introduction

The previous chapter introduced the basics of World Englishes, which are characterised by their diversity and variation. As an up-and-coming linguist or researcher interested in varieties of English, you probably have many burning questions already: Why do Indians seem to use *only* and *itself* so often? How often do

42 Corpus-linguistic approaches to language

Singaporeans use the famous word *lah*? And do Americans really use *like* more frequently than the Brits? You may have found out that a corpus may be the right tool for you, but you are now wondering how to proceed. This chapter serves as your gateway to the field of corpus linguistics by introducing its basics as well as some important terminology. This chapter is designed to show you what a corpus is, what it can do, and how you can get started with your study. As this book is an introduction, we cannot cover all the intricate details of statistical analysis of your data or present how to create a complex corpus. However, we will refer you to further, more in-depth literature on certain subjects, which you can find at the end of this chapter. From here on out, we primarily refer to the so-called 'concordance software' ***AntConc***. *AntConc* is freely available on the internet and can be downloaded via www.laurenceanthony.net/software/antconc/. Another useful tool for corpus analysis is ***WordSmith Tools*** (we will simply refer to it as *WordSmith*), which is commercial software for which individual or group licences can be obtained via www.lexically.net/wordsmith/. In order to ensure that you can work on the exercises in this chapter without any hassle, they have (mostly) been designed for *AntConc*. Occasionally, we also refer to *WordSmith*. Please note that some of the in-text exercises in this chapter require access to the *International Corpus of English* (ICE) for Hong Kong: A licence for the corpus as well as the corpus itself can be acquired free of charge via www.ice-corpora.uzh.ch/en/access.html; you can also check with your institution if a copy already exists.

3.2 Getting started: the basics

In this section, we introduce you to some theoretical and some practical basics. First of all, we clarify what we actually mean by 'corpus'. Then, we discuss some general approaches to doing corpus linguistics. Finally, we introduce the first corpus-linguistic tools and give you your first opportunity to do some hands-on work.

What is a corpus?

The word **corpus** comes from Latin and means, among other things, 'body'. From medieval times onwards, it was used more and more in the sense of a 'body of texts', ultimately referring to collections of texts, for instance all the texts written by one author or texts devoted to a specific topic. This development is also reflected in a modern definition of the term, since a corpus in corpus linguistics is, quintessentially, a collection of texts. In our context, the word **text** does not exclusively refer to written language; however, we also consider a phone call, a spoken exam, or the transcript of a TV broadcast a text. Working with such material can vary greatly. In some cases, reading an entire corpus is a valid (and possibly necessary) approach but, for many questions, using the advantages of modern technology is a fantastic asset and preferable. We will occasionally refer to those cases where manual corpus work is required, but our

Corpus-linguistic approaches to language   43

focus will be on working with software and digital corpora. Furthermore, we should note right from the outset that we are working with corpora in the written medium. That is, corpora in our study may be **transcriptions** of spoken interactions, but we access them in transcribed and machine-readable form. This does not mean that other kinds of corpora and studies based on them do not exist. Phonological analyses of spoken corpora, for which audio files would be required, have yielded plenty of interesting results for World Englishes and need to be acknowledged and celebrated. If you are interested in such work, we refer you to overviews and studies such as Durand et al. (2014), Fuchs (2016), and Wiechmann (2008), but we will not cover these here.

Using corpora for World Englishes

Corpora are such great tools because they allow us to investigate language use. Rather than focusing on possible structures, "we can investigate how speakers and writers exploit the resources of their language" (Biber et al. 1998: 1). In the context of World Englishes, this is particularly interesting for numerous reasons. First, the usage contexts of English for people in the Outer and Expanding Circle often clash with what they are taught in the classroom. A teacher may prefer Standard British or American English in their English lessons, even though this is not the kind of English locals might prefer when they are, for instance, talking to a friend in the market. In addition, English is often influenced by the other languages spoken in a country, which is why a particular set of sounds, words, and constructions is used. Thus, we are moving away from analysing the structures that are theoretically possible to actual structures used by people in speaking and writing. The kinds of corpora available today are as diverse as the varieties they represent and it is of utmost importance to be aware of the nature of the data you are working with. In general, "corpora can differ in a number of ways according to the purpose for which they were compiled, their representativeness, organization and format" (Kennedy 1998: 19). This is an issue we return to later as part of the typical design features of a corpus.

Corpus-based and corpus-driven approaches

Before we delve into the software you can use and the important design features of a corpus, a word in regard to two important approaches in working with corpora: the **corpus-based** and the **corpus-driven** approach. Deciding which of the two is right for you is particularly important in order to avoid frustration or results which are incompatible with your research question. These two terms have been famously introduced by Tognini-Bonelli (2001) and, in a sense, describe if (a) you wish to confirm a theory or hypothesis using a corpus or (b) if you use the data as an inspiration for building a theory. In other words, in a corpus-based approach, we take a theory or idea to the corpus and look for confirmation or rejection of it. It is therefore a **deductive** way of working with corpus data and stresses corpus

44 Corpus-linguistic approaches to language

linguistics as a methodology: we formulate predictions and hypotheses and then consider our dataset to see if we are able to verify these predictions and hypotheses based on our data. In an **inductive** and corpus-driven approach, on the other hand, the corpus is taken as the (perhaps only) basis for deriving theories about language: rather than being a tool, the corpus becomes the centre of research and theory-building. The question of how 'neutral' a corpus-driven approach can truly be has been subject to debate, but we recommend reading Meyer (2014) if you are interested in this problem.

–Takeaway Note–

Corpora contain spoken and/or written texts and are very important resources in World Englishes research. We distinguish corpus-based and corpus-driven approaches. Which one is appropriate for your own study should be clarified early on – pay attention to your research question!

First steps in a corpus analysis

In order to get started, you need a computer, concordance software such as *AntConc* or *WordSmith*, and a corpus. Although the presence of a computer is a given, bear in mind that certain tasks assigned to computers in corpus linguistics can be quite demanding of the hardware. For the purposes of our book, a standard modern laptop or PC will do just fine. *AntConc* can be downloaded as an executable file and does not require a licence. Once you open the program, you will see that it is ready to go without you having to change any settings. The creator of *AntConc*, Laurence Anthony, offers help with the program in a PDF file linked to the program and a series of YouTube tutorials (available via www.laurenceanthony.net/software/antconc/). Figure 3.1 shows you what the blank interface of the software looks like. We discuss some of *AntConc*'s functionalities throughout this and the following chapters.

AntConc is able to open different kinds of files, but it is preferable to use TXT or XML files, the two most common formats for corpus data. Thankfully, most PDF files and Microsoft Word documents can be converted to TXT quite easily using another tool by Anthony, the *AntFileConverter* (available via www.laurenceanthony.net/software/antfileconverter/). In *AntConc*, you can open one or more documents by clicking on *'Files'* and then selecting *'Open File(s) …'* or *'Open Dir …'*. With the latter, you can quickly load the contents of entire folders into *AntConc*, which saves you the hassle of individually selecting all the files in a folder. Once you have selected some files which can be opened by *AntConc* and pressed enter, they should all appear as a list in the column on the left-hand side. Opening files in *WordSmith* can be done by clicking on *'Concordance'*, *'Keyword'*, or *'WordList'* and selecting *'File'*. The basic interface of the tool is shown in Figure 3.2.

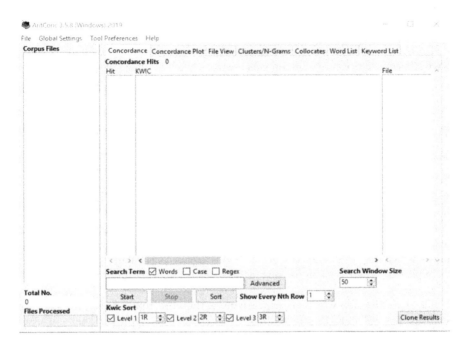

Figure 3.1 Screenshot of the *AntConc* interface

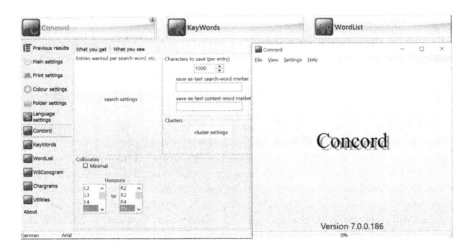

Figure 3.2 Screenshot of the *WordSmith* interface

46 Corpus-linguistic approaches to language

In order to illustrate some basic functionalities of *AntConc*, we ask you to open the accompanying file *'CommaGetsACure.txt'* from the book's website. *Comma Gets A Cure* (Honorof et al. 2000) is a short text frequently used in the study of English dialects and serves as our example text. You can read more about the text at www.dialectsarchive.com/comma-gets-a-cure. After loading the text file into *AntConc*, you can now start looking for words, creating a word list, and testing collocations.

⇒ With *Comma Gets A Cure* opened in *AntConc*, type the word *the* into the search screen and click on *'Start'*. How many instances of *the* show up? How does *AntConc* present the results to you and which information can we gather from the results screen?

◇ In total, there are 15 instances of the direct article *the* in *Comma Gets A Cure*. This number is shown above the concrete examples as *'Concordance Hits'* (more on concordances will follow in Section 3.4). In addition, we get all the instances from the text and some context to the left and to the right. The rightmost column also tells us in which file the examples occur – this is not particularly relevant in our example but, whenever you use several files, this is important information.

While searching for words or expressions is the core function of any software such as *AntConc* and *WordSmith*, these and similar tools typically offer an array of additional useful functions. *AntConc*, for instance, also provides word lists indicating *which* words occur in a text and *how often* they occur. In order to get the word list for a given file or set of files, simply click on the tab *'Word List'* in the *AntConc* interface.

⇒ Write down your expectations regarding the following questions: Which words and word classes are probably the most frequent in *Comma Gets A Cure*? How are words ordered when they are equally frequent? Once you noted your expectations, go to the *'Word List'* feature of *AntConc* and create the word list for the text. Compare the results to your expectations.

◇ Overall, the indirect article is the most frequent word in the text (25 times in the form of *a* and 5 times in the form of *an*). The direct article *the* is listed as the third-most frequent word at 15 occurrences; however, *AntConc* conflates occurrences of the second-most frequent word, *her*, as possessive determiner (as in *her car*) and personal pronoun (as in *they saw her*). This means that *the* is actually the second-most frequent word in *Comma Gets A Cure*. We will come back to this problem at a later stage. In terms of the order of words, *AntConc* lists words occurring equally frequently in a text alphabetically, but still assigns different ranks to them despite their identical frequency. Thus, if the words *that* and *the* both occur 20 times in a text as the most frequent words, *that* would be ranked at number 1 and *the* at number 2.

Another interesting feature of *AntConc* can be found in the tab '*Clusters/N-Grams*'. In addition to showing all the instances of a word in a file or several files, *AntConc* is also able to show in which combinations words are used and how often these combinations show up in a corpus. We might, for instance, be interested which words usually follow the direct article in the text.

⇒ Type in *the* in the tab '*Clusters/N-Grams*' and select a value of '*2*' for both '*Min.*' and '*Max. Cluster Size*'; then click '*Start*'. What kind of combination does this give us? How would you interpret these results?

◇ The resulting combinations are so-called **bigrams**, that is, sequences of two words, one of which is the direct article. In general, we refer to such sequences of words as **n-grams** and specify the value if necessary: bigrams for two words, trigrams for three words, and so forth. The most frequent bigram involving *the* in the text is *the goose*, which occurs four times.

You should now be aware of some essentials of doing corpus-linguistic research. The next sections serve to introduce basic corpus design features as well as more specific topics and terms relevant for your corpus study.

–Takeaway Note–

AntConc and *WordSmith* are two very powerful tools for corpus analysis. *AntConc* is freely available on the internet and is widely used in corpus-linguistic research. TXT and XML files are the preferable formats for corpora that we analyse using the two tools.

3.3 Basic corpus design features

In the following paragraphs, some important design features and criteria in corpus compilation and analysis will be discussed, with our focus being on the basics of working with corpora.

Representativeness and balancing

An important notion in corpus design, as we mentioned previously, is the **representativeness** of a corpus. A corpus is never going to be absolutely representative of a language or variety, since it always presents us with a snapshot of language. Still, many corpora are designed with the goal of representativeness in mind: "We are interested in a sample which is maximally representative of the variety under examination, that is, which provides us with as accurate a picture as possible of the tendencies of that variety, including their proportions" (McEnery & Wilson 2001: 30). A related aspect is that of balancing. We call a corpus **balanced** when it

48 Corpus-linguistic approaches to language

features texts from various genres and domains, spoken and written language (Kennedy 1998: 20), and, in some cases, an equal amount of contributions by people from different genders, backgrounds, and age groups. A balanced corpus is very useful in order to make comparisons between different varieties, since it is also going to be more representative of the variety. In any corpus project, it is important to be aware of what the corpus can and what it cannot tell you about a variety. For this reason, it is usually recommendable to discuss the representativeness and balancing of a corpus in your study.

–Takeaway Note–

Representativeness and balancing are important criteria in corpus design: you need to pay close attention to both of them when analysing and creating a corpus. In particular, you should know what kind of language and which text types are included in a corpus. Corpora designed for special purposes can be very useful for certain research questions, but they may not be representative and are, therefore, limited.

Types of corpora

Corpora come in many shapes and sizes: They may vary in their word count, their overall composition, their representativeness, and many other factors. Since it would be impossible to pay respect to all possible kinds of corpora in this introduction, we will stick to those corpora that feature predominantly in World Englishes research. For a discussion of corpus size and related methodological issues, we refer you to the first part of Chapter 4; information on the design of specific corpora is also provided in the next chapter. This section gives you some information on basic distinctions that need to be taken into account whenever you are creating a corpus or working with one.

Spoken and written corpora

First and perhaps most importantly, the distinction between **spoken** and **written** corpora needs to be considered. At first glance, the difference between spoken and written language seems obvious: a conversation between two people represents spoken language and a newspaper article represents written language. Drawing the line between the two is less obvious when we consider a printed interview, communication via WhatsApp, or a letter written to a friend: the reason for this lies in the difference between '**language of distance**' and '**language of immediacy**' (Koch & Oesterreicher 1985/2012) or 'conceptual orality' and 'conceptual literacy'. These terms refer to the fact that, despite being in either the spoken or written medium, language may in fact take on features typical of the other medium: a newspaper article is in the written medium and typically represents language of distance. A diary entry, on the other hand, is also written, but it may feature aspects associated with spoken language, such as forms of address, interjections, and so forth. This also works the other way round: a free conversation between two friends is in the spoken medium and represents a form of language of immediacy. A prepared speech, on the other hand, is also spoken, but may be more representative of language of distance since it lacks many of the typical features of spoken language.

⇒ First, think about the following spoken and written texts: Lectures, sermons, printed interviews, and diary entries. Where would you rank them on the continuum of conceptually written and conceptually spoken language? Then, consider your own intuitions about the linguistic features typical of spoken language. Which features and characteristics would you associate with language of immediacy but not with language of distance?

◊ Spoken texts such as lectures or sermons are close to the conceptually written end of the continuum and written texts such as printed interviews and diary entries are close to the conceptually spoken end. Printed interviews, for instance, are written versions of language that is originally spoken. With regard to the second question, there are many features that could potentially be listed here; a selection shall suffice: language of immediacy is characterised by, amongst other aspects, hyperbole, swear words, hesitation signals, direct speech, and interjections (Koch & Oesterreicher 1985/2012: 454). Overall, this kind of language is marked by spontaneity, a focus on the situation, and interaction with an audience or an interlocutor.

The fact that some written texts are close to the pole of language of immediacy has also helped a great deal in identifying what spoken language in the past must have been like, since we can use texts such as courtroom debates, fictional dialogue, and personal letters to trace linguistic features associated with (conceptually) spoken language in these texts. In this regard, Culpeper and Kytö (2010) differentiate 'speech-like' texts containing 'oral' features (e.g. second person pronouns), such as letters, 'speech-based' texts based on 'real' speech events, such as trial proceedings, and 'speech-purposed' texts supposed to be read out or performed, such as plays or sermons. In sum, the categories 'spoken' and 'written' may either refer to the channel of communication or to language of immediacy and language of distance (see also Hundt 2008), and any corpus linguist needs to be mindful of this distinction.

Text type, genre, and register

Related categories are **text type** and **genre**, two terms which, for quite a long time, have been "used vaguely, sometimes even interchangeably in the

Figure 3.3 Components in a register analysis (Biber & Conrad 2009: 6; reprinted by permission from Cambridge University Press)

literature" (Taavitsainen 2001: 139). We will focus here on the term 'text types'. Text types are characterised by a variety of factors, such as their structure, their purpose, their transmission, and so forth. Examples of some common text types included in World Englishes corpora are newspapers, conversations, and (student) essays. A problem in corpus linguistics becomes evident when we think about a text type such as the newspaper. Consider two of the most well known and most successful newspapers in the UK, *The Sun* and the *Daily Telegraph*: Would you immediately consider them as belonging to the same category? Despite being newspapers, they are both aimed at different audiences and their use of language is also quite different. Thus, despite technically belonging to the same category, there is a great deal of variation in these two newspapers. One difference that often plays a role relates to the **register** or the **degree of formality**. A text may be very formal and employ technical terminology, such as most academic books, or it may be relatively informal, as in, for instance, a casual conversation between friends. Different scales have been proposed over the years, often with a cline from a highly formal to a vulgar register. Generally, the situation in which a text was produced and its linguistic features need to be considered in a register analysis, as illustrated in Figure 3.3 from Biber & Conrad (2009: 6).

The issue of how to classify texts has taken centre stage in text linguistics for many years, which is why it is worth considering what kind of text(s) one is working with. In particular, it is important not to lump texts together that might actually be fairly different from each other. As Hundt (2008: 171) notes, a larger category such as 'academic writing' may, for instance, include texts from both the natural and the social sciences – whose writing conventions differ. Thus, the classification of text types and assigning texts according to their register is, at times, a subjective matter and needs to be approached carefully.

–Takeaway Note–

Depending on their formality and the text type, spoken and written language can meaningfully be conceptualised as 'language of immediacy' and 'language of distance'. This is something you should pay attention to, since this classification can have an impact on your analysis.

Corpus-linguistic approaches to language 51

> Furthermore, you need to consider the text types included in a corpus. Be aware of the fact that general external factors do not mean that all texts included in this corpus section are truly comparable: newspaper articles, for instance, can differ immensely from each other.

Annotation and metadata

Two further important components of a corpus are **annotation** and **metadata**. We call a corpus **unannotated** when we have nothing but the plain text and well call it **annotated** when it is "enhanced with various types of linguistic information" (McEnery & Wilson 2001: 32). The annotation of a corpus may range from simple in-text comments on aspects such as pauses to highly complex additions such as **parsing**, that is, the segmentation of a text into syntactic constituents. Annotation is often visible in the text in the form of tags in angled brackets. Typically, an opening tag is used first (e.g. <w>), then the expression follows (e.g. I'm), and then a closing tag, indicated by a slash, follows last (e.g. </w>). The two examples (3.1) and (3.2) illustrate in-text annotation.

(3.1) So <w> I'm </w> teaching there <,> uh in one of the <,> uh private college (ICE-IND:S1A-025#18:1:B)

(3.2) But anyway uh she she made <indig> kwento </indig> about Julio (ICE-PHI: S1A-081#40:1:B)

The annotation in these examples, also referred to as mark-up, is realised in the form of so-called 'tags'. These tags provide the information listed in Table 3.1. Please note that, in the running text, we use parentheses for the corpus references. In the actual corpus, angled brackets are used.

Table 3.1 Annotation examples from the *International Corpus of English*

Annotation/Mark-Up	Meaning
<ICE-IND:S1A-025#18:1:B>	• ICE-IND: Indian component of the *International Corpus of English* • S: Spoken section of ICE • 1: Dialogue section • A: Private dialogues • 025: Number of the file • #18: Number of the utterance in the conversation • 1: Subtext (often only 1 per file) • B: Speaker in the corpus
<w> I'm </w>	<w> and </w>: mark words with internal apostrophes
<,>	<,>: marks a short pause
<indig> kwento </indig>	<indig> and </indig>: mark an indigenous word, i.e. a word from a speaker's mother tongue

In some cases, you may want to hide tags in a corpus analysis. If you create word lists, for instance, *AntConc* would normally include any information provided by the tags. This is why 'ICE' shows up as one of the most frequent words in the ICE corpora despite not being a lexical item in this case. Hiding tags is relatively straightforward in *AntConc*: If you click on *'Global Settings'* and then on *'Tags'*, you get the option of hiding tags in your analysis (Figure 3.4). All tags will then be disregarded in word count analyses and in the word list. Depending on the design of the corpus, you may change the kind of tag you wish to exclude. It is recommendable to check in advance if *all* tags should be dismissed, since, in some cases, they may contain information relevant to your study.

Similar to annotation, **metadata** offer additional information on the text, albeit with a different focus. For historical texts, metadata may come in the form of information about the period a text was written in, the name of the author, the text type, and so forth. In the case of spoken corpora, metadata often include **variables** such as speaker age, gender, mother tongue, additional languages, and sometimes also proficiency. For many corpora, metadata is provided in additional files accompanying the corpus file. Thus, if you are interested in the age and gender of a certain

Figure 3.4 Hiding tags in *AntConc*

Corpus-linguistic approaches to language   53

speaker in the ICE corpora, for instance, you may open the accompanying file containing the metadata and look up some of their biodata. In certain corpora which can be accessed online, such as the ones available via **CQPweb** (cf. Hardie 2012), it is possible to select the metadata you are interested in. *CQPweb* is a corpus platform associated with the University of Lancaster. It is a major resource for corpus linguists and can be accessed via https://cqpweb.lancs.ac.uk/. For some corpora, licences need to be obtained; others are freely available to anyone with an account on the website.

It should be noted here that metadata can be incomplete or may not be available for certain corpora. In more recent times, awareness of the importance of good scientific practice is increasing and metadata as well as explicit consent of participants to be included in corpora becomes more common. For your own corpus study, you should read about the corpora you are using and ensure that you know the details of its compilation and the availability of metadata. With regard to important World Englishes corpora, Chapter 4 will give you more insight into annotation and metadata.

Limitations and caveats

Despite the fact that corpora are fantastic tools for studying World Englishes, they also come with certain flaws and caveats. Although we address this point again in Chapters 4 and 8, some important remarks should be made in this chapter already. First and foremost, neither manual nor automatic annotation and tagging of corpora should be treated as perfect. Consider, for instance, the case of **parts-of-speech** (POS) **tagging**: this process, which is usually done using software or a script, automatically detects word classes, but in World Englishes in particular, this is far from a trivial task.

⇒ Read the following example (3.3) from ICE-India. Which words in this example may cause problems in automatic POS-tagging?

(3.3) So uhm <,> her friend Laxshmi she was suffering from <,> her father was suffering from asthama <,> (ICE-IND:S1A-037#2:1:A)

◊ In example (3.3), two words would probably be an issue for an automatic POS-tagger: *Laxshmi* and *asthama*. Both words here might have been transcribed incorrectly, but there is also a chance that the transcribers wished to account for unusual pronunciation. At any rate, an automatic tagger might not be able to assign the correct word classes.

Another aspect worth thinking about concerns the 'naturalness' of spoken data. Imagine being interviewed for a popular TV show for the first time or, on a more personal level, remember the very first presentation you have ever given: There is

54 Corpus-linguistic approaches to language

a good chance that, in these situations, you feel self-conscious and are well aware of being observed. These might also be situations in which you take note of how you speak: You would probably try to avoid jargon or slang and even avoid dialectal speech. Whether or not this holds true, spoken data in corpus analysis come with a similar issue. Linguists are usually interested in the typical, everyday language of people; less in their ability to speak more standard-like. However, when people know that they are being recorded, they may feel that having less of a dialect or accent would actually be what the researcher wants. This phenomenon, referred to as the '**Observer's Paradox**', has been famously summarised by William Labov, who points out that:

> the aim of linguistic research in the community must be to find out how people talk when they are not being systematically observed; yet we can only obtain these data by systematic observation.
>
> (1972: 209)

Consider, as cases in point, the two examples in (3.4) and (3.5) from ICE-Hong Kong and ICE-Philippines:

(3.4) Yeah actually I'm the subject of the interview today (ICE-HK:S1A-089#3)

(3.5) *A:* You know what
   B: What
   A: I feel so embarrassed doing this thing
   B: Yeah
   A: Recording our voice
   B: A lot of people are looking at us
   A: Oh my gosh Okay anyway continue continue
   B: Don't mind them (ICE-PHI:S1A-039#278–286)

⇒ Think about the Observer's Paradox and how it affects data. What can linguists do to reduce its effects? What would your approach be?

◊ Different approaches have been suggested to cope with the effects of the Observer's Paradox. Usually, these approaches involve making the participants of the study feel comfortable. Fostering an engaging conversation also contributes to shift the focus away from the act of recording. A recent example is the 'cuppa coffee' method proposed by Rüdiger (2016), who applied it in the recording of Korean speakers of English and noted that "the simple act of framing the sociolinguistic interview as new acquaintances drinking a cup of coffee together helps to avoid a language learning and teaching framework, puts participants in a more relaxed mindset and finally results in more 'naturalistic' and richer conversational data" (2016: 49). Another strategy, which may

Corpus-linguistic approaches to language   55

be used in addition to methods such as the cuppa coffee method, is to remove the first critical minutes of the conversation.

–Takeaway Note–

Obtaining naturalistic spoken language remains one of the biggest challenges in corpus design: speakers may easily be distracted or aware of the fact that they are being recorded. For your research, this means that you need to be careful in the interpretation of your results: Ask yourself if the speakers are comfortable or not and if their language seems formal or informal.

Further limitations and caveats arise depending on the corpus you are using. Once more, what counts is a careful analysis of your data and the context of corpus compilation.

3.4 Accessing a corpus: concordances

You know some important basics about corpora now, but what actually happens when you search for an expression in a corpus? If the expression you typed into the software is actually present in your chosen corpus, *AntConc*, *WordSmith*, and similar tools usually show you **concordance lines**. In medieval times, concordances represented either parallel passages in the Bible or a sort of accompanying index for the Bible. This is quite comparable to what we understand as concordances in corpus linguistics in the present day: searching for a word in a corpus will, if it is present, result in the program giving you a list of where the word could be found and present the results in parallel lines. In the middle of each concordance line, you can find the item of interest. In Figure 3.5, for instance, you can see the first 18 concordance lines for the word *help* in the direct conversation files in ICE-Hong Kong.

Thankfully, *AntConc* and similar tools are able to do a lot more than simply showing instances of a word – they also provide the surrounding context as well as the name of the file in which the word could be identified. A concordance analysis thus presents us with a **Keyword in Context** (KWIC). Clicking on any of the examples opens the file in which the example could be found, making it possible to see even more of the context in which a word has been used.

The main advantage of a KWIC analysis is the opportunity to get insight into the grammatical and conversational contexts in which a word or structure is used. While this is a useful function in general, it is particularly helpful in World Englishes research. In varieties of English, a word that may follow a certain pattern in, for instance, British English (BrE), might be used very differently in Indian English (IndE). It should be noted that reading concordance lines is a manual task which often represents the first step of a more complex

56 Corpus-linguistic approaches to language

analysis. In addition, many words occur too frequently to study all occurrences in detail, which is why browsing through the data and reading only a sample may, at times, be the preferable option. The following exercise helps to illustrate some of the information we can gather simply by considering a number of concordance lines as presented above.

⇒ How many instances of *help* in Figure 3.5 are transitive (i.e. followed by a direct object) and how many are intransitive (i.e. not followed by a direct object)? Which problems are there when reading these concordance lines? Finally, what is the typical word class of the direct object following *help* (if there is one)?

◊ Disregarding one ambiguous case, there are eleven transitive instances of *help* (for instance in line 1 '[...] to help us') and six intransitive instances (for instance in line 15 '[...] and help out'). Line 5 poses a problem, since we do not know what the speaker says after *help*, indicated by the tag <unc> and the information that there are three unclear words. It can be counted as an intransitive example, since the beginning of the sentence strongly suggests it. The example in line 13 is more problematic: Technically, it is transitive, since *their homework* can be interpreted as a direct object. It seems more probable, though, that the speaker omitted certain parts of the full sentence, which might have been *Help them with their homework* or *Help with their homework*. This example shows that interpretation is often necessary; a good strategy here is to discuss

Figure 3.5 Concordance lines for the word *help* in the conversation files of ICE-Hong Kong

Corpus-linguistic approaches to language 57

Figure 3.6 Illustration of the 'Zap' function in WordSmith

such cases in your study. With regard to the last question, we can see that personal pronouns are the most frequent word class following *help*.

One advantage that *WordSmith* has over *AntConc* is the '*Zap*' function. Sometimes, you receive a number of examples which are not relevant to your study. You may, for instance, be interested in instances of the verb *to mean* in ICE-Philippines. However, searching for *mean* will also show instances of the adjective. By clicking '*delete*', you can simply '*zap*' these results and they will, for instance, not be exported if you wish to continue working with them. An example in which the first hit has been zapped is shown in Figure 3.6.

This section has shown that we can gather a lot of information simply by considering a set of concordance lines, for instance about grammatical patterns, unusual usages, discourse context, and so forth.

3.5 Handling frequencies

Having a set of concordances leaves you with many different directions to follow. You could read through the lines and identify patterns, or single out examples that seem particularly interesting to you. Depending on whether you already have

58 Corpus-linguistic approaches to language

a research question or are still looking for one, you can decide which step to approach next. Often, the data are approached from a **qualitative** perspective first, as in the previous section, and then from a **quantitative** perspective.

A qualitative approach means that the focus is not on how often any linguistic feature occurs. Instead, "the data are used only as a basis for identifying and describing aspects of usage in the language to provide 'real-life' examples of particular phenomena" (McEnery & Wilson 2001: 76). This step often comes before a quantitative analysis, since it allows us to get 'a feeling' for the data. Furthermore, it contributes to an understanding of 'what is there': Before we count and quantify linguistic features, it is usually necessary to investigate which phenomena there are or what forms and functions we can find in the data. This could be anything from the different spellings of a word to rare syntactic constructions in a corpus. The question of rarity is not an issue in this kind of analysis, since the ultimate goal is completeness and detail. A quantitative approach, then, focuses on counting frequencies and conducting statistical analyses, which can be relatively simple or complex, depending on the research question and the kind of data. Quantitative analyses focus on 'how often' features are used and what this can tell us about phenomena such as distribution and language change.

–Takeaway Note–

Qualitative analysis means that we look for individual examples and assess our data in detail. Quantitative analysis seeks to quantify results and encompasses statistical analysis. In a lot of the research carried out today, both approaches are combined, and this is also what you should strive to do. Generally, your research question should inform how you approach your data.

Quantifying your results and working with the **frequency** of an item is often a useful step. Essentially, this means you indicate how often a word or an expression occurs in a corpus. This sounds arguably simple, in particular since both concordance programs we suggest above instantly show you how often the item could be identified in the selected corpus files. However, the simplicity of this endeavour can be deceiving and bears many potential pitfalls. First of all, you need to identify which word class you are looking for: if you search for a single word, you need to make sure that it actually belongs to the word class you are looking for. One of the most notorious candidates in this regard is the word *that*.

⇒ Read the following five sentences and decide which word class each instance of *that* belongs to:

1. I love *that*.
2. I love *that* car.
3. I love *that* you have a new car.

Corpus-linguistic approaches to language 59

4. However, your new car is not *that* beautiful.
5. The new car *that* you bought is not very beautiful.

◊ In each of the sentences, you can find an instance of *that* with different word class membership: demonstrative pronoun in (a), demonstrative determiner in (b), subordinating conjunction in (c), adverb in (d), and, finally, relative pronoun in (e).

Of course, this raises the difficult question of how to deal with such ambiguity in a corpus analysis. We already introduced POS-tagging above and, if you select a good tagger, chances are that every instance of *that* will be assigned to the correct word class. Still, manually checking multi-word-class examples after using a POS-tagger can help ensure the correctness and quality of your data.

Another issue that arises is words that occur several times in an utterance or in a sentence. Consider, for example, the sentence: *The cat has left the building.*

⇒ Count how many words there are in total and how many different words there are in the sentence.

◊ There are six words in total but only five different words, since the definite article *the* occurs twice in the sentence.

In corpus linguistics, we use the terms **type** and **token** for this distinction: A type is the general existence of a word in a corpus, while a token is one instance. In the example sentence, we can identify five types and six tokens. Beware of confusing identical words as the same type: Words such as *bat* and *bat* can be two tokens of one type if they refer to the same thing, but if one refers to a flying animal and the other to a sports instrument, they need to be treated as different types. Related terms are **lemma** and **word-form**, which correspond to the pair of lexeme and word-form. The verb SEE, in its occurrence in a dictionary, is considered a lemma. This lemma, however, has several different word-forms or, to put it differently, actual realisations, such as *see, sees, saw, seen,* and so forth. Whether or not distinguishing type and token or lemma and word-form is useful depends on the specific research question, but it is highly important to be aware of these differences.

Indicating the frequency of an item is, as we mentioned before, not as straightforward as it might seem in the beginning. Of course, it is possible to simply write down how often a word occurs in a corpus, and in certain cases, this will be just fine; but in most cases, good scientific practice calls for a more elaborate and fine-tuned approach. The first problem that needs to be solved is that of comparability. In World Englishes, we often compare varieties: Otherwise, how would we know if the word *lah*, which is thought to be very common in Singapore English, really occurs more frequently in that variety than in, say, IndE? Comparing varieties sometimes entails that different corpora are used, which may or may not be comparable in size. Thus, it is important to differentiate **absolute frequency**, **relative frequency**, and **normalised frequency**. The absolute frequency of a feature refers to the

60 Corpus-linguistic approaches to language

number of instances this feature can be found in a corpus. Finding the absolute frequency of a feature is a good start, but it is usually not sufficient for comparisons. Even for corpora that are generally comparable in their size, the exact word count is usually different, which is why absolute frequencies can be misleading. Luckily, relative frequency and normalised frequency, both of which are more objective measures, can be obtained relatively easily. A very common way to indicate the relative frequency of an item is by using percentages. We could, for instance, compare how often a verb is used in the perfect and in the progressive in a corpus. For illustration, we are using the verb *go* in its perfective and its progressive form. First, we need to assess which forms are possible.

⇒ Which word-forms would we have to look for to find all tokens of *go* in the perfect and the progressive? Which problems could arise, for instance with regard to similar-looking constructions?

◊ We would have to consider the forms *am going, are going, is going, have gone,* and *had gone.* Two major problems would have to be addressed: (1) Additional words could be used between the auxiliary verb and the main verb, for instance in: *He had already gone.* (2) Realisations of the *going to*-future will also be shown.

For our fictitious example, let us assume that there are 25 tokens of *go* in the progressive and 36 in the perfect. This means that we have a total of $n = 61$ tokens. In order to calculate the percentage, we can simply divide the total number of tokens by the occurrences in the two forms. Performing this simple calculation tells us that roughly 59% of all tokens occur in the perfect and 41% occur in the progressive. We can easily apply the same formula to another corpus and then compare the percentages in order to identify whether there are differences.

We deal with normalised frequency when the number of occurrences is indicated in, for instance, per thousand words or per million words. This approach has two advantages: First, we can easily compare the frequency between corpora. Second, the dimensions of a feature are more evident compared to absolute or relative frequencies. Calculating the normalised frequency can be done using a simple formula:

nf = (number of examples of the word in the whole corpus ÷ size of corpus) × (base of normalisation)

This formula, taken from McEnery & Hardie (2012: 49), requires that you know how many examples there are in your corpus, the overall size of the corpus, and which base count you would like to receive (e.g. per hundred, thousand, or a million words).

Corpus-linguistic approaches to language 61

⇒ Let us use our example *go* again for illustration, but only the tokens in the progressive. Assume that we found the 25 tokens in a corpus of 24,368 words and, in a corpus we use for comparison, we found 132 tokens in 102,301 words. Which frequency is higher? In absolute terms, the frequency in the second corpus is higher. What we need, however, is a procedure that allows an objective comparison – we are interested in knowing how often these forms occur per ten thousand words. What would the calculation look like? Which results do we get?

◊ The calculation and the results would be the following:

- Corpus 1: $nf = (25 \div 24{,}368) \times (10{,}000) = 10.25$ instances per 10,000 words
- Corpus 2: $nf = (132 \div 102{,}301) \times (10{,}000) = 12.90$ instances per 10,000 words

We can see that the frequency is indeed higher in the second corpus, but by a much smaller degree than the absolute figures suggest. The calculated frequencies can easily be compared to further corpora and can be calculated regardless of corpus size, although, as mentioned above, the issue of representativeness always needs to be kept in mind. If you use corpora featured on *CQPweb*, the normalised frequency of a feature is indicated in the results screen for every word or pattern you look for.

–Takeaway Note–

Absolute frequencies can be interesting and, in certain contexts, may be sufficient. Most of the time, though, relative or normalised frequencies are more informative. They allow us to understand how often a linguistic feature occurs in different corpora despite the fact that the corpora differ in size.

So far, we considered frequencies under the assumption that a word or pattern occurs several times in a corpus. However, there are also words which occur only once: we call these **hapax legomena** (or, in the singular, **hapax legomenon**). Hapax legomenon is Greek for 'said (only) once' and refers to any word or expression which is present in a text or corpus exactly once. Although we might initially be tempted to think that hapaxes are obscure words, this does not have to be the case at all. Depending on the text type, the preferences of the involved speaker(s) or writer(s), the length of the text, and many other factors, words which would be considered fairly common could still be hapaxes in a corpus. An example of a frequency analysis including hapax legomena is provided in Figure 3.7.

Do not pay particular attention to the calculation involved – what matters here is that the line at the bottom (coloured red in the original) represents

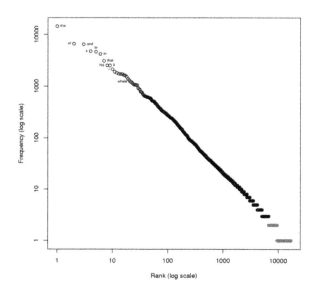

Figure 3.7 Frequency of hapax legomena in Herman Melville's *Moby Dick* (https://commons.wikimedia.org/wiki/File:Moby_Dick_Words.gif; public domain)

hapax legomena in Melville's *Moby Dick*. Perhaps surprisingly, 44% of all words in the novel only occur once; one example being *matrimonial*. The second line from the bottom (coloured blue in the original) marks words which occur twice in the book. As expected, the direct article (in the top-left corner) is the most frequent word in the book. Moving away from this first illustration, let us consider an example from a variety of English:

⇒ Intuitively, which of the following words would you expect to be hapax legomena in the ICE-New Zealand news files (consisting of 40,000 words): *welcome, speeches, odd, track, card, generally, handle, influence,* and *such*?

◊ The only words which are not hapax legomena in this list are *generally* (6 tokens), *track* (8 tokens), and *such* (29 tokens).

Hapaxes can be obtained in *AntConc* by using the word list function, which we already introduced above. You can scroll down in the word list and check all words which occurred only once in the corpus, but this function should be used very carefully: A word might have been spelled incorrectly or be a word-form of a lemma that is present more frequently. The word list for the abovementioned file will show you, for instance, that *recoveries* is only used once in the corpus. The word-form *recovery*, however, occurs four times in the corpus, which means that

Corpus-linguistic approaches to language 63

there are 5 tokens of this lemma in the file. Thus, once more, we stress the need to be thorough and careful in interpreting corpus findings.

Another aspect we should mention is that a careful treatment of corpus data is indispensable to obtain valuable and solid results. For the case of frequencies, there are numerous possibilities to follow examples of good practice. First and foremost, the interpretation of any results that you obtain should not be over-generalised: you can make statements about the corpus you work with and hypothesise about the larger population, but you should avoid making claims about, for instance, an entire variety based on the findings from one corpus. Furthermore, it is always a good idea to check how many people are respon-sible for a particular word or construction – in particular in a dialogic corpus. Idiolectal preferences, that is, preferences a speaker may have, can seriously distort the overall dataset. An example of this is given by Leech et al. (2001), who compared frequencies of the words *HIV*, *lively*, and *keeper* in the *British National Corpus* (BNC). The overall frequency of the words across 100 corpus files of the BNC is fairly similar.

⇒ Which word or words would you expect to be used in a higher number of different corpus files – *HIV* and/or *lively* and/or *keeper*?

◊ Clearly, *lively* and *keeper* occur in more corpus files than does *HIV*. Both *lively* and *keeper* are present in 97 out of 100 corpus files, while *HIV* is men-tioned in 62 out of 100 corpus files.

One way of dealing with this problem is by measuring the degree of **disper-sion**, which accounts for the potentially unequal distribution of an item. A simple example to illustrate the problem would be the overuse of a word by one speaker: If, in a corpus text, one speaker uses the word *collywobbles* 50 times but no other speaker does, its overall frequency in the corpus could still suggest that it is relatively frequent in a certain corpus and, by extension, a variety. There are various ways of measuring the degree of dispersion, but we recommend you focus on the three types of frequencies first before moving on to this measure. Simply counting in which files a feature is produced is already a good start and once you are familiar with these procedures, you may consider dispersion in more detail. A useful reference is the third section of Gries (2008), which offers a step-by-step explanation of how to calculate the degree of dispersion manually.

3.6 Collocations

In addition to assessing the frequency of a word, we may also be interested in the words that it occurs together with. Take, for example, the phrase *do your homework*. For German learners of English, a more intuitive translation would probably be *make your homework*, since a common and also more initially

64   Corpus-linguistic approaches to language

appealing translation of the German verb *machen* is *to make*. While *make your homework* can easily be understood, it would sound unidiomatic and probably mark the person who used this phrase as a non-native speaker. Studying these collocations or co-occurrences in World Englishes is a highly interesting endeavour. As David Crystal remarked, "[c]ollocations […] are likely to prove one of the most distinctive domains of varietal differentiation" (2003: 162).

You can examine collocations in *AntConc* by clicking on the *'Collocates'* tab in the interface. Here, you can enter the word or expression you are interested in and change a number of parameters. For instance, you can decide how many words to the left and right of your search term should be considered. Once you are done with your search, *AntConc* provides information on the overall number of co-occurrences of a word with your search term, frequency of occurrences to the left and to the right, and a probabilistic measure of association between the two words.

⇒ Open all files of ICE-Hong Kong in *AntConc* and click on the *'Collocates'* tab. How many words to the left and to the right would you choose to find out which verb *homework* co-occurs with? Once you found fitting parameters, conduct the analysis. What results do you get? Which verbs typically occur with *homework*?

3.7 Regular expressions

Having opened *AntConc*, you might have noticed that in addition to *'Words'* and *'Case'* you can also use *'Regex'* as a search term – this is short for **regular expression**. The complexity of what we look for in a corpus may vary quite drastically depending on our research question. Sometimes a word is enough, but we often look for more complex expressions. In other cases, looking only for a word would yield too many **false positives**, that is, hits that only superficially match what we were looking for. An incredibly helpful tool we may use to fine-tune our search term is a so-called regular expression: a search term enriched with limitations and specifications. These expressions have their own syntax, but understanding and mastering them will open up a vast field of possibilities to the researcher. In essence, we take a word or elements of a word and add symbols to it. These symbols can tell the software, for instance, to omit certain letters before or after a certain sequence.

For illustration, let us take a look at some examples, moving from simpler to more complex. In our example, we are interested in identifying different word-forms of *love* in IndE. This means that *love* would be fine and so would, for instance, *loves*, *loved*, and *loving*. What do you notice when you compare these examples? Indeed, some of them have an <e> in them, while one word does not.

A RegEx can help you deal with this problem. We use a question mark for optionality:

- RegEx: *love?*

The question mark in the RegEx tells *AntConc* that the last letter is optional; it can or cannot be there, but both cases should be shown to you. When you type in this RegEx and look for it in the spoken files of ICE-India, you should get 235 hits. The same result is yielded by typing in *lov.*, in which the dot acts as a sort of 'wildcard', that is, any letter or symbol may follow it. Scrolling through the concordances you received, you will notice that some unwanted words show up: *Czechoslovakia, beloved, gloveses*. These all contain the string *lov* but none of them matches what we were looking for. It is possible to get rid of all three of them with one simple addition to the RegEx, but there are different ways of approaching this to be on the safe side.

Examples like *Czechoslovakia* can be removed by aiming at the part that follows after *lov*. If you are sure that you know which elements may follow, you can specify which parts may stand after *lov* by using square brackets. The following RegEx is one way of retrieving only the forms *love, loves, loved, loving,* and *lovely*:

- RegEx: *love?[deil]*

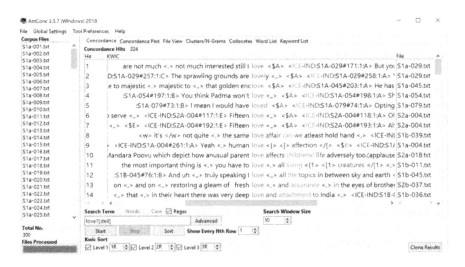

Figure 3.8 Example of a regular expression in *AntConc*

66 Corpus-linguistic approaches to language

What do we see in the RegEx? The question mark, as we know already, means that the *e* at the end of *love* is optional. The letters in the square brackets are those letters that may possibly follow after *lov* and *love* as completions of the potential word-forms (e.g. the *d* would follow in *loved*). The letter *e* is highly important in the square brackets and leaving it out would miss the base form *love* and significantly reduce the number of hits (although this may be just what you wanted). Having it in there means that *love, loves, loved, loving,* and *lovely* will all be found by the RegEx. The screenshot in Figure 3.8 shows you the RegEx typed into *AntConc* and the first concordance lines yielded as a result.

Now, the last step is to remove all examples in which other letters stand before *love*, such as *be-* in *beloved*. In order to do this, we use the boundary marker\b. This marker can be used at the beginning or the end of a RegEx and means that the RegEx only looks at the beginning or the end of a string, meaning that no other element will stand before it in this case.

- RegEx:*blove?[deils]*

After this step, only tokens relevant for your search should be shown in *AntConc*. Playing around with a RegEx and trying out different combinations is going to yield the best results, since their form is dependent on the results you would like to get. In order to create a meaningful RegEx for your own study, it is helpful to read through the set of symbols that can be added. You can browse tutorials and overviews such as the one provided by the University of Lancaster (http://corpora.lancs.ac.uk/clmtp/index.php) or *linguisticsweb* (www.linguisticsweb.org/doku.php?id=start) as well as RegEx 'cheat sheets' in order to gain a better understanding.

3.8 Statistics and significance testing

After identifying the frequencies of a feature and discussing some interesting examples, you may feel that you are finished with your corpus study. However, comparing frequencies of a feature in different corpora or text types and assessing which variables have an impact on a feature is a sophisticated next step. Thus, the last aspects we will touch upon in this chapter are statistics and significance testing. Despite its importance, we will only cover some essentials of statistics in this chapter and refer you to in-depth quality resources you can use to improve in this area on your own at the end of the chapter.

First, we need to clarify what statistics is and what it can do for you. A common distinction is between **descriptive statistics** and **inferential statistics**. Descriptive statistics, as the name suggests, seeks to offer a description and summary of the data as well as some first relations that can be found in a dataset. We may, for instance, be interested in how often certain age groups produce a certain feature in a corpus. If we visualise all frequencies for each of these age groups and find that it is much more present in speakers below the age of 20, we would have an example of descriptive statistics. We

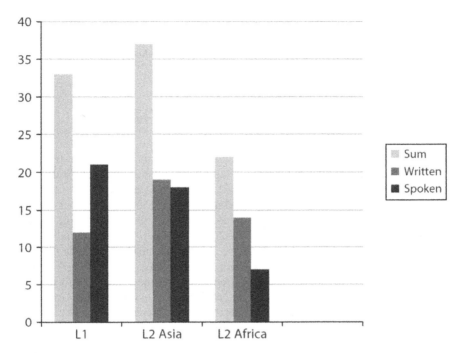

Figure 3.9 Creative word-formation in spoken and written first-language (L1) and second-language (L2) varieties (Biermeier 2014: 329; reprinted by permission from John Benjamins)

considered a simple relation between two variables, age group and a linguistic feature, and used visualisation to identify if there are any noteworthy tendencies. It should be noted that, in this example, it would be quite important to be aware of how many speakers there are in each age group. The most common visualisation is the bar plot, an example of which is given in Figure 3.9.

In Figure 3.9, Biermeier compares the amount of creative word-formations in spoken and written first-language and second-language varieties in Africa and Asia. Bar plots offer the advantage of being easy to read and understandable. A possible downside to them is that they can oversimplify matters and present incomplete pictures: We cannot gather, for instance, how many tokens or features were considered in Figure 3.9 without reading the accompanying text. As a consequence, you need to be cautious when working with bar plots and other visualisations both as an author and as a reader.

In contrast to descriptive statistics, inferential statistics seeks to provide statements about a larger **population** based on a (random) **sample**. A corpus cannot be fully representative and therefore always only gives us a sample. We

68   Corpus-linguistic approaches to language

Table 3.2 Frequency of *dicit* and *dixit* in the Gospel of Matthew and the Gospel of John

	Frequency of dicit	*Frequency of* dixit
Matthew	46	107
John	118	119

(www.lancaster.ac.uk/fss/courses/ling/corpus/Corpus3/3SIG.HTM)

might still be able to make assumptions about the population at large by using the methods of inferential statistics. A relatively straightforward statistical test is the **chi-squared test**. In simplest terms, this test can tell us whether there is a significant difference between expected and observed frequencies. Significant commonly means that "there is a 95% chance that our result is *not* a coincidence" (McEnery & Hardie 2012: 51; emphasis in the original). This difference is expressed in the **p-value**. An easy-to-understand example is given by the University of Lancaster (www.lancaster.ac.uk/fss/courses/ling/corpus/ Corpus3/3SIG.HTM). Comparing the frequencies of the Latin verb forms *dicit* (present form of 'to say') and *dixit* (perfect form of 'to say') in the Gospel of Matthew and the Gospel of John, we get the results shown in Table 3.2.

Even without doing any statistics, it seems as if *dicit* occurs significantly more frequently in the Gospel of John. Still, we are interested in finding out if this is statistically accurate and, therefore, perform a chi-squared test. Note that this test comes with numerous pitfalls and caveats: not all kind of data work well with the test, which is why it is usually a good idea to consult relevant literature and to talk to a statistician in order to select the right test for your data. That being said, the data in the example illustrate well the appropriate kind of data. Although there are different ways of performing a chi-squared test, using an online tool is perhaps easiest.

⇒ Open www.socscistatistics.com/tests/chisquare/default2.aspx, type in the data from Table 3.2 into this calculator, and perform the test. Which results do you get? What does the website tell you about the significance of the difference?

◊ The website should tell you that the chi-squared value is around 14.84 and that the p-value is lower than 0.005. This means that the observed differences in the usage of *dicit* and *dixit* are highly significant and that they are not due to chance. Commonly, a 0.05 value is considered sufficient to call the difference 'significant'.

World Englishes research offers both qualitative and quantitative studies, but quantitative and, specifically, statistical methods have become quite important in present-day linguistics. Thus, numerous sophisticated tools and visualisations have been developed and become popular. For this introduction, delving deeper into them is beyond what we are trying to achieve. However, we offer some suggestions for further reading at the end of this chapter and suggest that you consider both actual studies and textbooks on statistics. Important software for doing corpus linguistics, statistics, and data visualisation is *R*, which can be accessed at www.r-project.org/. *R* is a programming language and can also be downloaded as *R Studio*, which offers a more complex interface. We cannot offer an introduction to *R* here, but we list some practical introductions and textbooks in Section 3.11.

3.9 Summary

This chapter introduced you to the essentials of doing corpus linguistics. We focused on working with *AntConc* and *WordSmith* as well as important aspects of corpus design. We also showed you how data can be analysed. In particular, however, we hope that this chapter was able to take away some of the fear of working with a corpus. There are a vast amount of tools, books, and websites that help you develop and work on your corpus-linguistic research project. In Chapter 4, we build upon the insights from this chapter and give you more concrete examples of corpora and how to work with them.

3.10 Exercises

*Exercise 3.1

(a)   Count the types and the tokens in the following sentences:

(3.6) *Many years have passed since the unification of Germany.*

(3.7) *A child may play with a bow, but it shouldn't play with a bow.*

(b)   Which semantic phenomenon proves problematic in example (3.7)? What can we do to deal with such examples in a corpus analysis?

(c)   Consider the famous sentence *Buffalo buffalo Buffalo buffalo buffalo buffalo Buffalo buffalo*. Can you disentangle its meaning? Read up on the sentence in order to understand its structure. Why is this sentence a challenge in a corpus analysis?

Exercise 3.2

Preparation

Download and familiarise yourself with Anthony's *TagAnt* (2015), which is used for POS-tagging of corpus texts. Download the tool at www.laurenceanthony. net/software/tagant/and read about the annotation system at www.cis.uni-muenchen.de/~schmid/tools/TreeTagger/data/Penn-Treebank-Tagset.pdf (Santorini 1991).

70 Corpus-linguistic approaches to language

Table 3.3 Data for adverbs formed with and without -*ly*

	Adverbs formed with -ly	Adverbs with omitted -ly
Corpus 1 (C1)	27	195
Corpus 2 (C2)	68	112

(a) Manually apply the Penn Treebank Tagset to the short sentences in (3.8) and (3.9):

(3.8) *We saw the cat in our bedroom.*

(3.9) *He's never really been here with us.*

(b) Use *TagAnt* to apply POS-tagging to *Comma Gets A Cure* and search for all articles. What would you have to type into *AntConc* to do this? Do the frequencies you get as a result match the frequencies indicated by the word list function for the unannotated file in *AntConc*?

*Exercise 3.3

Preparation

Consider the data in Table 3.3. The table shows the absolute frequency of adverbs formed with -*ly*, such as *happily*, and adverbs which would typically be formed with -*ly* but for which the speaker did not attach this ending. The data have been gathered for two corpora. Corpus 1 contains 9,568 words and Corpus 2 contains 8,349 words.

(a) Calculate the normalised frequencies per 10,000 words of adverbs formed with and without -*ly* in the two corpora.
(b) Calculate the statistical significance for the difference between the two corpora using the chi-squared test.

3.11 Recommended reading

Corpus linguistics

McEnery and Hardie (2012), published as part of the *Cambridge Textbooks in Linguistics* series, has become a standard reference in corpus linguistics. It is not designed as a general introduction but instead the book's aim is "to introduce, explain and in some cases problematise the most fundamental conceptual issues underlying the use of corpora, as well as reviewing what we see as the major trends of research using corpora to date" (2012: xiii). Thus, this book is ideally consulted in addition to a more general introduction such as Meyer (2002), but it is of use for any researcher interested in corpus linguistics. Although many advances have been made in the field, Biber et al. (1998) remains an important source in corpus linguistics. O'Keeffe and McCarthy (2010), an edited collection, features 45 contributions covering the basics of corpus linguistics and applications of corpus linguistics in areas such as language teaching, the study of political discourse, and translation. Not all parts of this book will be immediately accessible to a beginner, but Sections 1 to 4 feature mostly excellent, easy-to-read overviews of important basics in corpus linguistics.

Relevant book series on corpus linguistics, some of them specifically with a World Englishes focus, are the *Varieties of English around the World* (VEAW) series by John Benjamins, and *Language and Computers* published by Brill Rodopi. Journals with a focus on (English) corpus linguistics are *Corpora* (Edinburgh University Press), *Corpus Linguistics and Linguistic Theory* (de Gruyter), *ICAME Journal* (Open Access; available online via https://content. sciendo.com/view/journals/icame/icame-overview.xml), and the *International Journal of Corpus Linguistics* (John Benjamins). These journals publish studies on World Englishes, but they also cover other areas. Journals with a focus on World Englishes are *English World-Wide* (John Benjamins) and *World Englishes* (Wiley). These journals, in turn, include corpus-linguistic studies, but they also accept studies using other methods and data. Please note that all of the listed journals publish high-quality original research, which is why not all articles will be accessible without solid background knowledge. Nevertheless, even for a beginner, getting an idea of the kind of research accepted in these journals can help with designing a corpus and a corpus-based or corpus-driven study.

Statistics and R

There are many books on statistics and working with R written specifically with linguists in mind. Many of them have in common that they require (at times extensive) background knowledge, which is why we would recommend working with these only if you have become familiar with the basics of corpus linguistics and the topic of your study. A good way to get started is to download the interface of R and read the information provided on www.r-project. org/. Once you have a basic idea of how R works, you may consult Gries (2013) and Levshina (2015), two excellent resources providing practical introductions for linguists interested in working with R. Another great but also relatively demanding source is Desagulier (2017); several online tutorials exist as well.

72 Corpus-linguistic approaches to language

References

Biber, Douglas & Susan Conrad (2009). *Register, Genre, and Style.* Cambridge: Cambridge University Press.

Biber, Douglas, Susan Conrad, & Randi Reppen (1998). *Corpus Linguistics: Investigating Language Structure and Use.* Cambridge: Cambridge University Press.

Biermeier, Thomas (2014). "Compounding and suffixation in World Englishes." In Buschfeld, Sarah, Thomas Hoffmann, Magnus Huber, & Alexander Kautzsch (eds.), *The Evolution of Englishes. The Dynamic Model and Beyond.* Amsterdam: John Benjamins, 312–330. doi: 10.1075/veaw.g49.18bie.

Crystal, David (2003). *English as a Global Language.* Second edition. Cambridge: Cambridge University Press.

Culpeper, Jonathan & Merja Kytö (2010). *Early Modern English Dialogues: Spoken Interaction as Writing.* Cambridge: Cambridge University Press.

Desagulier, Guillaume (2017). *Corpus Linguistics and Statistics with R. Introduction to Quantitative Methods in Linguistics.* Cham: Springer.

Durand, Jacques, Ulrike Gut, & Gjert Kristoffersen (eds.) (2014). *The Oxford Handbook of Corpus Phonology.* Oxford: Oxford University Press.

Fuchs, Robert (2016). *Speech Rhythm in Varieties of English: Evidence from Educated Indian English and British English.* Singapore: Springer.

Gries, Stefan Th. (2008). "Dispersions and adjusted frequencies in corpora." *International Journal of Corpus Linguistics* 13(4): 403–437. doi: 10.1075/ijcl.13.4.02gri.

Gries, Stefan Th. (2013). *Statistics for Linguistics with R. A Practical Introduction.* Berlin: de Gruyter.

Hardie, Andrew (2012). "CQPweb – combining power, flexibility and usability in a corpus analysis tool." *International Journal of Corpus Linguistics* 17(3): 380–409. doi: 10.1075/ijcl.17.3.04har.

Honorof, Douglas N., Jill McCullough, & Barbara Somerville (2000). "Comma gets a cure." URL: www.dialectsarchive.com/comma-gets-a-cure. (Last access: 28 February 2019).

Hundt, Marianne (2008). "Text corpora." In Lüdeling, Anke & Merja Kytö (eds.), *Corpus Linguistics: An International Handbook.* Berlin: de Gruyter, 168–187.

Kennedy, Graeme (1998). *An Introduction to Corpus Linguistics.* London: Longman.

Koch, Peter & Wulf Oesterreicher (1985/2012). "Language of immediacy – language of distance: Orality and literacy from the perspective of language theory and linguistic history." In Lange, Claudia, Beatrix Weber, & Göran Wolf (eds.), *Communicative Spaces: Variation, Contact, and Change. Papers in Honour of Ursula Schaefer.* Frankfurt: Lang, 441–473. doi: 10.15496/publikation-20415.

Labov, William (1972). *Sociolinguistic Patterns.* Philadelphia, PA: University of Pennsylvania Press.

Leech, Geoffrey, Paul Rayson, & Andrew Wilson (2001). *Word Frequencies in Written and Spoken English Based on the British National Corpus.* London: Longman.

Levshina, Natalia (2015). *How to Do Linguistics with R. Data Exploration and Statistical Analysis.* Amsterdam: John Benjamins.

McEnery, Tony & Andrew Hardie (2012). *Corpus Linguistics: Method, Theory and Practice.* Cambridge: Cambridge University Press.

McEnery, Tony & Andrew Wilson (2001). *Corpus Linguistics: An Introduction.* Second edition. Edinburgh: Edinburgh University Press.

Meyer, Charles F. (2002). *English Corpus Linguistics: An Introduction.* Cambridge: Cambridge University Press.

Meyer, Charles F. (2014). "Corpus-based and corpus-driven approaches to linguistic analysis: One and the same?" In Taavitsainen, Irma, Merja Kytö, Claudia Claridge, & Jeremy Smith (eds.), *Developments in English. Expanding Electronic Evidence.* Cambridge: Cambridge University Press, 14–28. doi: 10.1017/CBO9781139833882.004.

O'Keeffe, Anne & Michael McCarthy (eds.) (2010). *The Routledge Handbook of Corpus Linguistics.* London: Routledge.

Rüdiger, Sofia (2016). "Cuppa coffee? Challenges and opportunities of compiling a conversational English corpus in an Expanding Circle setting." In Christ, Hanna, Daniel Klenovšak, Lukas Sönning, & Valentin Werner (eds.), *A Blend of MaLT. Selected Contributions from the Methods and Linguistic Theories Symposium 2015.* Bamberg: University of Bamberg Press, 49–72.

Santorini, Beatrice (1991). "Part-of-speech tagging guidelines for the Penn Treebank Project." URL: www.cis.uni-muenchen.de/~schmid/tools/TreeTagger/data/Penn-Treebank-Tagset.pdf. (Last access: 3 March 2019).

Taavitsainen, Irma (2001). "Changing conventions of writing: The dynamics of genres, text types, and text traditions." *European Journal of English Studies* 5(2): 139–150. doi: 10.1076/ejes.5.2.139.7309.

Tognini-Bonelli, Elena (2001). *Corpus Linguistics at Work.* Amsterdam: John Benjamins.

Wiechmann, Anne (2008). "Speech corpora and spoken corpora." In Lüdeling, Anke & Merja Kytö (eds.), *Corpus Linguistics. An International Handbook.* Berlin: de Gruyter, 187–207.

Chapter 4

Corpora and World Englishes

Key terms:

Assessing corpora:
big data and small data; monitor corpora

Tools for building and analysing corpora:
BeautifulSoup; CLAWS Tagset; *Notepad++*; parsing; *Python*; *Sketch Engine*; spider; web crawling

Some important corpora for World Englishes research:
Brown family of corpora; *Corpus of Contemporary American English* (COCA); *Corpus of Historical American English* (COHA); *International Corpus of English* (ICE); *Global Web-based Corpus of English* (GloWbE)

4.1 Introduction: does size matter?

Choosing a corpus

You have a research question, you know the essentials of your topic, you are familiar with corpus linguistics, you are ready to go – but which corpus or corpora do you choose for your project? This problem is far from trivial, since there are hundreds of corpora freely available today, and countless more can be created for a specific purpose. Unfortunately, there is no one way to address this particular problem. Different corpora are useful for different studies and there is no corpus that perfectly fits every purpose. Critically assessing which corpus is right for you and your project is an essential step. What exactly constitutes the right corpus depends on a number of factors, such as:

Corpora and World Englishes   75

(1) your research question,
(2) the specific linguistic feature(s) you are interested in,
(3) the availability of a corpus and an accompanying manual,
(4) the quality of the transcription, annotation, metadata, etc.

When answering these questions, it is of the utmost importance to keep in mind that "[a] corpus (no matter how large) should never be regarded as a magic box which is able to provide fast and ready-made answers to any sociolinguistic questions we chose to ask" (Brezina & Meyerhoff 2014: 23). Brezina & Meyerhoff clearly have a sociolinguistic focus in mind, but their statement certainly extends to other linguistic research areas; corpora are an incredible tool for expanding our knowledge about language, but they cannot and should not be treated as the final answer to all questions asked in linguistics. Trying to capture linguistic variation in its entirety is like trying to catch lightning in a bottle; we can only ever collect bits and pieces in order to get an idea of language that is as comprehensive as possible.

In order to help you with your decision on a corpus, we introduce and discuss a selection of World Englishes corpora in this chapter. These corpora were not selected at random. Rather, they represent corpora that historically informed the corpus-linguistic study of varieties of English and have had a major impact on the field. We cannot realistically cover all World Englishes corpora, nor would this be a useful endeavour. Instead, we provide a detailed assessment of certain corpora in order for you to be able to assess not only these but also other data sources.

Small data and big data: what's the difference?

A general distinction to consider in any case is the one between **small data** and **big data**. There is no 'official' word count that would automatically qualify a dataset as belonging to one or the other. Generally, the word count of a corpus needs to be considered in context of the research question and in comparison to other corpora. Traditional corpora of 1 million words are now considered rather small, while a corpus of more than 50 million words is already quite big (although, as you will see later in this chapter, corpora of more than a billion words exist now as well). Clearly, the success story of the World Wide Web plays a big role in present-day linguistics, since gigantic amounts of text are uploaded to the internet every single day. However, as we show and discuss in this chapter, having access to a large amount of data does not equal that the data should be used or are adequate in every situation.

An advantage that comes with smaller corpora is that, more often than not, they are released with a lot of additional information. The reason for this is that a smaller dataset can be handled easier by one or more researchers and less overhead accumulates in their production: Relatively time-consuming tasks such as gathering detailed information about included speakers or authors can be carried out and adding metadata and annotation is a more realistic option. For very big corpora, the labour that would be involved in considering every single text individually is too demanding, which means that, unfortunately, some detail might be lost. This does not mean that big corpora are a terrible choice to work with in general or that every small corpus has been handled with sufficient care by its creators, but these are general points that should be considered.

As we mentioned in previous chapters, one of the major goals in the creation of World Englishes corpora is a high degree of representativeness. We are often interested in maximally balanced corpora which account for differences between spoken and written language, differences related to sociolinguistic variables, differences between text types and registers, and so forth. A corpus may not be an excellent source with regard to all of these criteria, but some certainly do a better job at being representative than others. Furthermore, some corpora are indeed created for a very specific purpose, which is why they might be less suited for others. For an illustration of some advantages and disadvantages of working with a bigger corpus, we refer you to Section 4.4 of this chapter.

What this chapter has to offer

In the following sections, we present and discuss the **Brown family of corpora**, the ***International Corpus of English*** (ICE), and the ***Global Web-based Corpus of English*** (GloWbE). For all of the corpora we discuss individually, we provide background on their structure and design, how to access them, their annotation and available metadata, as well as some advantages and disadvantages. At the end of this chapter, we will also discuss the option of building your own corpus and give you the basics of how to do that. For all the sections, we include shorter hands-on tasks in the running text, with more complex exercises as well as recommended literature at the end of the chapter. Please note that, like in the previous chapter, some in-text exercises require ICE-Hong Kong. If you wish to work with this chapter without the corpus, you can refer to the in-text answer.

4.2 The 'Brown family' of corpora

The first group of corpora we will consider in this chapter is the 'Brown family' of corpora. The term 'family' is used here because the first of these corpora, the *Brown University Standard Corpus of Present-Day Edited American English*, served as the model corpus for numerous follow-up corpora. Compiled by W. Nelson Francis and Henry Kučera in the 1960s, the original Brown corpus is a collection of (written) texts in American English (AmE) published in 1961. Some corpora modelled after Brown are the *Lancaster-Oslo/Bergen Corpus* (LOB), the *Kolhapur Corpus of Indian English*, the *Australian Corpus of English* (ACE), the

Corpora and World Englishes   77

Table 4.1 Overview of corpora included in the 'Brown family'

Corpus	Featured Variety	Year of Publication of Texts in the Corpus
Corpora Covering American English		
Brown Brown University Standard Corpus of Present-Day Edited American English	Written American English	1961
Frown Freiburg-Brown Corpus of American English	Written American English	1992
Corpora Covering British English		
LOB Lancaster-Oslo/Bergen Corpus	Written British English	1961
FLOB Freiburg-LOB Corpus of British English	Written British English	1991
Further Corpora Modelled after the Brown Corpus		
Kolhapur Corpus of Indian English	Written Indian English	1978
ACE The Australian Corpus of English	Written Australian English	1986

Freiburg-Brown Corpus of American English (FROWN), and the *Freiburg-LOB Corpus of British English* (F-LOB). Table 4.1 gathers the varieties covered by the different corpora as well as the publication dates of the texts featured in them.

In addition to these corpora, a series of new corpora looking back even further in time have been created or are currently in preparation. Two major examples are the 1930s BROWN Corpus (B-Brown, sampling texts from 1928–34) and the BLOB-1931 Corpus. However, as of early 2019, these two corpora are not yet available to the wider research community.

Structure and design

Each of the corpora listed in Table 4.1 features roughly 1 million words, split into 500 text samples of ca. 2000 words each. As mentioned before, the Brown corpora represent written English and do not include any spoken language. The corpora are divided into a section containing 'Informative Prose' (374 samples in Brown) and one containing 'Imaginative Prose' (126 samples in Brown). The former covers text types such as press texts and texts related to skills and hobbies, while the latter contains texts on areas such as Science Fiction, Adventure, and Western Fiction. An overview of the text types featured in the Brown corpus and the corpora built after Brown's model is given in Table 4.2.

78 Corpora and World Englishes

Table 4.2 Text types included in the Brown corpus

	Genre Group	Category	Content of Category	No. of Texts in Brown
I. Informative Prose (374)	Press (88)	A	Reportage	44
		B	Editorial	27
		C	Review	17
	General Prose (206)	D	Religion	17
		E	Skills, trades and hobbies	36
		F	Popular lore	48
		G	Belles lettres, biographies, essays	75
		H	Miscellaneous	30
	Learned (80)	J	Science	80
II. Imaginative Prose (126)	Fiction (126)	K	General fiction	29
		L	Mystery and detective Fiction	24
		M	Science fiction	6
		N	Adventure and Western	29
		P	Romance and love story	29
		R	Humor	9
Total				**500**

(adapted from www.helsinki.fi/varieng/CoRD/corpora/BROWN/basic.html)

The exact number of texts can vary slightly in corpora included in the Brown family, but the model is generally adhered to.

Accessing the corpora

There are different ways of accessing the Brown corpus and related corpora. A very convenient way of accessing the original Brown corpus is using the web tool **Sketch Engine** (https://app.sketchengine.eu/#dashboard?corpname=pre loaded/brown_1). Several functions of the website, such as creating word lists and concordances, can be accessed without having to register. A function provided by *Sketch Engine* going beyond the functions typically included in concordance software is the 'Word Sketch Difference'. This function, according to the website, "is an extension of the word sketch. It generates Word Sketches for two words and compares them making it a breeze to observe differences in use. The feature is especially useful for close synonyms, antonyms and words from the same semantic field" (www.sketchengine.eu/quick-start-guide/word-sketch-difference-lesson/). On the site, this function is visualised with two fisheye symbols. You can see what the interface of *Sketch Engine* looks like in Figure 4.1.

⇒ Open the Brown corpus in *Sketch Engine* and click on the tab for the 'Word Sketch Difference' function. Search for *quick* and *fast* as lemmas: What kind of result does *Sketch Engine* show you? How would you interpret the results in the column 'modifies'?

◊ At the top of the screen, the absolute frequencies of the two lemmas are provided: 70 tokens of *quick* and 36 tokens of *fast*. Numerous tables then provide more detailed information, for instance on the words that modify these words and words which are modified *by* them. The 'modifies' column tells us which words co-occur with *quick* and *fast* and how often they do so: We can see, for example, that *succession* occurs twice with *quick*, while *growth* occurs twice with *fast*.

The second way to access the Brown corpus itself as well as corpora from the extended family is by using *CQPweb*, which we introduced in the previous

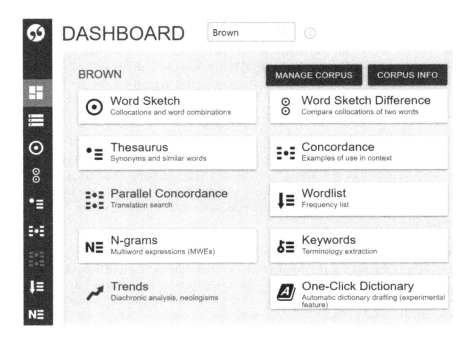

Figure 4.1 Functions of *Sketch Engine*

80 Corpora and World Englishes

chapter. All corpora which are part of the extended family can be accessed via this website, which also allows for more sophisticated searches than *Sketch Engine*.

Mark-up, annotation, and metadata

Accessing Brown or the Brown extended family via *CQPweb* has the distinct advantage of allowing much more complex searches and making use of additional annotation. Normalised frequencies of words are also indicated at the top of each search request, as we noted in Chapter 3. *CQPweb* allows for searches using the *CQPweb* syntax as well as POS tags. We might, for instance, be interested in usages of *quick* and *fast* as adverbs in Brown: It is well known that adverbs typically ending in *-ly* are sometimes used without this suffix in American varieties of English, which is why a search in older data could be insightful. Furthermore, Brown exclusively features written data. This makes the investigation quite interesting, since non-standard forms such as *quick* used as an adverb seem much more likely in spontaneous, informal speech. The tools we need for our little corpus study are the *CQPweb* interface as well as information on how adverbs have been tagged in the corpus. We can do that by taking a look at the so-called 'CLAWS' tagset, which is commonly used for the POS annotation of corpora.

⇒ Visit http://ucrel.lancs.ac.uk/claws7tags.html. Go through the list of tags and identify which tag would probably mark the usage of *quick* and *fast* as adverbs. Try the alternatives you identified in *CQPweb* by typing in 'quick_TAG' and 'fast_TAG', with TAG representing the tag you found on the website. Write down your expectations with regard to the frequencies and then compare which of the two words occurs more frequently as an adverb in the corpus.

◊ The only tag that should yield any results is 'RR', indicating 'general adverbs': *Quick* is used as an adverb only three times in the corpus, whereas *fast* is used 54 times in this function. This outcome confirms expectations, since *quickly* is the more common adverb corresponding to the adjective *quick*. A corpus search of *quickly* substantiates this assumption, since it occurs 89 times in the Brown corpus.

As the example task shows, using *CQPweb* to access the Brown corpora provides flexibility in the kind of study that can be carried out. Furthermore, comparisons between the different Brown components are easily possible. In terms of metadata, the Brown corpora do not provide a lot of additional information; for instance, the authors of the texts are not included.

Advantages and disadvantages

A major advantage of using the Brown family of corpora probably becomes evident just by looking at the tables featured in this section: in terms of general aim and size, the corpora included in the Brown family are structured very similarly, making them easily comparable. Due to the fact that updated versions exist for the American and British versions, diachronic studies chronicling change in written forms of these varieties are possible. The diachronic dimension of the original Brown corpus is potentially its most attractive feature now, since no studies of recent English are possible anymore using the corpus.

An aspect that comes with its own positives and negatives is the size of the Brown corpus and corpora created following its model. The clearest 'competing' corpora for AmE are the *Corpus of Contemporary American English* (COCA), published in 2008 (Davies 2009), and the *Corpus of Historical American English* (COHA) (Davies 2012). COCA, which has been enriched with more data since its publication, features more than 560 million words as of 2019 and also has sections containing spoken language. COHA, in turn, contains more than 400 million words and spans a timeframe roughly from the 1810s to the 2000s. These two corpora are obviously much bigger in size and may be preferable for numerous tasks. However, at the same time, the Brown corpora give you as a user a lot more control: reading larger segments of the corpora is possible and qualitative investigations can be carried out more easily. Thus, familiarity with the corpus and its contents is warranted. Furthermore, smaller corpora entail faster data processing. Finally, manually checking results yielded by a corpus search is much easier with a smaller corpus. Once again, whether you should choose one corpus over another depends largely on your research question and the design of your study.

–Takeaway Note–

The Brown corpus was the first 'big' digital corpus of written American English and has had enormous impact on the field of corpus linguistics. From a modern perspective, it is relatively small, but its strength lies in the comparability to its many follow-up corpora – the 'Brown extended family of corpora'.

4.3 The International Corpus of English (ICE)

The publication of the first component of ICE, which we already referenced in earlier chapters, represents another milestone in the history of World Englishes corpora. Initiated by Greenbaum in 1990 and then made widely known by Greenbaum (1996), the ICE corpora still represent essential resources for World Englishes researchers. A major advantage offered by these corpora is

Table 4.3 Structure of the ICE corpora (adapted from www.ice-corpora.uzh.ch/en/design.html)

Spoken (300)	**Dialogues (180)**	**Private (100)**	**S1A** **Face-to-Face Conversations (90)** **Phone Calls (10)**
		Public (80)	**S1B** Classroom Lessons (20) Broadcast Discussions (20) Broadcast Interviews (10) Parliamentary Debates (10) Legal Cross-Examinations (10) Business Transactions (10)
	Mono-logues (120)	**Unscripted** (70)	**S2A** Spontaneous Commentaries (20) Unscripted Speeches (30) Demonstrations (10) Legal Presentations (10)
		Scripted (50)	**S2B** Broadcast News (20) Broadcast Talks (20) Non-Broadcast Talks (10)
Written (200)	**Non-printed** (50)	**Student Writing (20)**	**W1A** Student Essays (10) Exam Scripts (10)
		Letters (30)	**W1B** Social Letters (15) Business Letters (15)
	Printed (150)	**Academic Writing (40)**	**W2A** Humanities (10) Social Sciences (10) Natural Sciences (10) Technology (10)
		Popular Writing (40)	**W2B** Humanities (10) Social Sciences (10) Natural Sciences (10) Technology (10)
		Reportage (20)	**W2C** Press News Reports (20)
		Instructional Writing (20)	**W2D** Administrative Writing (10) Skills/Hobbies (10)
		Persuasive Writing (10)	**W2E** Press Editorials (10)
		Creative Writing (20)	**W2F** Novels & Short Stories (20)

Corpora and World Englishes 83

their inclusion of spoken and written sections and their comparable design: each ICE corpus contains roughly 1 million words and is structured identically to the other ICE corpora. This means that comparisons across different varieties of English are easily possible. In this chapter, we introduce ICE by presenting its overall design and structure, how to access it, and some of the advantages and disadvantages of working with it.

Structure and design

We generally refer to the country-specific ICE sections as 'components' (or 'subcorpora'). Thus, ICE-India would be an ICE component, and so would ICE-Great Britain. Each ICE component contains 500 texts, with 300 of these in the spoken part and 200 in the written part. All texts are supposed to be roughly 2,000 words in length, although the exact number may vary slightly from corpus to corpus. Speakers included in ICE should be 18 years of age or older and have experienced English-medium education. Exceptions are acceptable when the inclusion of a speaker seems warranted without applying these criteria: a famous example is Queen Elizabeth II., who, having been home-schooled, does not fit the criteria for being included in ICE, but is certainly worthy of being an exception to the rule. The model structure of ICE components in terms of the included text types is illustrated in Table 4.3, which also indicates how many texts are featured in each section.

As Table 4.3 shows, there are more spoken texts included in the corpus than written texts. This distribution certainly reflects the desire of World Englishes scholars to work with authentic speech material. It is important to stress that working with the same text type across different corpora does not guarantee that these are similar in all respects. The direct conversations and phone calls, for instance, are generally designed to be free, undirected conversations amongst peers. However, consider the example from ICE-Philippines in (4.1):

(4.1) *A:* Uhm good afternoon Sir uhm
    B: Good afternoon
    A: So Sir how are you
    B: I'm fine I'm I'm okay (ICE-PHI:S1A-093#4–7)

⇒ Which problem can you see with this example, bearing in mind that the private dialogues are supposed to contain undirected, free speech?

◊ You probably notice that one of the interlocutors addresses the other person as *Sir*, which suggests an unequal relationship. Although the conversation that follows is friendly, it seems unlikely that either of the two speakers talks the same way they would with a close friend.

84 Corpora and World Englishes

The issue of unequal relationships in this particular corpus component has been noted in the release notes of ICE-Philippines:

> There were technical difficulties in taping from the phone, even with a gadget for the purpose, and friends who were asked to tape their distanced conversations balked at the suggestion. Finally, graduate students were tapped to collect phone conversations as a requirement for their graduate class. The interlocutors in these conversations include nine males and 11 females, with seven dyads made up of friends and three dyads made up of students talking to their teachers.
>
> (Bautista 2004: 12)

What the example in (4.1) and the quote from Bautista (2004) show us is that, despite all efforts, sometimes corpus compilers have to take routes that they could not anticipate. Thus, it is always recommendable to read the release notes to a corpus and have a look at the metadata (discussed a little further below), if any are available. If, in this specific case, you use the phone calls from several corpora and compare them without having a critical look at them, you would get results from data that are not truly similar in terms of how they were collected. Comparisons between ICE components are, however, generally possible and the ever-growing number of available ICE corpora certainly invites cross-corpus investigation. Table 4.4 provides an overview of available and in-preparation ICE corpora.

Table 4.4 Available ICE components and ICE components currently being compiled (as of June 2019)

Available ICE Corpora	ICE Corpora in Preparation
Canada	Bahamas
East Africa	Fiji
Great Britain	Ghana
Hong Kong	Malaysia
India	Malta
Ireland & SPICE Ireland	Namibia
Jamaica	Pakistan
New Zealand	South Africa
Nigeria (written)	Sri Lanka (spoken)
The Philippines	Trinidad and Tobago
Singapore	Uganda
Sri Lanka (written)	
USA (written)	

Corpora and World Englishes   85

In addition to the components in compilation right now, there are corpora which have been or are currently created after the model of ICE. These include historical corpora of World Englishes as well as corpora for Learner Englishes. We will address some of these in Chapter 8 in a section dealing specifically with the creation of new corpora.

Accessing the corpora

Currently, the ICE corpora are hosted by the University of Zurich (www. ice-corpora.uzh.ch/en.html). In order to get access to the corpora, a licence is required. Note that many linguistic institutes already have acquired the necessary rights to work with the corpora, so that you would not need to fill in these documents – at any rate, it makes sense to double-check with your supervisor or colleagues. If the licences have not been obtained, you need to fill in the document at www.ice-corpora.uzh.ch/en/access.html. This licence works for most of the ICE components; different procedures apply for ICE-Great Britain, ICE-New Zealand, ICE-Sri Lanka, and ICE-Nigeria.

After obtaining the licence and downloading the corpora, the concordance software introduced in Chapter 3, such as *AntConc* or *WordSmith*, can be used to work with the ICE components. Since the corpus texts come in TXT format, any general text editor may also be used to open them. Many options are available here, but **Notepad++** (https://notepad-plus-plus.org/) has become the customary word processor for many linguists. Using word-processing software in addition to tools such as *AntConc* may be useful if you wish to remove unnecessary tags in the annotation, for instance tags marking pauses (see the next section for more information). *Notepad++* also offers many practical functions, such as the use of colour-coding for different text elements.

We should note that the development of a digital ICE platform is in the works as of 2019 – it is worth checking the website from time to time for the release of ICE-online.

Mark-up, annotation, and metadata

There are two mark-up manuals documenting the conventions for in-text annotation of information, one for the spoken and one for the written sections. Both can be downloaded via www.ice-corpora.uzh.ch/en/manuals.html. The following sections address the spoken components first and then the written components, with some background on metadata in ICE following at the end. It should be noted right away that not all mark-up symbols are used in every ICE corpus: The manuals provide a list of essential, recommended, and optional mark-up as a guideline for teams compiling ICE components.

Table 4.5 Mark-up symbols used in the spoken sections of the ICE corpora (adapted from the ICE manual available at https://www.ice-corpora.uzh.ch/en/manuals.html)

Larger Category	Mark-Up Tag	Meaning / Function	Brief Explanation
Corpus Structure	<$A>, <$B>, ...	Speaker tag	Identifies speaker (see metadata below)
	<X>...</X>	Extra-corpus text	Marks text produced by non-corpus speakers
	<&>...</&>	Editorial comment	Additional comments not captured by other tags
	<I>...</I>	Subtext marker	Marks cases in which different texts are part of the same file
	<#>	Text unit marker	Indicates the part of the corpus
	<O>...</O>	Untranscribed text	Used to mark coughing, sneezing, etc.
	<?>...</?>	Uncertain transcription	Indicates uncertainty in transcription, but is based on a good guess
Word Structure	<@>...</@>	Changed name or word	Indicates name changes for the sake of anonymity
	<w>...</w>	Orthographic word	Marks all words with internal apostrophes (e.g. in *the cat's*)
	<.>...</.>	Incomplete word	Used to mark incomplete words whose complete meaning cannot be guessed
	<mention>...</mention>	Mention	Indicates words which are cited
	<foreign>...</foreign>	Foreign word(s)	Marks unusual words of foreign origin
	<indig>...</indig>	Indigenous word(s)	Describes non-English but indigenous words, e.g. Malay words in Singapore
	<unclear>...</unclear>	Unclear word(s)	Marks completely unclear words
	<(>...</(>	Discontinuous word	Indicates insertion of a word in another word (e.g. *fanbloodytastic*)
	<)>...</)>	Normalised disc. word	Shows the normalised version of disc. word (e.g. *bloody fantastic*)
Discourse Flow	<,>	Short pause	Pauses in the length of a syllable
	<,,>	Long pause	Pauses in the length of more than one syllable
	<[>...</[>	Overlapping speech	Marks overlapping strings
	<{>...</{>		

Corpora and World Englishes 87

Larger Category	Mark-Up Tag	Meaning / Function	Brief Explanation
		Overlapping speech set	Marks the segment in which the overlapping occurs
Other	<->...</->	Normative deletion	These are used to normalise original corpus text, e.g. for parsing purposes
	<+>...</+>	Normative insertion	
	<}>...</}>	Normative replacement	
	<=>...</=>	Original normalisation	

Mark-up in the spoken ICE components

The spoken parts of the ICE corpora feature in-text mark-up to indicate a number of phenomena related to corpus structure, word structure, and the flow of the discourse. In the following, we will discuss some examples and then provide an overview in Table 4.5. First, consider the brief exchange shown in (4.2). Unlike most other corpus examples from ICE featured in this book, we did not modify the text or the tags.

(4.2) <$A>
        <ICE-SIN:S1A-052#156:1:A>
        <{> <[> No </[>

        <$C>
        <ICE-SIN:S1A-052#157:1:C>
        <[> No </[> </{>

        <$A>
        <ICE-SIN:S1A-052#158:1:A>
        <unclear> word </unclear> Denash knows as well

In this example, <$A> and <$C> tell us that speakers A and C are contributing to the discussion. These labels provide anonymity for the speakers but can be used to identify the metadata corresponding to these speakers for some ICE corpora; more on that follows below.

⇒ Take a look at which utterances are enclosed in the tags <[> and <{>. Which part(s) of the utterances are enclosed by which tags – and what might

88 Corpora and World Englishes

we conclude about this part of the discussion, considering this is an undirected, spontaneous conversation?

◊ Both speakers say 'No', with each token enclosed by the square bracket <[>. The braces, <{>, enclose both utterances, however. These tags are used to mark overlapping speech: The utterances which overlap are individually enclosed in square brackets and the larger segment of the conversation in which the overlapping occurs is enclosed in braces. Using both symbols may seem redundant, but this strategy can also affect cases in which only parts of words actually overlap. If there is overlap of multiple words in a speaker's turn, the square brackets are numbered.

Finally, there is a tag marking a word as <unclear> in the example. Such tags indicate that transcribers were unable to understand one or more words and marked them accordingly in the corpus. Having unclear words in the data is, of course, unfortunate in some cases. An example would be in the analysis of certain syntactic constructions, for the analysis of which a complete sentence would have been necessary. However, unclear words are not particularly common in the ICE corpora and it is usually the best strategy to discard examples that would involve them. It might be worthwhile to discuss such instances in your text or to mention that you discarded certain examples.

Very important tags to be aware of are <X> and its closing tag </X>. These mark extra-corpus text in ICE. Not all conversations included in ICE are necessarily only held between speakers of the variety of interest; any speaker from a different place additionally receives the label <Z> and all of their utterances are tagged in <X> and </X>. The most obvious problem that comes with extra-corpus text relates to the question of authenticity: the presence of speakers from another place may lead to the locals speaking differently, since there might be a certain degree of accommodation towards the interlocutor. Another problem arises when automatic searches are done and the results are interpreted as representative of a variety when potentially many hits actually stem from extra-corpus speakers. Take, for instance, tokens of the discourse marker *yeah* in the direct conversation files included in ICE-Hong Kong.

⇒ Open the direct conversation files in ICE-Hong Kong in *AntConc*, search for *yeah*, and note its frequency. Then, search for 'Z> yeah'. Ensure that some context to the right is allowed in *AntConc*, since there may be additional tags between the speaker label and *yeah*. How many tokens do you get and what does this tell you about interpreting frequencies shown for ICE?

◊ The first query should yield 7998 tokens; the second one 3024 tokens. Figure 4.2 is a screenshot of the first concordance lines resulting from the second query. In terms of interpretation, the results tell us that almost 38%

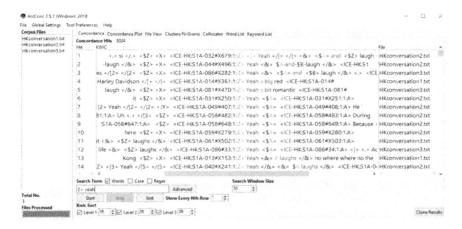

Figure 4.2 Some tokens of *yeah* produced by extra-corpus speakers in the direct conversations in ICE-Hong Kong

of all tokens of *yeah* in the direct conversations in ICE-Hong Kong are produced by speakers who are not from Hong Kong. Thus, the frequency produced by the first search is incredibly misleading and warns us to be very careful.

–Takeaway Note–

Pay close attention to mark-up conventions and consult the tagging manuals whenever you decide to work with a corpus! Extra-corpus text by speakers of other varieties can seriously distort your findings, which is only one of several reasons why you should be careful.

The presence of extra-corpus text in ICE raises two questions: First, why is it even included in the corpus and, second, how can we deal with it? The first question can be answered by considering the logistics of corpus creation as well as the nature of conversations. By logistics, we refer to the fact that World Englishes are naturally located in regions where multilingualism and the presence of multiple ethnicities are common. Hong Kong is still a place where people of different origin meet regularly, despite being a bit of an outlier in comparison to some other places where non-standard varieties of English are spoken. In addition, the teams who compile ICE components have a daunting task on their hands, and discarding conversations solely because speakers from other places contribute as well is probably out of the question. 'The nature of

90 Corpora and World Englishes

conversations' refers to the fact that there is an abundance of phenomena, for instance in discourse pragmatics and syntax, for which insight into the behaviour of the interlocutors is highly relevant: a syntactic construction may be shaped differently due to one of the speakers reacting to a claim made by another, or a certain discourse marker may be used to express approval or disapproval to a statement made in the conversation. Furthermore, reading segments of the corpus would be a lot more tedious if all of the extra-corpus text had been erased. Thus, once again, knowing about the presence of extra-corpus text and interpreting it appropriately is key to ending up with a valid study.

Dealing with tags in ICE can be handled differently and also depends on what you are trying to achieve. If you wish to normalise frequencies, you need the raw word count without any tags or superfluous material distorting it. For this purpose, all tags and information between the tags can be removed using regular expressions. We included the regular expressions necessary for cleaning the tags with a brief manual in the online files accompanying this book's website. We should mention right away that the mark-up in ICE or any other corpus may be faulty: there is always a risk that a closing tag has not been included or mistyped, which is why it is important to check that you are not removing too much text from the file.

An overview of mark-up used in the spoken ICE corpora is provided in Table 4.5; a full list can also be found in the official manual. The tags are categorised according to the linguistic level or the overarching phenomena they describe.

In addition to the mark-up symbols shown in Table 4.5, *uh* and *uhm* in the corpus are used as orthographic representations of audible pauses.

Mark-up in the written ICE components

The phenomena which need to be marked in written texts are, as you probably expected, not identical to those in spoken texts.

⇒ Compare spoken and written language in general and the text types included in ICE in particular (see Table 4.3). Which phenomena will probably need additional mark-up tags for the written sections included in ICE and which of the tags listed in Table 4.5 will also be useful for written texts?

◊ The mark-up tags shared amongst spoken and written texts are numerous and relate to various aspects concerning corpus structure, individual words, and the normalisation of text. For reasons of space, it is easier to list those tags that are used for spoken texts only: speaker tags, unclear word(s), short and long pauses, and the markers for overlapping speech. Perhaps the most obvious differences in written text relate to the typescript (fonts, font style) and structural aspects, such as footnotes, headings, etc.

Consider the example in (4.3), taken from the press editorials in ICE-Hong Kong. Once again, we did not modify the example in order to show you what kind of tag structure is actually used in the corpus.

(4.3) <I> <h>

    <ICE-HK:W2E-001#1:1>
    <bold> Home truths </bold> </h>

    <p>
    <ICE-HK:W2E-001#2:1>
    Even though mortgage rates have fallen to three%, the lowest in as many years, and flat prices have more than halved since the peak of 1997, tens of thousands of vacant flats are still looking for buyers.
    </p>

A first difference you might notice is that the line informing us about the corpus now features a W instead of a S, which tells us that we are looking at corpus material from the written sections. Furthermore, there are tags which do not occur in the spoken sections. <h> and its corresponding closing tag mark *Home truths* in the example as the headline, while <p> and </p> designate the beginning and end of a paragraph. Finally, <bold> and </bold> represent words written in bold font. Similar to Table 4.5, Table 4.6 gives an overview of mark-up tags used in the written sections of ICE. We only included tags which have not already been described above.

The tags referring to typesetting and layout are all listed in the optional section of the mark-up manual, although they can, in certain cases, reveal interesting aspects. Further information can be gained by considering corpus examples and the manual itself.

ICE metadata

The availability of metadata for ICE varies: Some of the ICE components come with detailed metadata (e.g. ICE-India), while none are readily available for others. ICE metadata are usually stored in files named like the files they accompany, except that they frequently have the .HDR file extension. These documents can be opened with regular editors such as *Notepad++*. More detailed information on the availability of metadata for the various ICE components is provided in Appendix B.

In terms of the information included in these files, let us consider the private conversations part of ICE-India.

⇒ What kind of metadata could be useful for a corpus of spoken English, that is, what would we like to know about a speaker and their life? You may also consider the specific context of Indian English (IndE).

92 Corpora and World Englishes

Table 4.6 Additional mark-up symbols used in the written sections of the ICE corpora (adapted from the ICE manual available at www.ice-corpora.uzh.ch/en/manuals.html)

Larger Category	Mark-Up Tag	Meaning/ Function	Brief Explanation
Text Structure	<l>	Line break marker	Marks end-of-line hyphens
	...	Paragraph marker	Marks paragraphs
	<h>...</h>	Heading	Marks headings
	<footnote>... </footnote>	Footnote	Marks footnotes
	<fnr>...</fnr>	Reference to footnote	Marks references to footnotes in the text
	<space>	Orthographic space	Marks unusual spacing, e.g. before punctuation
	<marginalia>... </marginalia>	Marginalia	Marks authorial comments at the margin which relate to the text
Typescript and Layout	<sb>...</sb>	Subscript	Segment in subscript
	<sp>...</sp>	Superscript	Segment in superscript
	<ul>...</ul>	Underline	Underlined segment
	<it>...</it>	Italics	Segment in *italics*
	<bold>... </bold>	Boldface	Segment in **bold**
	<typeface>... </typeface>	Change of typeface	Segment in significantly different typeface
	<roman>... </roman>	Roman type	Segment not in italics *in a text that is predominantly in italics*
	<smallcaps>... </smallcaps>	Small capitals	Word(s) in SMALL CAPITALS

◊ Information on 'typical' sociolinguistic variables should always be included. These are age, gender, occupation, and region. Ideally, details on the speaker's education and their proficiency are also obtained. Considering that World Englishes are spoken in multilingual environments, including the other languages spoken by the interlocutors is also very important. Finally, a comment on the relationship between the speakers should be interesting, since a conversation can follow very different paths depending on whether the people talking are, for instance, friends, co-workers, or teacher and student. An aspect of relevance to the Indian community would be a speaker's caste. However, this information is not normally obtained, since it carries a lot of social and political weight. If you are interested in the kind of information that may get speakers to cooperate (or to stop cooperating entirely), we recommend you read Chapter 3 on the sociolinguistic interview in Tagliamonte (2006).

The metadata available for (most of) the speakers in the private conversations in ICE-India are the following:

- Speaker ID in ICE,
- Communicative role,
- Surname,
- Forename,
- Age,
- Gender,
- Nationality,
- Birthplace,
- Education,
- Educational level,
- Occupation,
- Affiliation,
- Mother tongue,
- Other languages,
- Free comments.

It is important to stress that not all bits of information are provided for every speaker, which is why you need to check the availability carefully. Similar to the annotation, it is worth double-checking the information given in the accompanying files containing the metadata. Recently, Hansen (2017) pointed out that some of the speaker information given in the metadata files for ICE-India do not align correctly with the speaker tags in the files. Thus, if you plan on including this kind of information, you should ensure that it is correct.

Advantages and disadvantages

The ICE corpora represent the most popular corpora in World Englishes research, and certainly for good reason. Similar to the extended Brown family of corpora, ICE components are easily comparable since they are all structured following the same model. In addition, more and more ICE corpora are being compiled, which means that even more complex and cross-corpus comparisons become a possibility. This is particularly exciting, as the teams who compile the new ICE components have much more sophisticated technology at their disposal compared to the original teams. Thus, we can expect more complex annotation, parsing, and precise transcriptions.

As a consequence of the ICE project's popularity, there is an abundance of research based on these corpora. This means that follow-up studies are always an option, but there is also a large body of literature to read with regard to what the

94 Corpora and World Englishes

corpora can be and cannot be used for. Finally, a major advantage of ICE is the fact that the corpora are easily available and relatively easy to handle.

Although there are many positive aspects, certain disadvantages of working with ICE should be pointed out. We already covered one of these in Chapter 3: incorrect or ambiguous transcriptions, that is, transcriptions which either contain typos or are, for some reason, unclear. This problem does not only affect ICE, however. In manual corpus transcription, errors are very difficult to avoid, and rarely are they severe enough to make working with the corpus a bigger problem. Perhaps more importantly, the English featured in ICE has traditionally been close to the standard and produced by educated people. While this is not a problem per se, it does not necessarily reflect the reality of the English spoken in a country.

⇒ Read online about the difference between 'Singlish' (or Colloquial Singaporean English) and 'Standard Singaporean English'. There is also an abundance of YouTube videos with Singlish speakers presenting and discussing their variety. Which of the varieties would you expect in ICE-Singapore and which variety is a more accurate description of 'everyday' English in Singapore?

Another problem concerns the comparability of ICE components. We listed this aspect as one of the main advantages of ICE, so why is there a problem? Of course, the structure and the generally similar approach means that the ICE components are indeed comparable to a certain extent. Consider, however, that some ICE components were created in the 90s and others are being compiled right now: Language is constantly changing and, in many countries, demographics have changed significantly in the last two to three decades. Thus, we could say that older ICE components have a diachronic dimension to them (see also Hundt 2015). Corpora always represent a snapshot of language at a certain point in time, which is why a corpus created in 1994 does not reflect language at the same stage as a corpus that features language from 2014.

An issue which is sometimes difficult to avoid has been mentioned before: the Observer's Paradox. You can read about this in more detail in Chapter 3. In particular, it is noteworthy that, as we discussed above, the teams who collected data for the ICE components sometimes did not get enough people to participate, which is why they gathered data from their students. This is not inherently a problem if their students fit the criteria for being included in the corpora. However, making the participation in a corpus a part of an examination can result in anxiety and students thinking that they need to speak a certain way in order to 'pass'. In order to be aware of such cases, reading the accompanying release notes for the corpora can be very helpful.

Once again, these issues should certainly not keep you from working with ICE. Instead, you should keep them in mind and address them in the methodology section of your study.

Corpora and World Englishes 95

> **–Takeaway Note–**
>
> Despite their relatively small size, the various components of the *International Corpus of English* are still a key resource in World Englishes research – not least due to the large spoken section in each segment. The biggest advantages of ICE are the large number of varieties covered by the project (more are still added) and its active use in the linguistic community. Close attention should be paid to the release notes for each ICE component you work with.

4.4 GloWbE and large (web-based) corpora

In the introduction to this chapter, we briefly pointed to the fact that, in addition to smaller corpora, there are also larger corpora. These corpora frequently use internet sources as material, since this kind of data is readily available and can be collected using programming languages and software. The prime example of this is GloWbE, released in 2015 by Mark Davies with a release note by Davies & Fuchs (2015). We will take a closer look at GloWbE in this section and discuss other (also non-web-based) corpora below.

Structure and design

GloWbE contains a total of ca. 1.9 billion words, distributed across the wide range of varieties listed in Table 4.7. In addition to the word count for each of the included countries, the table also indicates the abbreviations used in the corpus.

In terms of content included, Davies & Fuchs (2015: 4) report that GloWbE consists of 60% informal blogs and 40% more formal texts.

Accessing the corpus

GloWbE can be accessed via www.english-corpora.org/glowbe/, which offers users an easy-to-use interface. Figure 4.3 shows the results of a search for *furnitures*, which is known for being occasionally used as a count noun in World Englishes.

The results in the figure tell us that 206 tokens of *furnitures* could be found in the corpus. Speaking in absolute frequencies, *furnitures* occurs most often in the texts from Malaysia, the Philippines, Singapore, and Hong Kong, while no tokens are present in the South African section. In general, the frequencies are relatively low. However, the fact that the highest frequencies show up in Southeast Asian varieties confirms previous studies indicating that the lack of a mass-count distinction is typical of this area. In order to see normalised

Table 4.7 Countries included in GloWbE and abbreviation and word count for each country (adapted from Davies & Fuchs 2015: 6; Loureiro-Porto 2017: 450)

Country	No. of Words	Country	No. of Words
United States (US)	386,809,355	Singapore (SG)	42,974,705
Canada (CA)	134,765,381	Malaysia (MY)	42,420,168
Great Britain (GB)	387,615,074	Philippines (PH)	43,250,093
Ireland (IE)	101,029,231	Hong Kong (HK)	40,450,291
Australia (AU)	148,208,169	South Africa (ZA)	45,364,498
New Zealand (NZ)	81,390,476	Nigeria (NG)	42,646,098
India (IN)	96,430,888	Ghana (GH)	38,746,231
Sri Lanka (LK)	46,583,115	Kenya (KE)	41,069,085
Pakistan (PK)	51,367,152	Tanzania (TZ)	35,169,042
Bangladesh (BD)	39,658,255	Jamaica (JM)	39,663,666

Figure 4.3 Search results for the word *furnitures* in GloWbE

frequencies, 'per mil' or 'per mil+' need to be selected in the *'Options'* drop-down menu.

For most queries, the web interface is sufficient to work with GloWbE. If you intend to work with the corpus offline or cite material, buying a licence would be required. Since the licences are priced relatively highly, you should check whether your university already has a licence for the corpus or if obtaining one is an option.

Mark-up, annotation, and metadata

Due to the size of the corpus, no detailed metadata or annotation are available. In the release article, Davies & Fuchs (2015) only point out that information on the URLs of the included websites, the country of the text's origin, and the title of the page have been stored.

Advantages and disadvantages

GloWbE represents a fascinating new resource that, amongst its uses as a corpus, was also helpful in intensifying the academic conversation about large web-based corpora. The article accompanying its release by Davies & Fuchs (2015) was published in an issue of the journal *English World-Wide* alongside four response articles by established World Englishes scholars (Mair 2015; Mukherjee 2015; Nelson 2015; Peters 2015). We will cover some advantages, but also problems mentioned in these articles and elsewhere here.

The most obvious advantage of GloWbE – which is simultaneously one of its biggest disadvantages – is its size. We are able to find examples of words or constructions that might not be featured even once in ICE or the Brown family of corpora, possibly even in a large quantity. Furthermore, the fact that so many different varieties are included and frequencies are visualised directly on the web interface means that both impressionistic and more in-depth comparisons are easily possible. The size of the corpus is a disadvantage in the sense that the sub-corpora vary quite drastically in terms of their word count and higher frequencies mean that a lot more work goes into handling the data.

Perhaps the biggest problem with GloWbE, however, lies in the fact that many of the included sources are ambiguous for one reason or another: In some cases, the websites are no longer available (which is a problem that any web-based corpus has to deal with); in others, the origin of the author is not clear. As Davies & Fuchs themselves point out, "in GloWbE we only know that a website is from a particular country, but there might be speakers from other countries who have posted to that website" (2015: 26). Furthermore, different varieties may be used in the same text and the formality of some texts is unclear.

Further large corpora

GloWbE is, of course, not the only 'large' corpus available today. Further important examples include COCA, the *British National Corpus* (BNC), and so-called **monitor corpora**. The BNC is not only a highly relevant source in research on British English (BrE) due to its size, but also because there are two versions now: the BNC1994 and the BNC2014. Similar to corpora in the Brown family and ICE, comparisons between the older and the more recent version can be carried out in order to track change in BrE. For a closer look at the old and new versions of the BNC and what you can do with it, we refer you to Aston & Burnard (1998), Love et al. (2017), and Jones and Waller (2015). Monitor corpora are another interesting kind of corpora that should be mentioned here. They are special in that "[t]exts are constantly being added to it, so that it gets bigger and bigger as more samples are added" (McEnery & Wilson 2001: 30). In contrast to many other corpora, monitor corpora are dynamic and cover large samples over time.

> **–Takeaway Note–**
>
> The *Corpus of Global Web-based English* provides very useful and interesting data, but should be used with caution – as should any other corpus. The decision between 'small data' and 'big data' should be informed by your research question and you should always motivate your data choice (as well as the pros and cons of your corpus) in the methodology section of your paper or thesis.

4.5 Creating your own corpus

In addition to using already existing corpora, there is always the option of creating your own corpus. We suppose that this idea might make you wonder about a couple of problems, starting with: How do I approach this task? Which texts do I choose? How many texts should I include? In light of the technical challenges associated with this process, building your own corpus may seem a daunting task, but, for small-scale projects in particular, creating your own corpus and working with it can be a great alternative. A big plus of building a corpus is that you will end up a more skilled researcher: we would predict that there will be some moments of frustration, but also many moments of satisfaction in corpus compilation, all of which contribute to your experience in one way or another. Furthermore, building a corpus requires a very diverse skillset that will prove very handy in linguistics and beyond. The question remains, of course, where to begin and how to proceed, which we will address in the following paragraphs. As we cannot cover all the intricacies of corpus creation here, we have provided some necessary basics to get you started and refer you to further literature at the end of the chapter.

We should point out right away that building a corpus does not necessarily equal collecting 'new' texts. As soon as you decide on a selection of texts, you are, essentially, working with a corpus specially designed for your purposes. Thus, using texts from different existing corpora and combining them in new ways would also be an example of corpus creation. The focus of this section, however, is on creating corpora 'from scratch'. Table 4.8 gives an overview of the major steps and questions you need to consider before, during, and after building your corpus; these will be addressed one by one below.

Deciding on a research question

The inevitable starting point for creating your own corpus is deciding whether you would like to do a corpus-based or a corpus-driven study (see Chapter 3.2) and which linguistic aspects you are interested in. If you wish to explore

Corpora and World Englishes 99

Table 4.8 Major steps in corpus compilation and potential issues

Component/Step in Corpus Compilation	Issues for Discussion
What would I like to know? Deciding on a research question	Which project is this for – a term paper, a final thesis, a dissertation?
Which data do I use? Text type selection and corpus size	What kind of text is appropriate for my study – spoken, written; fictional, academic; etc.? How many texts should I choose?
How do I get the data? Text collection	Do I need to clear the copyright of any texts, especially for those taken from the web?
How do I prepare my data? Text processing	Is there superfluous information in the texts that distorts the word count? Do I need any annotation and, if so, what kind and to what level of detail?
What happens with my data? Making corpora available	Should I make the corpus available to allow replication of my study?

a hitherto under-researched variety, a corpus-driven approach could be the right choice but, often, a corpus-based approach is preferable. In any case, knowing which linguistic features you would like to investigate as well as the theoretical background to your study should be clear. In other words, you should ideally have a good idea about the topic and the research question of your study.

The importance of the research question can hardly be stressed enough. Although the exact question may change in the process of finding and analysing your data, it is important that you have a clear idea from the get-go. Research questions should be modified according to the length and time you have for your project. A topic for a PhD dissertation, for instance, is going to be a lot more complex than one for a term paper or a Master's thesis. In Chapter 6, we discuss several case studies in which you can see what kind of research question is appropriate for journal articles and chapters in edited collections. Further information can be gained by discussing the topic with your supervisor and colleagues or your fellow students and, if possible, by having a look at some term papers or theses that have been handed in at your institute before.

–Takeaway Note–

The success of a corpus-linguistic project depends to a large extent on the quality of your research question. This question should be modified to fit the requirements of your project – the longer the paper, the more complex it can be. Spend enough time on it and discuss it with your supervisor!

Finding your data

The next step would be to assess what kind of text type you need for your project. Some text types are more difficult to acquire than others: written text types, in particular those available on the internet, can be gathered and prepared for corpus research much more easily and quickly than, for instance, recordings of free conversations. However, they sometimes lack the kind of metadata that help us contextualise information or cannot be used without obtaining copyright. Although a corpus of original recorded speech (and the corresponding transcription) is always exciting, this might be something you should use for your final thesis or even a dissertation rather than a term paper or a course project.

McEnery et al. perhaps formulate it best when they note that "[c]orpus building is of necessity a marriage of perfection and pragmatism" (2006: 73). The type of data you use for your study should be appropriate for the research question, but it should also have dimensions that you can realistically handle. Making the choice to build your own corpus is a bold move in itself, since there is a plethora of corpora readily available for research purposes. It should be expected that your supervisors take this into account when reading your work, since corpus compilation is time-consuming and demanding work. Go into this task aware of the following key questions: (1) How much time and funding (if any) do you have for your project? (2) How balanced and representative do you want your corpus to be and how balanced and representative does it *have* to be with regard to your research question? (3) Where and how can you realistically get the texts you need to include for your study?

For the first question, allow plenty of time for acquiring the various skills necessary for compiling your corpus. We briefly comment on programming languages and their usefulness below, but chances are that you will have to do at least some basic programming. Post-processing of your data, that is, the preparation of your files for the actual analysis, can also be more time-consuming than expected and, lastly, the linguistic analysis itself should also get enough space in your outline. For questions of representativeness and text type selection, we refer you to the previous chapter. Here, the brief comment shall suffice that your corpus should yield enough tokens of the feature you are interested in and it should be somewhat representative. If you, for example, look for instances of the word *however* in academic literature, you may want to include not only final theses but also journal articles. Then, these articles could cover a broader base than only the sciences or only the humanities; instead, a mixture of academic disciplines, journals, and, if possible, decades might yield more interesting and robust results than focusing on only one journal. Once again, the research question should, to an extent, dictate what kind of data you need.

–Takeaway Note–

Representativeness, balancing, text type selection, and corpus size are four crucial elements in building a corpus. Your choices regarding these aspects should fit your research question and you should not plan on doing more than you can handle. Prepare a clear outline and schedule!

Obtaining your data

Once you decided on using certain data, you can think about the actual process of building a corpus. Let us take news websites as an example: Many newspapers now offer online versions of their articles, many of which can be accessed without registering on the website or paying for them. Thus, it is possible to download news articles manually. Of course, there are more sophisticated ways of creating a corpus. One approach you might be interested in is using programming languages such as **Python**. *Python* allows you to use scripts which automatically download texts and process them in a way that makes them useful for your research. The process of gathering relevant texts from the internet is often referred to as **web crawling**, with tools that do so referred to as **spiders**. The actual downloading of texts from websites is commonly referred to as **parsing** (be careful: do not mix this up with syntactic parsing!). A popular script written in *Python* for parsing HTML and XML websites is ***BeautifulSoup***, documented at www.crummy.com/software/BeautifulSoup/bs4/doc/.

Yet another approach (and one that is much easier to use for beginners) is by employing websites such as *Sketch Engine* (which we introduced above). *Sketch Engine* is a tool used predominantly in research on the lexicon, but many other linguistic features can also be studied using it. The main advantage of *Sketch Engine* is that, in addition to giving you access to many corpora, it also allows you to build your own corpus by typing in the URLs of the websites you would like to investigate. However, *Sketch Engine* might only be a realistic alternative if your institution is able to pay for it.

A corpus can also be built by accessing text archives and using sections from them. Many older texts are freely available and may even be used for commercial purposes. We should note again that 'creating your own corpus' does not necessarily equal that you use entirely 'new' material: you can also combine parts from different corpora or only use certain parts of corpora and rearrange them or apply a specific tagging procedure on them.

–Takeaway Note–

How you get your data depends on the kind of data you need: spoken language can be obtained by recording people or using material from

102 Corpora and World Englishes

> TV shows, the radio, etc., and typically requires transcription. Written language can be obtained by crawling the web, downloading texts, and by using OCR. OCR refers to optical character recognition and can be used, for instance, in scanning texts: This technology creates machine-readable texts out of hardcopy documents (but often requires manual corrections).

Preparing your data

You now have your data and are ready to go – but are the data in adequate shape? Before you begin with your analysis, you should prepare the texts. Once again, different text types require different procedures: For audio material, you would need transcriptions; files from the web often need to be cleaned from superfluous links and advertising; and you might want to add annotation or metadata to your files. Let us consider an example to see how simple processing works.

⇒ Download the text from the article on https://timesofindia.indiatimes. com/elections/lok-sabha-elections-2019/maharashtra/news/1-471-voters-added-to-pune-baramati-constituencies/articleshow/68587942.cms (or another article from the *Times of India*) into a TXT file. What kind of post-processing would you do to ensure that no superfluous information is included? What kind of metadata should be included?

◊ Websites containing news articles often contain advertising or links to other articles, which you should not include in the corpus files. In terms of metadata, the date of publication of the article should always be included. Of course, the URL itself may also be relevant. Furthermore, it could be useful to provide information on the larger topic: For instance, all texts dealing with 'Sports' or 'Religion' could be grouped by including this information in the metadata.

Part of why you need to search your data for irrelevant material is that, for any quantitative analysis, you will need the word count of your corpus. This word count should not include metadata or in-text mark-up, since it is not part of the original text. In addition, this means that you need to have a clear idea what counts as a word in your corpus.

⇒ Consider contractions such as *I've, she's, the cat's*, etc. How would you expect word processors to count these? Are they one word or two words? How do we have to treat them if we want to differentiate between *the cat's cute* and *the cat's scratching post?*

◊ Word processors such as *Microsoft Word* typically count such contractions as one word if they are written together (*I've*) but as two words if there is a space between them (*I 've*). This is why contractions are often written with a space between the noun or pronoun and the verb, such as in the ICE corpora. Since *the cat's scratching post* contains a genitive, writing *cat's* together works, while it should be separated in *the cat 's cute* if you want the contraction to count individually.

> **–Takeaway Note–**
>
> Do not rush to the linguistic analysis once you have your data, even if it is tempting – your data should be carefully prepared first. Regular expressions (see Chapter 3.7) are quite useful if you need to remove superfluous information, such as advertising on websites. Identify to what extent metadata, annotation/mark-up, and 'cleaning' of the files are necessary! Store different versions of your corpus texts and keep record of all changes you made to each version.

Storing your data

Another aspect you may want to consider is making your corpus available to others, either at your institute or even the research community at large. Whether this is a realistic option or not depends on your individual project and the corpus but, in general, new corpora are usually received very well. The reason for this is the increased replicability of studies: calls for good scientific practice have led to demands that studies should be replicable in order to allow the rejection or verification of results. Also, the hard work you put into creating your corpus would be for the benefit of others instead of only going into one single project. Many universities now have their own cloud services and data repositories; larger repositories also exist.

> **–Takeaway Note–**
>
> Consider making your corpus available to others: your work will be seen and appreciated by other people and your study can be replicated. Always be sure to save any new version of your corpus!

4.6 Summary

This chapter brought corpus linguistics and World Englishes together by introducing important World Englishes corpora, such as the Brown family of

104   Corpora and World Englishes

corpora, the ICE corpora, and GloWbE. Apart from giving you an idea of the history and development of these corpora, the chapter also served

- to highlight methodological aspects, such as considering metadata and annotation,
- to introduce further tools and websites you can use for your research,
- and to illustrate some difficulties and limitations, but also opportunities associated with certain corpora.

In addition, we showed you advantages and disadvantages of working with 'small' and 'big' corpora. Finally, we listed and discussed important aspects you need to take into account when creating your own corpus. Overall, you should be able to make a more informed decision now when selecting a corpus for your study on World Englishes. Important points you should always consider are the following:

- Your corpus should fit your research question, not vice versa!
- The fact that two corpora have roughly the same size or structure does not automatically mean that they are directly comparable. You also need to take into account the time when they have been compiled, sociolinguistic factors such as the age of the people included in the corpus, the kind of language featured in the corpus (e.g. standard-like or colloquial), etc.
- Corpus size plays a role, since it can affect the level of detail in terms of metadata, annotation, and, sometimes, quality of the data. For the study of certain linguistic phenomena, bigger corpora are more suitable.
- You should always pay close attention to corpus manuals and release notes. Often, these provide important information that might be relevant to your study.
- Good scientific practice entails being open about your methodology and approach. Do not hesitate to be explicit about your methodological choices in your research papers and always motivate your choice of data!

4.7 Exercises

Exercise 4.1

In the section on the Brown corpora, we used the words *quick/quickly* and *fast* as examples. We hypothesised that non-standard occurrences of *quick* used as an adverb in AmE increased over time, in line with a trend suggesting a lower frequency of adverbs ending in *-ly*. You can take this analysis further by conducting a corpus-based diachronic analysis. The central question here is: Are there noticeable differences in frequency between the middle of the 20th century and today?

(a) Go through the corpora mentioned in this chapter. Which corpora would you use to conduct this study – and why? Are there other corpora that we did not mention that might be useful for this purpose?
(b) Discuss whether spoken or written language is more promising for this study. You can also take into account our remarks on spoken and written language in Chapters 3 and 5.
(c) Carry out a corpus analysis using your selected dataset. Be careful to look for the correct part of speech!
(d) Find other examples of adverbs that are used without the suffix -*ly* and corroborate your results.
(e) This task is a bit more complex, but could be quite interesting. Check other World Englishes, such as those in the ICE corpora, for instances of adverbs used without the -*ly*. Try to find reasons why you can or cannot find examples in certain varieties by considering the following aspects: How do speakers of a certain variety learn English? How big is the impact of AmE in the respective country?

Exercise 4.2

Find at least two nouns that would be considered non-count nouns in standard varieties of English (such as *furniture* in the example above).

(a) *Search for occurrences of the non-count nouns with a plural marker in GloWbE. Do the results suggested by *furnitures* (as being most frequent in East and Southeast Asian Englishes) hold up?
(b) Search for occurrences of *furnitures* and other non-count nouns in ICE-Hong Kong. Are the tendencies similar to those you identified for GloWbE?

4.8 Recommended reading

The article by Kirk and Nelson (2018) provides an update on the ICE project and is worth reading both for insights into the management of a decade-spanning and multinational corpus project as well as the future of ICE. We also suggest you have a look at Loureiro-Porto (2017) who compares the ICE corpora and GloWbE. Her goal is to assess how small and big data compare in studies on World Englishes and where we run into limitations.

Apart from tackling many general issues of corpus design that we also addressed in Chapter 3 and this chapter, McEnery et al. (2006) offer further insight into building your own corpus. They also describe usage scenarios of

List of Corpora

Brown:

Francis, W. N. & H. Kučera (1964). *Manual of Information to Accompany a Standard Corpus of Present-Day Edited American English, for Use with Digital Computers*. Providence, Rhode Island: Department of Linguistics, Brown University. Revised 1971. Revised and amplified 1979. URL: http://clu.uni.no/icame/manuals/BROWN/INDEX.HTM#bc3. (Last access: 2 July 2019).

Corpus of Contemporary American English (COCA):

Davies, Mark (2009). "The 385+ million word Corpus of Contemporary American English (1990–present)." *International Journal of Corpus Linguistics* 14(2): 159–190. doi: 10.1075/ijcl.14.2.02dav.

Corpus of Historical American English (COHA):

Davies, Mark (2012) "Expanding horizons in historical linguistics with the 400 million word *Corpus of Historical American English*." *Corpora* 7: 121–157. doi: 10.3366/cor.2012.0024.

F-Lob:

Hundt, Marianne, Andrea Sand, & Rainer Siemund (1999). *Manual of Information to Accompany the Freiburg – LOB Corpus of British English ('FLOB')*. Freiburg: Department of English. Albert-Ludwigs-Universität Freiburg. URL: http://khnt.aksis.uib.no/icame/manuals/flob/INDEX.HTM.Last access: 2 July 2019).

Frown:

Hundt, Marianne, Andrea Sand, & Paul Skandera (1999). *Manual of Information to Accompany the Freiburg – Brown Corpus of American English ('Frown')*. Freiburg: Department of English. Albert-Ludwigs-Universität Freiburg. URL: http://khnt.aksis.uib.no/icame/manuals/frown/INDEX.HTM. (Last access: 2 July 2019).

GloWbE:

Davies, Mark & Robert Fuchs (2015). "Expanding horizons in the study of World Englishes with the 1.9 billion word Global Web-Based English Corpus (GloWbE)." *English World-Wide* 36(1): 1–28. doi: 10.1075/eww.36.1.01dav.

International Corpus of English:

International Corpus of English (ICE). URL: www.ice-corpora.uzh.ch/en.html. (Last access: 2 July 2019).

Kolhapur corpus:

Shastri, S. V., C. T. Patilkulkarni, & Geeta S. Shastri (1986). *Manual of Information to Accompany the Kolhapur Corpus of Indian English, for Use with Digital Computers.* URL: http://clu.uni.no/icame/manuals/KOLHAPUR/INDEX.HTM. (Last access: 2 July 2019).

LOB:

Johansson, Stig, Geoffrey Leech, & Helen Goodluck (1978). *Manual of Information to Accompany the Lancaster-Oslo/Bergen Corpus of British English, for Use with Digital Computers.* Oslo: Department of English, University of Oslo. URL: http://clu.uni.no/icame/manuals/LOB/INDEX.HTM. (Last access: 2 July 2019).

References

Aston, Guy & Lou Burnard (1998). *The BNC Handbook: Exploring the British National Corpus with SARA.* Edinburgh: Edinburgh University Press.

Bautista, Ma. Lourdes S. (2004). "An overview of the Philippine component of the International Corpus of English (ICE-PHI)." *Asian Englishes* 7(2): 8–26. doi: 10.1080/13488678.2004.10801139.

Brezina, Vaclav & Miriam Meyerhoff (2014). "Significant or random? A critical review of sociolinguistic generalisations based on large corpora." *International Journal of Corpus Linguistics* 19(1): 1–28. doi: 10.1075/ijcl.19.1.01bre.

Davies, Mark & Robert Fuchs (2015). "Expanding horizons in the study of World Englishes with the 1.9 billion word Global Web-Based English Corpus (GloWbE)." *English World-Wide* 36(1): 1–28. doi: 10.1075/eww.36.1.01dav.

Greenbaum, Sidney (ed.) (1996). *Comparing English Worldwide: The International Corpus of English.* Oxford: Oxford University Press.

Hansen, Beke (2017). "The ICE metadata and the study of Hong Kong English." *World Englishes* 36(3): 471–486. doi: 10.1111/weng.12282.

Hundt, Marianne (2015). "World Englishes." In Biber, Douglas & Randi Reppen (eds.), *The Cambridge Handbook of English Corpus Linguistics.* Cambridge: Cambridge University Press, 381–400. doi: 10.1017/CBO9781139764377.022.

Jones, Christian & Daniel Waller (2015). *Corpus Linguistics for Grammar.* London: Routledge.

Kirk, John & Gerald Nelson (2018). "The International Corpus of English project: A progress report." *World Englishes* 37(4): 697–716. doi: 10.1111/weng.12350.

Loureiro-Porto, Lucía (2017). "ICE vs GloWbE: Big data and corpus compilation." *World Englishes* 36(3): 448–470. doi: 10.1111/weng.12281.

Love, Robbie, Claire Dembry, Andrew Hardie, Vaclav Brezina, & Tony McEnery (2017). "The Spoken BNC2014: Designing and building a spoken corpus of everyday conversations." *International Journal of Corpus Linguistics* 22(3): 319–344. doi: 10.1075/ijcl.22.3.02lov.

Mair, Christian (2015). "Response to Davies and Fuchs." *English World-Wide* 36(1): 29–33. doi: 10.1075/eww.36.1.02mai.

McEnery, Tony & Andrew Wilson (2001). *Corpus Linguistics. An Introduction.* Second edition. Edinburgh: Edinburgh University Press.

McEnery, Tony, Richard Xiao, & Yukio Tono (2006). *Corpus-Based Language Studies. An Advanced Resource Book*. London: Routledge.

Mukherjee, Joybrato (2015). "Response to Davies and Fuchs." *English World-Wide* 36(1): 34–37. doi: 10.1075/eww.36.1.02muk.

Nelson, Gerald (2015). "Response to Davies and Fuchs." *English World-Wide* 36(1): 38–40. doi: 10.1075/eww.36.1.02nel.

Peters, Pam (2015). "Response to Davies and Fuchs." *English World-Wide* 36(1): 41–44. doi: 10.1075/eww.36.1.02pet.

Tagliamonte, Sali (2006). *Analysing Sociolinguistic Variation*. Cambridge: Cambridge University Press.

Chapter 5

Tracing variation and change in World Englishes

Key terms:

Language variation and change:
actuation and propagation; change from below; gender paradox; index; linguistic variable; overt and covert prestige; registers; rhoticity; speech community; style-shifting; variation (social variation, regional variation, variation according to use, variation according to the user); vernacular

Language contact:
borrowing; calque; cline of bilingualism; code-switching; feature pool; Founder Principle; interference; interlanguage; koinéisation; matter and pattern replication

Processes of language change:
analogy; generalisation; grammaticalisation; reanalysis; redundancy; regularisation

5.1 Introduction

'Standards are going down', 'The internet is destroying the language', 'I don't understand these young people any more' – we all have heard such complaints before. People worry about (real or imagined) language change, perceived as a kind of threat to the 'order' of language, and possibly even to society at large. In the context of World Englishes, these concerns may take the form of a fear that standard English may disappear altogether when World Englishes are 'allowed' to set their own standards. But people who keep complaining about the language of the younger generation always look only one way. They never say things like 'my parents' language was so much better than mine!' Younger people and linguists know that variation and change in language are way more natural than its opposite. They are a testimony to the liveliness of a language and the creativity of its speakers; only dead languages do not change.

110 Tracing variation and change in World Englishes

The preceding chapter has taken you on a grand tour around World Englishes corpora big and small; the exercises have given you a first indication of what to expect from investigating specific aspects of varieties of English. In doing so, we are bound to find differences between varieties. While these are surely worth knowing in themselves (remember the *biscuit-cookie* example from the introduction), linguists are also keen on finding explanations for such differences. This chapter spells out some of the most basic assumptions that are implicit in tracking down differences between World Englishes with corpus-linguistic methods. These questions will concern us in this chapter:

- Variation in language is all around us, but how and when does variation turn into language change?
- What do we know about speakers' gender and age as factors in language change within a given speech community?
- How do we draw the line between *innovation* and *mistake* when we see something new happening in Englishes around the world?
- Which processes drive variation and change in World Englishes?
- And finally, why are scholars of World Englishes interested in spoken language?

5.2 From variation to language change

A song in the Hollywood musical *Shall we Dance* (1937) features the famous line 'You like *to-may-do*, and I like *to-mah-to*' – a comment on pronunciation differences concerning the word *tomato*, which in the context of the movie is one of many which might even keep the main protagonists from marrying each other (the video clip is available on YouTube). Variation in language is all around us, and even if several types of variation tend to overlap in practice, in theory we might try to distinguish **variation according to use** and **variation according to the user**. The first category covers different degrees of formality as well as different **registers**. Picture a university student who also plays hockey: She might greet her fellow students with 'Hey buddies', but, for addressing her professor, she will switch to a more formal style. Registers are related to hobbies or professions and are mostly about specialised vocabulary; in our example, the student will know and use technical terms from hockey which are unknown to a cricket player, or technical terms from her course and life on campus in general that are useless to a police officer. Our hockey-playing student might be enrolled for a degree in English at a university in Hyderabad in the south of India. She might come from an affluent family in Delhi, in which English was spoken on a daily basis; her roommate might come from a rural area in Gujarat, and her parents were not able to send her to an English-medium school so that she only acquired English in college. In this example, **social** and **regional variation** go together to determine a speaker's position on the **cline of**

bilingualism (see Chapter 2.3). The student from Delhi has English as a Second Language (ESL) in her repertoire, while the student from Gujarat speaks English as a Foreign Language (EFL) and is more likely to integrate specific regionally marked usages into her variety of English.

Standard English

In Inner Circle countries with an established standard variety, the relationship between social and regional variation might play out differently. The standard is **supra-regional**, that is, speaking with the standard accent does not reveal your place of origin – even though standard forms of a variety typically emerge from specific local and social contexts. A good example for this is British English (BrE) **Received Pronunciation** (RP). The scholar Alexander Ellis is credited with introducing the term when he wrote:

> In the present day we may, however, recognize a received pronunciation all over the country, not widely differing in any particular locality, and admitting a certain degree of variety. It may be especially considered as the educated pronunciation of the metropolis, of the court, the pulpit and the bar.
>
> (Ellis 1869: 23)

At the time, "*received* was already in use with the meaning 'acceptable in polite society'" (Beal 2004: 183). Note that Ellis' description captures several crucial features: RP is spoken all over the country (it is **supra-regional**), but it can be traced to the metropolis (London) and further to highly prestigious groups of users, namely royalty (the court), the clergy (the pulpit), and the judiciary (the bar). About half a century later, the phonetician Daniel Jones published the first *English Pronouncing Dictionary* and explained whose pronunciation he was going to take as his model: "that most usually heard in everyday speech in the families of Southern English persons whose menfolk have been educated at the great public boarding schools" (Jones 1917). Again, the regional (southern England) and social (upper class) roots of RP are clearly indicated. We will hear more about standards and standardisation later; right now the important point is that the absence of regional dialect traces is typically correlated to belonging to a higher social group, and not being able to switch from a regional to the standard dialect marks you out as belonging to a lower social group. But – why? Why and how do speakers' linguistic choices acquire social meaning, or come to indicate or *index* membership in a specific social group? Regional variation has been studied in the UK or the US for a long time. The informants for such large-scale surveys were typically elderly people from rural areas who had ideally never left their village, making them 'authentic' representatives of their local dialect. But what happens to traditional dialects in the age of industrialisation, population movement, and mass migration? Variation will probably still persist, but how do we make sense of it?

112   Tracing variation and change in World Englishes

⇒ Read the information about lexical variation in the UK on the dedicated website of the British Library (www.bl.uk/british-accents-and-dialects/articles/lexical-variation-across-the-uk). Scroll down to *nain* – a term for grandmother in Welsh English. Make a list of the kinship terms you use for (a) parents and siblings, (b) your wider family. Pick some of these terms and trace their distribution in the *Corpus of Global Web-based English* (GloWbE).

Sociolinguistics

The linguist William Labov can be credited with tackling this very problem and more or less single-handedly founding the discipline of sociolinguistics in the process. He noticed early on that even in big cities where people from many different places come together, patterns of variation emerge which acquire social meaning. That is, even cities like New York, or megacities like Mumbai or Lagos with millions of inhabitants, become **speech communities**:

> The speech community is not defined by any marked agreement in the use of language elements, so much as by participation in a set of shared norms; these norms may be observed in overt types of evaluative behavior, and by the uniformity of abstract patterns of variation which are invariant in respect to particular levels of usage.
>
> (Labov 1972: 120–21)

Labov's definition stresses that not all members of a speech community talk the same way; rather, they share an understanding about the norms of their particular variety, so that they recognise each other as New Yorkers or Mumbaikars when they talk to each other. 'Norms' in this context only refer to the specific speech community's language – they are typically not written down anywhere and may even be opposed to what you find as rules in grammar books or dictionaries. A New York pattern may be non-standard within the wider context of General American English (GA), but firmly established in its speech community. The last part of the definition points out how norms work even if people are not consciously aware of them. Labov observed that all speakers in general engage in **style-shifting**, that is they command a range of different styles from the most informal – the **vernacular** – to formal styles. When Labov and his researchers tried to elicit these different styles, they invariably found that the vernacular hosts more local patterns, which then become fewer when people shift to a more formal style. Such 'abstract patterns of variation' thus display a specific direction and are not random; they show that 'in respect to particular levels of usage', that is, in different styles, speakers are sensitive to the ranking of their variety within the larger communicative context. They prefer their community dialect for informal occasions and become more 'standard' in formal settings.

Tracing variation and change in World Englishes   113

⇒ Discuss the following question: Which linguistic features (vocabulary items, grammatical constructions) would you use (a) only in formal, (b) only in informal and/or colloquial contexts? Can you identify reasons for your choices?

We will trace Labov's pioneering studies in New York City to explain the concept of the **linguistic variable** and the kind of insights we can gain when we correlate the linguistic with the **independent variables** such as age, gender, or ethnicity, as Labov set out to do.

The linguistic variable

Labov and his research team were interested in the language of New Yorkers in the 1960s. Earlier studies as well as their own observations in the speech community prompted them to single out some pronunciation variables for further study. One of these is fairly easy to spot in peoples' speech, namely **rhoticity**. New Yorkers at the time went against the GA pronunciation trend in frequently pronouncing words like *car* without the final – *r*-sound. The variable (r) has thus two realisations: [r] and zero. Labov and his team then collected speech samples in different settings, representing different styles from formal to **vernacular**. They also asked participants about their age, gender, ethnicity, and social class. Their hunch that these **independent variables** might have an impact on peoples' realisation of the variable (r) as either [r] or zero turned out to be correct. The higher the social status, the closer speakers generally came to the GA standard pronunciation.

–Takeaway Note–

Sociolinguistics is concerned with linguistic variables and their social meaning. Different realisations of a particular variable are correlated with independent variables such as social class, gender, or age.

The gender paradox

In this and later work, Labov and his associates noticed an intriguing pattern, which they labelled the **gender paradox**:

> Women conform more closely than men to sociolinguistic norms that are overtly prescribed, but conform less than men when they are not.
>
> (Labov 2001: 293)

That is, women are typically leaders of change from below – they favour innovative incoming forms. On the other hand, women are more likely to uphold already existing norms. This pattern has been confirmed in many studies for quite different speech communities in and beyond Western industrialised societies. But Labov himself has pointed out that we should not take this kind of relation between language and gender for granted in all societies; rather, we should be prepared for "unexpected findings that respond to the wider range of social relations" in non-Western societies (Labov 2015: 21).

⇒ Which factors might influence each gender's relation to the norms of the standard language?

◊ An important aspect is *access to education*. For most of the history of English, women were excluded from higher education, or even education in general. For example, studies of women's writing from the Early Modern English period show more non-standard forms than men's writing.

Labov has also been criticised by the next generation of sociolinguists for his *essentialist* notion of gender. In his study designs, the biological category 'sex' and the social category 'gender' were one and the same thing, while more recent approaches generally stress that the important point about gender is not its biological roots, but the social and cultural consequences of being a man or a woman – or a person above and beyond this dichotomy. In the 'third wave' of sociolinguistics (Eckert 2012), gender becomes something we *do* rather than something we *are*. We choose the kind of male, female or other person we want to be and take our pick among linguistic choices accordingly. This perspective stresses the performativity of gendered identities; its related method of ethnographic field work among speech communities has uncovered how people go about creating their social identities. Eckert's fieldwork with adolescents in a US-American high school took a bottom-up perspective – rather than taking predefined categories such as *male-female, (upper) middle class – working class*, she observed how young people dressed, how they spent their time, which attitudes they had towards school, and then also their language use. In this way, the categories that were eventually useful in explaining the patterns of linguistic variation were created and maintained by the adolescents themselves, including the very specific intermingling of the categories *gender* and *social class*.

–Takeaway Note–

William Labov's approach to sociolinguistics has been labelled *variationist sociolinguistics* or the *First Wave*. The *Third Wave* in sociolinguistics is associated with a more ethnographic approach, and stresses the performative aspect of language in creating local identities.

Unfortunately, this third wave approach to sociolinguistics is not easily transferrable to corpus-linguistic work. After all, in working with corpora we are

Tracing variation and change in World Englishes 115

mostly far removed from the original speech community in time and space, and we do not even have access to speaker data for all available corpora, ICE and otherwise. Corpus-linguistic studies of World Englishes thus frequently focus on the variables *national variety* and, where possible, *text type* or *register*. We will come back to the importance of text types in Section 5.5.

5.3 Variation, mistake, innovation

Chapter 2.2 has sketched the spread of English across the world. We have chosen a regional overview, focusing on areas connected by the Atlantic, the Pacific, and the Indian Ocean. Other accounts depict the expansion of English (speakers) as a time line (for example Trudgill 2017), and many handbooks take the current English-speaking nation-states or regions as their point of departure and work their way backwards to the history of the individual contact situations (for example Kortmann et al. 2004). However we want to conceptualise World Englishes through time, we will always come back to BrE as the **historical input variety** (reminder: with the exception of Philippine English).

Stereotypes about non-native Englishes

Differences between BrE and English as spoken and written in the colonies were noticed early on and were at best treated with curiosity, at worst with imperial condescension. Many examples are readily available from the long history of English in India. The British journalist Arnold Wright came to work for the *Times of India* in the second half of the 19th century. In 1891, he published *Baboo English as 'tis Writ: Being Curiosities of Indian Journalism*, in which he asserted that the large majority of Indian newspapers in English "are contemptible as organs of public opinion. They are for the most part edited by aspiring native students, whose imperfect knowledge of English leads them to perpetrate most ridiculous blunders" (1891: 17). *Baboo* or *Babu*, originally a respectful Bengali term for a male person, later came to be used for Indian clerks working for the British colonial administration; *Baboo English* became a stereotype for stilted, unnatural and verbose writing – a stereotype Wright exploited commercially and helped to spread further. Other authors developed a remarkably modern approach to variation in Indian English (IndE), for example George Clifford Whitworth, a member of the colonial Indian Civil Service, who published *Indian English: An Examination of the Errors of Idiom Made by Indians in Writing English* in 1907. His systematic observations on IndE usage allow us to trace back many IndE patterns, which in turn might provide clues about their origin. An example concerns question formation: "Where, for example, an Englishman would say 'Ask him where his father is,' an Indian would say 'Ask him where is your father?'" (Whitworth 1907: 149–50). This syntactic feature, labelled 'lack of **inversion** in questions', is still around in contemporary IndE; we will come back to it in Chapter 6.4.

116　Tracing variation and change in World Englishes

Mistake or innovation?

Note that Wright and Clifford talked about 'blunders' or 'errors', whereas we referred to 'variation' with respect to the observable differences between a variety and its historical input variety BrE. How do we tell one from the other? This question has profound implications that go far beyond the theoretical concerns of World Englishes researchers. After all, the teaching of English is a multi-million Pound- or Dollar business! Let us assume that you are Australian and have taken up a job as English teacher in Japan. If one of your students writes in their essay *'she don't know'*, you will consider this an error and provide the correct *'she doesn't know'*. If in doubt about a particular point of usage, you will probably consult the Australian *Macquarie Dictionary*, or the *Oxford English Dictionary* (OED), or the American *Merriam-Webster* – that is, you will apply native speaker norms as codified in grammars and dictionaries. Your students are learners of English, trying to get as close as possible to the target language English in pronunciation and grammar. In the process of language acquisition, they are bound to make mistakes due to **interference** from their mother tongue. They may find specific sound sequences of English hard to pronounce because they have no equivalent in Japanese, or they may carry over Japanese patterns into English. If your students are highly motivated, they will become more and more native-like in their acquisition of English, but if they cannot be bothered that much, they might be quite content with their **interlanguage** (Selinker 1972). This term from early research in Second Language Acquisition (SLA) is a label for learners' personal version of a target language which falls short of 'the real thing'. Many people around the world learn just as much of another language as they need to get by in their daily lives, where efficient communication is more important than correctness – after all, not everybody using English wants to do a university degree or aspires to reading Shakespeare in the original.

–Takeaway Note–

The terms *interference* and *interlanguage* had a negative connotation for a long time and were avoided by World Englishes scholars, because they implied lack of proficiency in English. Many researchers in the field of language contact are now using *interference* in a neutral way.

Let us further assume that you have found a new job in India, say in Kolkata. Your new Indian colleagues might ask you after you have settled in *'Are you enjoying?'*, and you might look at them and ask *'Enjoy what?'* For you, the question addressed to you is an incomplete sentence – the verb *enjoy* is transitive, that is, it requires a direct object which indicates what it is that you are enjoying. However, it would be quite awkward to lecture your new colleagues on the 'correct' use of the verb *enjoy*, since they are not learners of English, but teachers like you, and probably more experienced and anyway more familiar than you with their variety of English. Unfortunately, there is no Dictionary of Indian English comparable to the *Macquarie Dictionary* yet. If you could just look up 'enjoy' to find out that the verb can be used without an object in IndE, you would be content to have learned about another difference between your and somebody else's variety of English. But what do you, or Indians for that matter, refer to in the absence of a dictionary?

Native and non-native Englishes

We have already mentioned in Chapter 2.3 that the linguist Braj Kachru fought for the acceptance of Outer Circle Englishes as varieties in their own right. One of his opponents was the grammarian Randolph Quirk (best known for his work on the monumental *Comprehensive Grammar of the English Language*), who published a short paper which triggered what came to be known as the Quirk-Kachru debate. For Quirk, the English-speaking world was neatly divided into native Englishes and learner Englishes, and the "relatively narrow range of purposes for which the non-native needs to use English (even in ESL countries) is arguably well catered for by a single monochrome standard form that looks as good on paper as it sounds in speech" (Quirk 1985: 6). However, even in 1985, English was a pluricentric language, with the two fully codified varieties British and American English. But Quirk continued in this vein and basically denied the existence of an Outer Circle when he wrote:

> The problem with varieties in this branch is that they are inherently unstable, ranged along a qualitative cline, with each speaker seeking to move to a point where the varietal characteristics reach vanishing point, and where thus, ironically, each variety is best manifest in those who by commonsense measures speak it worst.
>
> (Quirk 1990: 5–6)

That is, all English speakers beyond the Inner Circle are lumped together as learners who are stuck with their interlanguages. If their variety of English betrays a West African or South Asian origin, then they have missed the target of 'proper' English. This whole line of thinking was vigorously contested by Braj Kachru, as we saw in Chapter 2.3.

English in the Outer Circle

What Quirk did not take into account was that many speakers in the Outer Circle use English the way they do not because they cannot 'do better', but because they do not want to. Their localised and nativised variety of English has become a marker of identity. After all, nobody would dare to tell a New

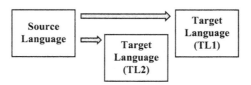

Figure 5.1 Acquisition of English in multilingual Outer Circle contexts (based on Thomason 2001: 75)

Zealander to talk more like an Australian, or a Canadian to sound more American. Figure 5.1 illustrates how we might conceptualise the acquisition of English in typically multilingual Outer Circle contexts, following the contact linguist Sarah Thomason. Note that the term 'acquisition of English' may cover both the early period of the establishment of English in a new territory and the current on-going spread of English. Thomason basically distinguishes two contact scenarios; one in which fluent bilinguals interact with each other, and another in which one group of speakers acquires another language:

> First, learners carry over some features of their native language into their version of the TL, which can be called TL2. Second, they may fail (or refuse) to learn some TL features, especially marked features, and these learners' errors also form part of the TL2. If the shifting group is not integrated into the original TL speech community, so that (as in the case of Indian English) its members remain as a separate ethnic or even national group, then the TL2 becomes fixed as the group's final version of the TL.
> (Thomason 2001: 75)

In such a scenario, the shifting speakers are most likely to carry over features of their original language's pronunciation and grammar into their version of English as the target language. A well-known example of a language-shift variety is Irish English (IrE). A speaker of IrE might say 'I'm after dinner' meaning 'I've just had dinner' – speakers of Irish shifted to English on a large scale in the 19th century, integrating the 'hot news-' or 'after-perfect' found in Irish into their variety of English.

However, language shift is definitely not what we see in Outer Circle countries, where English just joins the already multilingual club. Thomason is fully aware of this and has added a clarification on this point:

> One complication here is that a significant amount of shift-induced interference is sometimes found in a long-term contact situation in which imperfect learning was important early on, but then bilingualism was established and maintained for a considerable period of time: the shifting

group's version of the target language was fixed at a time when the level of bilingualism was low among members of the shifting group, and (possibly for attitudinal reasons [...]) it never converged toward the target language as spoken by the original target-language speech community.

(Thomason 2010: 37)

The two quotes mention in passing two different reasons why a speech community may not go all the way towards perfect mastery of a target language. The first quote refers to the lack of integration: a speech community may find itself at a social distance or geographical distance from the historical input variety, and in the case of Postcolonial Englishes (PCEs) it was typically both. The second quote alludes to 'attitudinal reasons'. As already mentioned, the speech community itself may give higher prestige to its own national variety, and less to BrE, perceived as the coloniser's language.

–Takeaway Note–

Speakers of English in the Outer Circle typically use English for intra-national and not for international purposes. They either do not need to follow an Inner Circle model, or they do not want to because their variety has become a marker of identity.

From innovation to standardisation

We have now rejected the idea that everything we find in a variety of English that happens to be absent from Quirk's 'single monochrome standard' is an error by definition – but we still have not come up with a principled distinction between mistake and innovation in PCEs, especially those in the Outer Circle which are not codified yet. We cannot just take the opposite view and declare all divergent usages to be innovations, either. Remember the notion of the cline of bilingualism in the Outer Circle, which means that we are bound to come across speakers with low proficiency in English as well as fluent bilinguals. It is ultimately up to the speech community in question to decide which features to consider acceptable. Recall from Chapter 2.3 that it is precisely this process of acknowledging one's own indigenous variety which takes centre stage in phase 4 of Schneider's Dynamic Model. The outward signposts of this process are literary creativity in the new variety and the publication of dictionaries and grammars. However, this development towards an autonomous variety of English hardly ever goes uncontested. The label 'bad English' for nativised English does not only come from outsiders such as Randolph Quirk (see above), but also from inside the speech community: "questions of linguistic norm acceptance are frequently social group struggles in disguise" (Schneider 2007: 52). In stage 4, the balance between conservative speakers who cling to an exonormative model and progressive speakers who embrace indigenous usage has finally tilted towards the local norm, but this does not mean that the complaint tradition has vanished overnight. Speakers may still pick upon their fellow speakers' expressions, accusing them of lowering the standards, being uneducated, ruining the language/the nation/the future of their children, and so on.

This is where corpus-linguistic investigations of World Englishes can prove very important, since they allow us to give an account of the frequency and distribution of a specific innovative feature in a specific variety. The ICE corpora, featured in Chapter 4, are particularly well-suited for this, not only because of their wide coverage of varieties, but also because of their composition. Sidney Greenbaum, the initiator of the ICE-project, wrote in an early report: "I envisaged the new corpus having as its components regional corpora sampling the standard varieties in countries where English is a first language and the national varieties in countries where it is an official additional language" (Greenbaum 1990: 79). For the latter, that is, Outer Circle countries, he added that the national variety may not be standardised yet, but "[t]he standard language, as elsewhere, would tend to be non-regional and represent the consensus of educated speakers" (Greenbaum 1990: 82). Since the ICE corpora aim to sample data from adult speakers who have (minimally) completed their secondary education through the medium of English, they represent acrolectal national varieties of English. To put it another way: The (emergent) standard is part of the ICE-DNA.

We know already that not all ICE corpora come with speaker metadata, but a careful analysis of raw corpus data for a specific feature can go a long way. A feature that occurs 20 times in the speech of five speakers and not at all elsewhere is obviously skewed in its distribution and thus unlikely to be acceptable for the overall speech community. A feature that is well represented in the spoken language but absent from the written registers may represent **change from below**. However, it might still not make it into the emergent standard; a point we will discuss further in Section 5.4. We may also arrive at a more realistic picture of 'typical features' of a variety that crop up in textbooks – we may find that such features are not so frequent after all. 'Realistic' may also refer to the usage of the speech community. We know from sociolinguistic studies about the gap between what speakers think they should be saying and what they actually say. Speakers may be fully convinced to use a standard form when, in fact, they do not, or they may claim to go more for non-standard usage than they really do. Such over- and under-reporting was described by Trudgill (1972) and linked to the notions of **overt** and **covert prestige**: The standard is associated with upward social mobility and has overt prestige; the non-standard carries connotations of toughness and street credibility and has covert prestige. In Outer Circle context, speakers may be fully convinced that they follow the standard of the historical input variety and deny the existence of a local norm, even if they actually appear to be following it.

Before we move on to the sources of innovations in PCEs, we need to acknowledge that, after everything we said in favour of a corpus-linguistic search for emerging standards in Outer Circle Englishes, the last word on this issue always rests with the speech community concerned.

5.4 Contact and the feature pool

Contact obviously plays a big role in World Englishes, both in the past and in the present. The spread of English around the world involved two types of contact: dialect contact between English speakers from different regions who met on board the ships to foreign lands, or later in already established settlements, and language contact between these English speakers and the local population. The linguist Salikoko Mufwene has adapted the biological metaphor of the **feature pool** to visualise what happens in such contact situations. Linguistic features – morphemes, lexical items, usage patterns, or more abstract structures – from different varieties and/or languages come together in a 'pool' and then undergo competition and selection as in evolutionary biology (Mufwene 2001: 4–6). Some features win out over others and make it into the new composite or restructured variety. Just as in biology, this is a complex process which is not yet fully understood in all its details. One important conditioning factor is the sheer number of speakers of a particular language or variety. We have seen that in settlement colonies such as Canada or Australia, speakers of local languages hardly had a chance to contribute much to the feature pool. Exploitation colonies such as India, on the other hand, supplied a host of local languages as input to the feature pool. Another important notion which goes back to Mufwene is the **Founder Principle**: "newcomers adjust to norms established by earlier generations, so the earliest settlers, the founders of a new community, will establish a strong convention which is bound to persist" (Schneider 2007: 111). The US can serve as a fitting example: millions of southern and Eastern Europeans and East Asians migrated to the US, but the language of the original colonisers persisted and the new arrivals made sure to become English speakers as fast as possible.

Language contact and language change

However, language contact as a factor shaping varieties of English around the world is not restricted to the past. Especially those varieties that we have come to know as New or Outer Circle Englishes are in continuous contact with surrounding languages. As a speaker of English in Ghana or Sri Lanka, you are very likely to switch between all the languages you know – English is just one part of your multilingual repertoire. Language contact is thus a factor that is very likely to play a role in making World Englishes special, but it is also not the only one. Figure 5.2 quite aptly captures the complex and interconnected network of processes that are apparent in the emergence of World Englishes. Schneider points out "that by containing empty cells the diagram suggests that

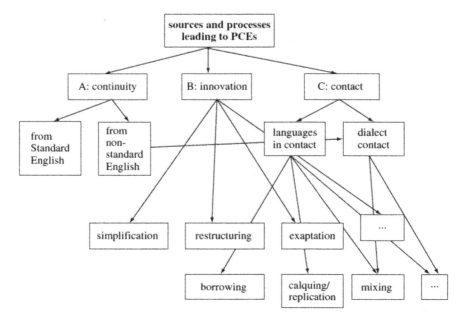

Figure 5.2 Sources and processes leading to PCEs (Schneider 2007: 100; reprinted by permission from Cambridge University Press)

the listings are not exhaustive, and the arrangement is definitely not the only possible one; the figure just suggests one way of systematising a set of complex interrelationships" (Schneider 2007: 100). Let us look at each box in turn with a focus on those processes that crop up most frequently in the World Englishes literature (Schneider 2007: 97–112 has all the details).

Continuity

Box A with the label 'continuity' has two branches, indicating that all PCEs are descendants of their historical input variety. They also may have retained some of its features which have become obsolete in the homeland in the meantime. A prominent example of this process is already familiar to you from Chapter 2.4, namely rhoticity: BrE was still rhotic when it was first transported to North America, and while rhoticity disappeared from Standard BrE, it was retained in AmE. We find an equally classic case of retention of a non-standard feature in Australia. Since many of the convicts who involuntarily became the Australian first settlers were from London and spoke the Cockney dialect, some originally Cockney sounds were adopted into today's 'broad Australian', for example *'today'*

Tracing variation and change in World Englishes | 123

sounding more like '*to die*'. Not only pronunciation may be retained, but also lexical items and grammatical structures.

Innovation

Box B, 'innovation', is intended to capture "the results of internal change and linguistic creativity, something that, as was stated earlier, characterises all languages at all times" (Schneider 2007: 102). Its first branch comprises processes of simplification and regularisation which are also active in SLA. Researchers frequently evoke universal cognitive processes in second-language learning when they find diverging patterns in PCEs. After all, Outer Circle Englishes did not only start their life as learner Englishes, they were also sometimes taught by non-native speakers of English. Furthermore, many speakers of English in Outer Circle countries find themselves at the EFL end of the cline of bilingualism and are likely to resort to the same language acquisition strategies as the very first people who were exposed to English in the country.

'Simplification' with respect to language appears intuitively obvious, even though the notion that languages can be more or less 'simple' is highly contested. Researchers have come up with different terms and go into more or less detail with their classifications, but all agree that simplification in language has to do with **regularisation**. This term refers to "any changes which result in surface forms which are less diverse or contain fewer exceptions to the basic, canonical patterns of the target system" (Williams 1987: 170). Regularisation thus applies when speakers get rid of irregular forms or exceptions to rules in the language. Consider the following examples (5.1) to (5.10) from a range of ICE sub-corpora. All are taken from the spoken language sections, so be prepared for repetitions, incomplete sentences, and the like:

(5.1) *B:* Did you see him thief the donkey
    E: Yes m'Lord
    C: Are you not aware that Mr Smith **own** donkeys of his own
    E: No madam
    C: Are you not aware that Mr Smith **own** donkeys of his own
    E: No madam he **don't** own no donkey is steal him steal that donkey
    (ICE-JA:S1B-067#204–209)
(5.2) Is a ya and they are not willing to disclose too many **informations** so that could be (ICE-SIN:S1A-070#50:1:B)
(5.3) The consumption tax will the tax on the daily necessities of what you and I would use shoes **clothings** food drinks everything under the sun (ICE-SIN:S2A-022#22:1:A)
(5.4) You know if a country **is having** a lot of population then definitely there will be no employment (ICE-EA spoken S1B001T)
(5.5) Were you **knowing** this accused by name Sharma? (ICE-IND:S1B-064#227:1:B)

124 Tracing variation and change in World Englishes

(5.6) Because when this Mount Pinatubo erupted there were a lot of people who were affected **isn't it** (ICE-PHI:S1A-021#103:1:A)

(5.7) I mean it depends on what <,,> uh all of us agree upon **isn't it** <,> (ICE-IND:S1A-014#44:1:B)

(5.8) Yeah in general term I can uh say <,> there is uh <,> a layer **called as** Ionosphere <,> in the in earth's upper atmosphere (ICE-IND:S1A-069#46:1:B)

(5.9) Actually there are many people <,> uhm **discussing about** this question (ICE-HK:S1A-090#696:1:A)

(5.10) I suppose I can't **enter into** university, but I'm sure I can be a college student as its requirements are lower (ICE-HK:W1B-004#50:1)

Example (5.1) from a court case in Jamaica illustrates that speakers may simplify English verb morphology (see Chapter 2.4) by omitting the marker -*s* for third person singular and thus making the inflection of verbs more regular. Examples (5.2) and (5.3) do not show the loss, but the addition of an inflectional form: in the historical input variety, nouns such as *information, clothing,* or *luggage* are non-count nouns which are never marked by a plural -*s*. We can argue in these cases that the speaker has extended the general rule of plural formation to all nouns. A similar case of **generalisation** seems to be at work in examples (5.4) and (5.5). Stative verbs such as *have* or *know* are treated just like active verbs and can take the progressive form. Examples (5.6) and (5.7) feature *tag questions* at the end of the utterance. Such tag questions generally map the form of the clause they are attached to, so that example (5.7) would be '*I mean it depends on what* <,,> *uh all of us agree upon* **doesn't it**'. The tag *isn't it* is thus in both cases invariant, that is, it is generalised to all contexts, making the rules of forming tag questions drastically simpler.

Some processes actually involve addition of new material rather than loss, and very often the likely explanations for a specific feature overlap. Examples (5.8) to (5.10) all have an additional particle following the verb. One explanation that covers all three examples is **redundancy**, the "unmotivated repeated (or double) marking of the same piece of information" (Schneider 2012: 65). Another way of looking at these examples would be to refer to **analogy**, "the transfer of some principle or procedure from a source domain to a target domain" (Schneider 2012: 66). *Called as* is not found in BrE, but *known as* is, and the verb-particle combination *discuss about* might have been inspired by the nominal form '*a discussion* **about** *something*'. Come to think of it, placing *as* after *call* might also be a case of extending a rule from verbs like *know (as)* to others. With several options for explaining a pattern, we need to look very closely at the contexts of such patterns of variation, and we should be careful not to jump to conclusions on the basis of isolated examples.

Tracing variation and change in World Englishes 125

⇒ Consider the following example sentences (5.11) and (5.12), again from different ICE sub-corpora. Try to pin down the innovative feature and discuss possible explanations.

(5.11) so what I am planning to do is to finish up my first degree first then [...] I will look for ways to write or to get certified in the aspect of professional exams (ICE-NIG con_51)

(5.12) *A:* And I feel bad also but the thing is uhm we're having a tournament coming up you see
    B: Is it
    A: organised by the School of Physical Education and you know So I was gearing my boys up for the for the championship actually
    B: So you got chance or not
    A: Well I'll rate our chances as fifty fifty (ICE-SIN:S1A-058#187–192)

The remaining two boxes, 'restructuring' and 'exaptation', comprise more general processes in language change. Restructuring may involve **reanalysis**, which occurs when "subsequent speaker generations analyse and understand the same constituent sequences differently" (Schneider 2007: 105). It may also involve **grammaticalisation**, the 'recycling' of content words as function words (see Chapter 2.4), or the re-use of lexical items as grammatical markers. Let us consider a classic example of reanalysis first, namely the *hamburger*. According to the OED, *hamburger* is short for *Hamburg steak* or *Hamburger steak*, where *Hamburg* refers to the city in Germany. In both German and English, the suffix *– er* added to a location creates a new noun that designates someone or something coming from that location (*Hamburger, New Yorker*). So the original morphological structure of the *Hamburger steak* goes like this:

Hamburg {-er} (steak)

However, now we have not only *hamburgers*, but also *cheeseburgers, veggieburgers*, and so on. That is, over time the morphology of the *hamburger* was **reanalysed**; both *ham* and *burger* became independent words which were then able to enter into new combinations:

hamburg {-er} -> {ham-} {burger}

Examples for **grammaticalisation** are easier to come by in the context of World Englishes. Take example (5.13) from ICE-Nigeria:

(5.13) if my my mum eat that thing the the woman *go fit* vomit (ICE-NIG con04.txt)

We can turn to the *Atlas of Pidgin and Creole Language Structures Online* for more information about *Nigerian Pidgin*, the Nigerian English *basilect*. The survey article (https://apics-online.info/surveys/17) tells us that *'fit'* is a modal marker which

126 Tracing variation and change in World Englishes

means 'can, be able to' – the lexical verb 'fit' has become a grammatical marker. Similarly, the verb 'go' in Nigerian Pidgin English has shifted its meaning – from full verb indicating a kind of movement to yet another grammatical marker with verbs, indicating conditional or future. Now that we have grasped the meaning of the sentence, we should feel sorry for the speaker's mom!

Contact

Box C, 'contact', brings us back to the idea of the feature pool. If speakers of many different languages contribute to the feature pool, then 'language contact' is an appropriate label. If speakers of different English dialects predominate, then dialect contact will lead to **koinéisation**, that is, "mixing and subsequent levelling of previous dialect differences as well as the development of interdialect forms. Koinéisation happens because speakers of different dialect backgrounds tend to accommodate to each other in their speech behavior" (Hundt 2016: 318). Actually, this happens all the time when people from different linguistic backgrounds get together. Consider the last time you interacted with somebody in your common mother tongue English, but both of you spoke different dialects. You are likely to stumble across pronunciation features or lexical items that your dialects do not share, and you will typically go for the common ground – you will accommodate your speech to each other. You do that by levelling, that is, by dropping those features that are peculiar to your dialect and may draw looks of incomprehension from other speakers. This common ground is what is meant by the Greek word *koiné*, and the "outcome of koinéization would be a relatively homogenous variety with fewer dialect features than found in the input varieties" (Hundt 2016: 318).

Borrowing and code-switching

The network of arrows with the box 'languages in contact' at its centre already indicates the interconnectedness of processes of change in PCEs. Language contact is a straightforward explanation for a new feature when it comes to lexical items borrowed from a source language into the target language, for example the term *barangay* ('village, neighbourhood, community') in Philippine English, borrowed from the local language Filipino. Linguists interested in language contact often make a distinction between borrowing or **matter replication** and **pattern replication** (for example Matras 2009: Chapters 6 and 9); or material borrowing ("borrowing of sound-meaning pairs") and structural borrowing ("copying of syntactic, morphological or semantic patterns", Haspelmath 2009: 38). The former is easy to spot; try it yourself with this humorous excerpt from a website devoted to Colloquial Singapore English or *Singlish*. You will probably gather straight away that this is about *The Lord of the Rings*. You can retrieve the meaning of loanwords and other Singaporean expressions from the original website 'Tolkien for Bengs' at http://72.5.72.93/html/article.php?sid=1275.

Tracing variation and change in World Englishes   127

Last time got this short-short person with si-beh hairy legs called Bilbo, lor. He, hor, got this ring that last time belong to some monster.

But then, hor, one day suay-suay the monster want it back, and send his kah kiah to Bilbo's house to settle, lah.

But the ring, hor, acherly can make people very powderful. But then, hor, if you wear too long will also kena sai. Si beh hiong one, so better faster go and destroy it, lor.

This text with its many words derived from local languages brings us to another problem which continues to haunt linguists, namely the distinction between **code-switching** and **borrowing**. Simply speaking, a borrowing is an expression that has started its life as a code-switch and has grown up in the target language. Code-switching is a linguistic behaviour that requires fluent bilingualism; once an expression from a source language is routinely used in the target language and can be understood by its monolingual speakers, then it has become a borrowing or loanword – a misleading term, since the speech community is unlikely to return the word! Holding on to that thought, the speakers of the source language may not even want it back – borrowings are typically more and more integrated into the target language over time, in pronunciation as well as in their morphosyntax. The history of English provides thousands of examples for the integration of French loanwords.

'Calquing' is another term for loan translation and may refer both to matter and pattern replication. A famous example of a **calque** is *Superman*, a literal translation of *Übermensch* ('uber-human') as coined by the German philosopher Friedrich Nietzsche.

⇒ Determine the history of the prefix *uber-* in English with the help of the OED, then go to GloWbE and/or the *Corpus of Historical American English* (COHA) and check its distribution across time/national varieties. In which linguistic contexts is *uber-* used (only as a prefix or also as separate lexical item)?

'Pattern replication' or 'structural borrowing' means that multilingual speakers transfer patterns from their source languages into English. This process is much less obvious to speakers themselves, and harder to trace for linguists. Consider the example (5.14), again from Colloquial Singapore English or *Singlish*:

(5.14) I mean they're like there is guy who must be about sixty over then always *kena* teased by this other guy uhm (ICE-SIN:S1A-079#149:1:A)

The information from the *Atlas of Pidgin and Creole Language Structures Online* runs as follows: "*Kena*, from Malay 'to suffer', marks a non-prototypical passive-like construction, which may simply indicate non-volitional actors" (https://apics-online.info/valuesets/21-90). That is, a lexical item from Malay, one of the official languages of Singapore, is used to express the passive with a specific

128 Tracing variation and change in World Englishes

meaning: The *kena*-passive indicates that the patient (the person or entity at whom or which the action is directed) is indeed at the receiving end of some action, typically with undesirable consequences.

Summary: language change in World Englishes

We have now reviewed and illustrated sources and processes which trigger innovations in PCEs. The list is neither exhaustive nor unique – other researchers may apply different labels to processes, and/or a different emphasis on individual phenomena – but pretty much all World Englishes scholars would agree on the following shorthand for the processes under discussion:

- **Internal change**: all varieties undergo change over time, and this change just happens at a different pace in a particular PCE, that is a PCE may lead or lag behind a change;
- **External change** may be driven by the following factors:
  - **Cognitive processes:** universal cognitive strategies in SLA may lead to restructuring of specific aspects of the language;
  - **Contact:** contact-induced language change is most obvious (and also least remarkable) at the level of the lexicon, that is loanwords, but may also involve structural borrowings from multilingual speakers' other source languages.

These processes are much easier to keep separate in theory than in practice. A lot of work on World Englishes concludes that it is very hard to hit upon one single explanation for what is happening in a particular variety; rather, several processes interact and conspire in the emergence of innovations.

Still, everything we said this far presupposes that a new form is sufficiently widespread in a speech community that we consider it worthy of our attention. Linguists find it really frustrating that they cannot study the **actuation** of a new feature, only its **propagation**. Someone, somewhere says something for the first time ever, finds a new way of saying things – but we are unlikely to be around for that. We can only investigate this feature once it has caught on in the speech community, on its way to creating variation and possibly also change. Luckily for us, so much is happening in Englishes across the globe that we as linguists will not easily be bored. Chapters 6 and 7 will be your points of departure for venturing into the hotspot of linguistic innovation in World Englishes.

5.5 Spoken and written language

Chapter 3.3 has already drawn your attention to the distinction between spoken and written language. Linguists have become more interested in typical features of spoken language, and more and more corpora are available now to feed that

Tracing variation and change in World Englishes 129

interest. Corpus linguistics has indeed come a long way from the first-generation corpora in the 1960s, which contained printed written language only!

Recall from Chapter 3.3 that you were asked to think about the differences between spoken and written language. One important issue is the situational context and its linguistic consequences. Consider the following excerpt from the text S1a-010 in ICE-Great Britain. Speaker A is female and belongs to the age group 26–45, speaker B is also female, age 66+. We have simplified the textual mark-up to make the dialogue easier to read. While reading the dialogue, take down examples of

- features that you think are unique to spoken language;
- features that are not unique, but more frequent in spoken language.

(5.15) *A:* What was that <,> building on the corner <,> just past Chapel Street on the right where it used to be Lyon's <,,>
What was it called the <,>
Well it w it wasn't called Lyon's Corner House but it was
B: Chapel Street
A: Well you know Chapel Street
B: Yeah up at Islington
A: Yeah <,>
If you go on a bit you come to <,> a corner shop a big which used to be a big Lyon's <,> with a
Oh you don't know oh
B: Well as I say I don't know it <,,>
No I don't know <unclear-words> I didn't know Islington until I moved there but
A: And it used to have <,> uhm it used to have a name like uhm <,> like uhm <,,> uhm not the Trocadero but you know how they they uhm they acquire funny names for their places uhm uhm lifting them out of the tea shop <,> brigade
B: Uhm no uhm <unclear-words>
Mm
Mm
Mm <,>
A: Well that was slightly above the average tea shop
B: Oh
A: You know you paid a halfpenny more for tea and things like that <,,>
B: Oh yes <,> I don't know I don't I mean I didn't know Islington at all until I moved there really

You will probably find this text difficult to read. The reason for this is simple: It was never meant to be transferred one-to-one to the written medium. Conversation is interactive and happens in the here and now. The speakers share

130 Tracing variation and change in World Englishes

this here and now and can freely refer to *Chapel Street, Lyon's Corner House*, and *Islington* because it is common knowledge between them. Speakers, unlike writers, do not have time for planning and refining their utterances. Thus, conversations are full of *dysfluencies*. Take speaker A's fourth turn, where she says '*it used to have*' twice, then continues with '*a name like uhm <,> like uhm <,,> uhm not the Trocadero*'. She repeats herself, starts again searching for the name, and keeps going with pauses and *fillers* such as *uhm*. While A is speaking, B utters *non-clausal units* such as *mm* to signal that she is listening. *Discourse markers* such as *oh, well, you know* are abundant in the text and absolutely typical of spoken language.

Speakers further typically go for *shortcuts*: Note the contracted forms *wasn't, don't*, and *didn't* in the transcript. Just try once to talk without contractions, saying *going to* rather than *gonna*, or *would not* rather than *wouldn't*, and be prepared for the funny looks of your conversation partners! Speaker B's second utterance '*Yeah up at Islington*' is also a shortcut. On its own, it is not a complete sentence, but in the context of the conversation this does not matter as long as it fulfils its communicative function. Note also speaker A's last utterance, when she refers to '*tea and things like that*'. You will notice many more example of *vague reference* such as this one in everyday speech: *kind of …, sort of …, … and stuff*, and others.

If we compare this conversation to a newspaper article, we are bound to find more first and second pronouns in speech. Sentences tend to be shorter and less complex: conjunctions such as *nevertheless* or *moreover* are more appropriate for the written medium. The newspaper article is also more likely to use more verbs in the passive than spoken language does. You will find such systematic differences between spoken and written language in all varieties of English, since they arise from the situational contexts and communicative functions of linguistic registers. Furthermore, all speakers are more likely to use informal, colloquial, and innovative features in their spoken language first. As a multilingual speaker, you are also more likely to introduce elements from your other language(s) into your English – you will be engaged in **matter** or **pattern replication** on a daily basis. However, you might hesitate to use such features of your everyday linguistic repertoire in your more formal writing. Your teachers or your colleagues might point out to you that this particular form of phrase is not 'standard English' as they learnt it. The Indian linguist Jean d'Souza has pointed out how speakers of PCEs might actually benefit from the standardisation (or codification) of their variety:

> Without codification the varieties of English will continue to lack *locus standi*, not only in the eyes of the world, but also in the eyes of the speakers of the varieties. Without codification British English becomes the unnamed but ever present standard resulting in a learner mentality with New Variety English (NVE) speakers denied the freedom to use the language in new and innovative ways. If, when in doubt about

a particular usage or point of grammar, an Indian speaker of English has to refer to exonormative materials, it inevitably undermines any kind of innovation that has gained ground within Indian English.

(D'Souza 1999: 272)

We as corpus linguists should thus always be aware of the huge potential of looking separately at spoken and written registers. World Englishes might not be so terribly different from each other at the written level, but some of the most noticeable features may work their way up from everyday creative language use. Such **change from below** may one day be codified and become part of a speech communities' standard English, a unique marker of identity.

5.6 Summary

This chapter has introduced you to the key ideas in the study of linguistic variation and change. Our emphasis moved from variation in language generally to the reasons for variation in the context of PCEs. Keeping everything we said in mind, we can set up the following checklist for our corpus-linguistic work. If we think we have found an innovative feature in a variety of English, we should consider these points if possible (that is, if we have speaker metadata):

- Is the feature a mistake or an innovation? Check its distribution in the speech community:
  - Is it pan-regional or supra-regional?
  - Is it used by educated speakers?
  - Is it used by younger and/or female speakers? Then we might speculate about a change from below in progress.
  - Is it already found in the written language? Then it might be on its way to becoming part of the variety's codified standard.

- What are likely explanations for the emergence and spread of the new feature?
  - Is it a case of *retention*? Make sure to consult earlier records of the historical input variety, for example the OED or historical corpora.
  - Could universals of SLA such as **generalisation** play a role?
  - Could **language contact** play a role?

Do not worry if you cannot come up on the spot with the ultimate explanation for the feature you investigated. Discuss your findings and pool your resources with others, try to follow what is going on in the field, and remember that scholarship is a group activity where everybody's contribution counts!

5.7 Exercises

Exercise 5.1

Consider the graph (Figure 5.3) which illustrates the results of Labov's famous *Fourth Floor* study in three New York City department stores. It plots the realisation of the linguistic variable (r) by shop assistants in 3 different kinds of shops: *Saks* is an expensive store, *Macy's* has a medium price range, and *Klein* offers cheap products. Labov asked his researchers to enter the shops and elicit the response 'fourth floor', for example by asking 'Excuse me, where can I find …?' He assumed that the shop assistants would match their speech patterns to the social class of their customers. What does the graph reveal about Labov's assumption – and about style-shifting?

5.8 Recommended reading

Sociolinguistics

Meyerhoff (2006) covers all relevant aspects of sociolinguistics in a very accessible manner, while never losing sight of larger theoretical issues. Trousdale (2010) is a more concise introduction to the field. For those who want a hands-on introduction to actually doing sociolinguistics, Meyerhoff et al. (2015) offer a step-by-step guide to current and time-tested sociolinguistic methods.

Language contact and contact-induced language change

Both Matras (2009) and Thomason (2001) cover all aspects of language contact phenomena in their introductory textbooks, ranging from borrowing and code-switching to contact-induced language change.

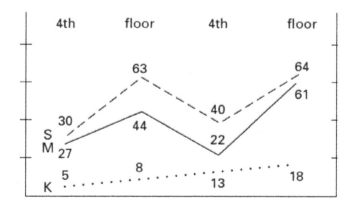

Figure 5.3 Realisation of the variable (r) first in casual and then in emphatic speech by shop assistants in *Saks* (S), *Macy's* (M), and *Klein* (K) (Labov 2006: 48; reprinted by permission from Cambridge University Press)

Spoken and written language

The paper by Quaglio and Biber (2008) provides a good starting point for getting an overview of the features of spoken and written language.

References

Beal, Joan C. (2004). *English in Modern Times*. London: Arnold.

D'Souza, Jean (1999). "Afterword." *World Englishes* 18(2): 271–274. doi: 10.1111/1467-971X.00139.

Eckert, Penelope (2012). "Three waves of variation study: The emergence of meaning in the study of sociolinguistic variation." *Annual Review of Anthropology* 41(1): 87–100. doi: 10.1146/annurev-anthro-092611-145828.

Ellis, Alexander John (1869). *On Early English Pronunciation Vol. 1*. London: Asher & Co. URL: https://archive.org/details/onearlyenglishp02winkgoog/page/n7. (Last access: 5 July 2019).

Greenbaum, Sidney (1990). "Standard English and the International Corpus of English." *World Englishes* 9(1): 79–83. doi: 10.1111/j.1467-971X.1990.tb00688.x.

Haspelmath, Martin (2009). "Lexical borrowing: Concepts and issues." In Haspelmath, Martin & Uri Tadmor (eds.), *Loanwords in the World's Languages*. Berlin: de Gruyter, 35–54. doi: 10.1515/9783110218442.35.

Hundt, Marianne (2016). "Global spread of English: Processes of change." In Kytö, Merja & Päivi Pahta (eds.), *The Cambridge Handbook of English Historical Linguistics*. Cambridge: Cambridge University Press, 318–334. doi: 10.1017/CBO9781139600231.021.

Jones, Daniel (1917). *An English Pronouncing Dictionary*. London: J.M. Dent.

Kortmann, Bernd, Kate Burridge, Rajend Mesthrie, Edgar W. Schneider & Clive Upton (eds.) (2004). *A Handbook of Varieties of English: Volume 2: Morphology and Syntax*. Berlin, New York: Mouton de Gruyter.

Labov, William (1972). *Sociolinguistic Patterns*. Philadelphia, PA: University of Pennsylvania Press.

Labov, William (2001). *Principles of Linguistic Change, Volume 2: Social Factors*. Malden, MA: Blackwell.

Labov, William (2006). *The Social Stratification of English in New York City*. Second edition. Cambridge: Cambridge University Press. First edition 1966.

Labov, William (2015). "The discovery of the unexpected." *Asia-Pacific Language Variation* 1 (1): 7–22. doi: 10.1075/aplv.1.1.01lab.

Matras, Yaron (2009). *Language Contact*. Cambridge: Cambridge University Press.

Meyerhoff, Miriam (2006). *Introducing Sociolinguistics*. London: Routledge.

Meyerhoff, Miriam, Erik Schleef, & Laurel MacKenzie (2015). *Doing Sociolinguistics: A Practical Guide to Data Collection and Analysis*. London: Routledge.

Mufwene, Salikoko (2001). *The Ecology of Language Evolution*. Cambridge: Cambridge University Press.

Quaglio, Paulo & Douglas Biber (2008). "The grammar of conversation." In McMahon, April & Bas Aarts (eds.), *The Handbook of English Linguistics*. Malden, MA: Blackwell, 692–723. doi: 10.1002/9780470753002.ch29.

Quirk, Randolph (1985). "The English language in a global context." In Quirk, Randolph & Henry G. Widdowson (eds.), *English in the World: Teaching and Learning the Language and Literatures*. Cambridge: Cambridge University Press, 1–10. URL:

www.teachingenglish.org.uk/article/english-world-teaching-learning-language-litera tures. (Last access: 5 July 2019).

Quirk, Randolph (1990). "Language varieties and standard language." *English Today* 21: 3–10. doi: 10.1017/S0266078400004454.

Schneider, Edgar W. (2007). *Postcolonial English. Varieties around the World*. Cambridge: Cambridge University Press.

Schneider, Edgar W. (2012). "Exploring the interface between World Englishes and Second Language Acquisition – and implications for English as a Lingua Franca." *Journal of English as a Lingua Franca* 1(1): 57–91. doi: 10.1515/jelf-2012-0004.

Selinker, Larry (1972). "Interlanguage." *International Review of Applied Linguistics in Language Teaching* 10(3): 209–231. doi: 10.1515/iral.1972.10.1-4.209.

Thomason, Sarah G. (2001). *Language Contact: An Introduction*. Washington, DC: Georgetown University Press.

Thomason, Sarah G. (2010). "Contact explanations in linguistics." In Hickey, Raymond (ed.), *The Handbook of Language Contact*. Malden, MA: Wiley-Blackwell, 29–47. doi: 10.1002/9781444318159.ch1.

Trousdale, Graeme (2010). *An Introduction to English Sociolinguistics*. Edinburgh: Edinburgh University Press.

Trudgill, Peter (1972). "Sex, covert prestige, and linguistic change in the urban British English of Norwich." *Language in Society* 1(2): 179–195. doi: 10.1017/S0047404500000488.

Trudgill, Peter (2017). "The spread of English." In Filppula, Markku, Juhani Klemola, & Devyani Sharma (eds.), *The Oxford Handbook of World Englishes*. Oxford: Oxford University Press, 14–34. doi: 10.1093/oxfordhb/9780199777716.013.002.

Whitworth, George Clifford (1907). *Indian English: An Examination of the Errors of Idiom Made by Indians in Writing English*. Letchworth, Herts: Garden City Press.

Williams, Jessica (1987). "Non-native varieties of English: A special case of language acquisition." *English World-Wide* 8(2): 161–199. doi: 10.1075/eww.8.2.02wil.

Wright, Arnold (1891). *Baboo English as 'tis Writ: Being Curiosities of Indian Journalism*. London: T. Fisher Unwin.

Chapter 6

Interpreting variation and change in World Englishes

Key terms:

Verb Phrase (VP):
aspect (simple – progressive); auxiliary verbs; dative alternation; mood & modality (epistemic – deontic); particle verbs; stative verbs; tense; transitive, intransitive, and ditransitive verbs; verb complementation

Noun Phrase (NP):
definiteness; definite and indefinite article; determiner; generalisation; pre- and post-modifier; quantifier

Sentence structure:
compound and complex sentence; conjunctions; fronting; interrogative/subject-auxiliary inversion; left-dislocation; pronoun copying; right-dislocation; sentence types (declarative; interrogative (polar and constituent); imperative; exclamative); topicalization

Lexicon:
borrowing; clipping; compounding; neologism; prefixation; productivity; suffixation

Pragmatics:
face (positive and negative); intensifiers; politeness; speech acts

6.1 Introduction

Now that you have accumulated so much theoretical and practical know-ledge about corpus linguistics and World Englishes, you are well equipped to go ahead and find your own research topics. This chapter will help you to get started. Its structure matches the levels of language from Chapter

2.4: We will look at research concerning inflectional morphology in the verb phrase (VP) and the noun phrase (NP) in the first two sections. On the level of sentence structure, we will consider studies that tackle lack of inversion in questions. Section 6.5. will focus on vocabulary in World Englishes, and the final section will deal with pragmatic aspects of language, such as intensifiers and discourse markers.

We will introduce each section with a brief reminder of technical terms that you might need. Throughout the chapter, we use sample sentences from the book *The New Englishes* by John Platt et al. (1984) for illustration of the relevant feature. Their book was the first comprehensive study of what is 'new' in the New Englishes, and many of their original observations have triggered corpus-linguistic research. Whenever you see the reference '(PWH: page number)' after an example sentence, it is taken from their book.

When we set out to choose the studies to present to you, we had several aspects in mind. We tried to pick studies that are quite well known and basic in their particular research direction, which means that they are quoted a lot by others. We also looked for studies that are accessible to you once you have worked your way through the first five chapters of this book. Finally, we chose studies that can in principle be done by a single person within a reasonable time frame, rather than by a whole team of people doing the data retrieval. Furthermore, we would like to emphasise that we do not seek to reprint the contents of entire studies here; rather, we focus on aspects of each study that we deem particularly important or interesting.

6.2 Researching the verb phrase

Let us start our investigation into properties of the VP in varieties of English with a line from an old song by the British rock band *Queen*:

(6.1) *I want to ride my bicycle.*

The sentence consists of two NPs, the pronoun 'I' and the pre-modified noun 'my bicycle', and the verb phrase 'want to ride'. The VP-slot could take other options, for example:

(6.2) *I ride my bicycle*
(6.3) *I am riding my bicycle*
(6.4) *I can ride my bicycle*
(6.5) *I should ride my bicycle*
(6.6) **I am having a new bicycle*
(6.7) *I am getting off my bicycle*
(6.8) *I have to put up with your bicycle*

Example sentences (6.2) and (6.3) only differ in **aspect**: 'ride' is the **simple** and 'riding' the **progressive** form, expressing an on-going action. Example (6.6) is marked with an asterisk to indicate that there is something peculiar about the construction. In Inner Circle Englishes, (6.6) is ungrammatical or at least unusual. **Stative** verbs such as 'have' generally do not occur in the progressive – but the examples (6.9) and (6.10) from Outer Circle Englishes show that such a restriction might not hold for them:

(6.9) Indian English: *Mohan* is having *two houses* (PWH: 72)
(6.10) East African English: *She* is knowing *her science very well* (PWH: 73)

Example sentences (6.4) and (6.5) feature **modal** verbs, which are one way of expressing **mood** or **modality**. Modal verbs in English and many other languages express two kinds of modal meanings. 'I *can* ride' tells others about the speaker's judgment, they might also say 'I know I am able to ride'. This kind of modality is about speakers' degree of certainty about what they believe to be true. The technical term is **epistemic modality** from the Greek word for 'knowledge'. 'I *should* ride', on the other hand, implies some kind of obligation placed on the speaker. **Deontic modality** thus concerns permission or obligation. English modal verbs are a subgroup of **auxiliary** verbs, with some special properties: Their behaviour in terms of inflection is quite different. There is no such form as **yes, he cans*, and *yes, he could* is not the past tense of *yes, he can*.

Example sentences (6.7) and (6.8) represent multi-word verbs or **particle verbs** (PVs). Reference grammars of English will tell you more about phrasal verbs, prepositional verbs, and how to distinguish between the two types. A phrasal-prepositional verb combines with two particles, as in example sentence (6.8). Such combinations are typically less transparent: You cannot work out the meaning of the whole expression by adding up the meanings of the individual parts of the verb phrase.

World Englishes display highly interesting patterns of variation in the area of tense, mood, and aspect. New studies continually add to our understanding of motivations for such variation, be it general language change, language contact, or other driving forces. We take a closer look at one of the pioneering corpus studies concerning the verb phrase in the next section.

Example study: particle verbs (Schneider 2004)

Background of the study

Edgar Schneider published a first paper concerned with his Dynamic Model in 2003; his monograph *Postcolonial English* appeared in 2007 and had an enormous impact on the field of World Englishes, as we saw in Chapter 2.3. Schneider's study on PVs appeared before his 2007 book, but its terminology and research agenda are already driven by his new model. The paper

138 Interpreting variation and change in WEs

was also among the first to make use of some of the recently released ICE corpora.

Aim of the study and research questions

Schneider first explains how a mix of factors has led him to his topic in the first place. To begin with, PVs belong to that 'lexico-grammatical borderline area' where a lot of variation is simply expected (2004: 229). PVs also arose quite late in the history of English as a native alternative to verbs of Latin origin, and might thus also display social variation in usage. Finally, other researchers had already hinted at new, variety-specific verb-particle combinations and meanings.

The immediate aim of the study is then to uncover patterns of structural nativisation (see Chapter 2.3) concerning phrasal verbs in World Englishes. The list of more specific research questions looks like this:

- *Incidence and frequency of use*: Are PVs in general, or certain PVs in particular, preferred in certain WEs? [...]
- *Structural behavior*: Is there any evidence for particular PVs being used and categorized grammatically differently in different varieties? [...]
- *Productivity range*: Is the propensity to coin new PVs stronger in some varieties than in others, or are certain new PV uses characteristic of any specific WE [=World English]? (Schneider 2004: 233)

Schneider's interest thus ranges from quantitative preferences to qualitative differences in the choice and formation of PVs. We pick out a quantitative and a qualitative aspect of the study and explain his procedure in our next step.

Method

The basis for the study are the ICE corpora from Singapore, the Philippines, and East Africa (Kenya and Tanzania considered separately), plus ICE-Great Britain for comparison. Data are presented as normalised frequencies per million words for the spoken and written sub-corpora separately. The spoken component of ICE-Philippines was not available at the time of writing.

⇒ Schneider's first research question concerns the frequency of PVs. How would you go about finding them in a corpus? What problems do you expect in narrowing down results?

◊ To find all types and tokens of particle verbs is a daunting task, as a glimpse at any *Dictionary of Phrasal Verbs* would tell you. You could start with the most frequent verbs, for example *give*, and set your concordance programme options to sort all hits according to the first word to the right of the search word. You

Interpreting variation and change in WEs 139

would thus see all instances of *give away, give in, give up*, and so on immediately, and you could zap away (see Chapter 3) all irrelevant concordance lines. You would have to make sure to include cases where the particle is separated from the verb, as in 'she *gave* her old bike *away*'. You could also compile a list of all possible verbs: In *AntConc*, click on '*Advanced Search*', check the box '*Use Search Term(s) from List Below*', and enter your list. In *WordSmith*, you have to turn your list into a separate file and then load it into the search window. Your life would be much easier with a tagged corpus! You would not have to specify each individual verb, but could search for the combination of [VERB] plus [PARTICLE].

Findings

To follow up on his first research question, Schneider put together a list of 20 PVs, including some very common and some less common ones. Nine items on his list did not show up at all in his data: "in other words, rare PVs are rare everywhere" (Schneider 2004: 235). Table 6.1 displays the results for the remaining 11 PVs.

⇒ How do you interpret the findings represented in the table? Pay special attention to the differences between spoken and written language.

◊ It is interesting to note that Singapore English (SinE) outranks the historical input variety British English (BrE) when it comes to the overall frequency of

Table 6.1 Frequencies of PVs normalised to 1 million words and rounded (Schneider 2004: 236; reprinted by permission from Wiley)

Lexical item/PV	GBspo/wri	SINspo/wri	PHIwri	INDspo/wri	EA-Kenspo/wri	EA-Tanzspo/wri
back off	0/2	5/2	2	0/0	0/0	0/0
cloud over	0/0	0/0	0	0/2	0/0	0/0
crop up	0/0	11/2	4	0/7	0/5	0 7 %
drop out	3/0	8/2	9	3/7	10/22	9/2
leak out	2/2	0/0	0	3/4	0/0	0/0
pull ahead	0/0	3/0	0	0/0	0/0	0/0
rush off	0/2	0/7	2	0/0	0/0	0/0
show up	5/14	9/11	9	0/4	0/10	0/7
sign off	0/7	2/7	0	1/7	0/0	0/2
sign up	2/5	9/23	4	0/2	0/0	0/0
turn up	46/19	26/9	4	9/7	25/20	14/15
sum	57/52	71/63	35	16/40	35/57	23/32
sum per region	55	68	35	26	46	29

140   Interpreting variation and change in WEs

PVs. Schneider adds that "Singaporean English shares with BrE the stylistic marking, with PVs being predominantly informal, i.e. occurring more frequently in spoken than in written texts, while in India and East Africa the stylistic signaling function is reversed" (2004: 235–36).

However, if we think about structural nativisation in connection with PVs, we might expect not only quantitative, but also qualitative differences between World Englishes. Some varieties may have extended the range of meanings of already existing PVs, or they may have come up with altogether new combinations of verb and particle. Schneider tackles this question under the heading 'productivity range', zooming in on semantic productivity. He first selected three PVs, namely *close up, put up,* and *cross over,* and then determined the range of meanings for each verb with the help of dictionaries. *Put up,* for example, may have 16 different meanings according to dictionaries of standard BrE, among them 'build', 'increase', or 'provide someone with a place to stay' (Schneider 2004: 243). First establishing all meanings and then matching them to actual corpus examples is a lot of work and not without ambiguities. Still, the results of this aspect of the study are displayed in Table 6.2.

The table "indicates the range of semantic types (out of the total number) and the overall token frequency for each variety" (2004: 243). For example,

Table 6.2 Range of meanings of selected PVs (meaning types/tokens) (Schneider 2004: 236; reprinted by permission from Wiley)

Lex-ical item/ PV	GB spo	wri	SIN spo	wri	PHI wri	IND spo	wri	EA-Ken spo	wri	EA-Tanz spo	wri
close up (6)	2/2	0/0	2/7	1/1	0/0	1/1	1/1	0/0	0/0	0/0	0/0
put up (16)	7/12	3/3	12/36	7/23	6/15	9/17	6/7	6/13	5/12	5/11	4/8
cross over (8)	0/0	2/2	4/5	4/5	0/0	1/1	0/0	0/0	0/0	0/0	2/2
sum (typ-es/ toke-ns)	9/14	5/5	18/48	18/48	6/15	11/19	7/8	6/13	5/12	5/11	6/10
sum per region		13/19	20/74		6/15	14/27		8/25		8/21	

out of 16 possible meanings for *cross over*, 7 occur in the spoken section of ICE-Great Britain, and these are realised by 12 tokens. SinE again turns out to be highly productive with respect to exploiting the range of meanings of PVs. A closer look at the individual tokens also reveals some innovative meanings that were so far not attested in dictionaries. At this stage, Schneider remains cautious about generalising his findings because the token frequencies are so low.

Evaluation and follow-up research

Schneider's study clearly spells out its research questions, its method, and its conclusions and thus remains a very instructive step-by-step introduction to the topic, especially since it includes both quantitative and qualitative aspects. Since then, a host of other corpora have become available for further studies. Schneider himself notes:

> However, token frequencies of individual forms were too low throughout to allow for significance testing or hard-and-fast acceptance of the results, so the correlations just referred to need to be interpreted with caution. They may represent emerging innovations, but whether they really are is impossible to tell. This will require either substantially larger corpora or, simply, the test of time.
>
> (2004: 247)

A huge corpus such as GloWbE would then be a suitable database for a follow-up study.

The more general label 'verb complementation' covers the combination of verbs with other constituents in a sentence, mainly objects. Schneider focused mostly on intransitive particle verbs; the following examples illustrate other verbal patterns (with or without particle):

(6.11) transitive: *She tried out the software*
(6.12) ditransitive: *I gave her the book/I gave the book to her*
(6.13) complex-transitive: *I consider her a genius*

Example (6.11) shows a **transitive** verb, requiring one direct object. The examples in (6.12) display the two possible patterns with a **ditransitive** verb. The first sentence has the beneficiary of the action or indirect object before the direct object. The order is reversed in the second sentence, but then the preposition *to* has to be added. The technical term for this is **dative alternation**. The term might strike you as odd – once you start looking for a dative case in English. Many European languages have kept a distinction between the four cases nominative, genitive, dative, and accusative, but English is not among them. Both 'her' and 'to her' are in the objective case (as opposed to the

142 Interpreting variation and change in WEs

subjective 'she'), so the term 'dative alternation' is a kind of fond memory of earlier stages of the language and a common European grammatical tradition. Example sentence (6.13) illustrates the **complex-transitive** construction: *genius* is the object complement referring to the object *her*.

Verb complementation in World Englishes continues to be extensively studied. For example, Mukherjee and Hoffmann (2006) is a pilot study about ditransitives in Indian English (IndE); further studies have since appeared which include more varieties. Complex transitives in World Englishes and Learner Englishes have been studied by Koch et al. (2018). There are still many more studies of verbal patterns out there for you to explore!

Replication task

Schneider also drew up a list of possible verb-particle combinations for "three base verbs of medium productivity" (2004: 242). He found these combinations:

- *count against / among / down / for / in / off / (up)on / out / toward / up*
- *help along / off with / on with / out / up,*
- *sign away / for / in / into / off / on / out / over / up / with*

Use GloWbE to retrieve these PVs and determine their normalised frequency in all varieties represented in GloWbE. How do you interpret the differences in distribution?

6.3 Researching the noun phrase

Recall our example (6.14) for a noun phrase (NP) from Chapter 2.4:

(6.14) *the frumious Bandersnatch*

An NP consists minimally of its head noun, in this case 'Bandersnatch', but can be **pre-modified** by other words and **post-modified** by prepositional phrases and/or a relative clause, for example (6.15):

(6.15) *the five ugly frumious Bandersnatches on bicycles who scared the hell out of me*

All noun modifiers are optional, but if they occur with a noun, they do so in a fixed order. First comes the **determiner**, in this case the definite article 'the'. Other forms in this slot could be demonstrative pronouns such as 'this/ these', possessive pronouns such as 'my', or words indicating a quantity such as 'every, some, many' (so-called **quantifiers**). The next pre-NP slot is for words carrying additional or more specific information about the noun, typically adjectives such as 'ugly' and 'frumious', but also the numeral 'five'. There is no

Interpreting variation and change in WEs 143

limit to the number of adjectives except the speaker's creativity (and the listener's patience)!

Post-modifying relative clauses may vary with respect to the relative pronoun introducing them. The options here are *who*, *which*, *that*, or zero, depending on a variety of factors. Now consider the following example sentences (6.16) to (6.19) from World Englishes:

(6.16) Nigerian English: I lost all my *furnitures* and valuable *properties* (PWH: 50)
(6.17) Philippines English: He has many gray *hairs* (PWH: 50)
(6.18) Singaporean English: I want to buy *[ø]* bag (PWH: 56)
(6.19) Irish English: So it means that I'm getting pissed on *the* Tuesday and all day on *the* Wednesday <#> Youse are all coming out as well on *the* Tuesday <#> I'm giving youse three months' notice (ICE-IR S1A-017:A)

Example sentences (6.16) and (6.17) may remind you of Chapter 5.4, where we discussed the loss of the distinction between count nouns and non-count nouns as a case of **generalisation**. Examples (6.18) and (6.19) obviously have to do with the unexpected presence or absence of articles with NPs. This topic has received a lot of attention from scholars, and we will take you through one of the studies that has investigated this phenomenon across a range of World Englishes.

Example study: definite articles (Sand 2004)

The feature we consider in more detail with regard to the NP is article usage. More precisely, we ask how the **indefinite article** *a/an* and the **definite article** *the* are used in World Englishes. Perhaps, this may not seem like an obvious choice at first: How much variation can there truly be in article usage? However, as our example study by Sand (2004) and follow-up studies are able to show, there is quite substantial variation in how the indefinite and definite articles are used in varieties of English. Furthermore, the study of articles entails certain methodological challenges worthy of mention. Thus, Sand's paper published in *World Englishes* serves as our focus for this section on NPs. In order to limit ourselves, we describe the general outline and method for all types of articles, but only discuss the results for the definite article.

In order to give you an idea of how article usage may vary, consider the sets of nouns with and without the different possible articles in (6.20):

(6.20) a. *society; a society; the society*
     b. *university; a university; the university*
     c. *people; a people; the people*

⇒ Based on the examples, which criteria seem to affect the presence of the indefinite and the definite article? Can you explain the difference between the three members of each set? Do they achieve the same effect for every example?

◊ The main aspect affected by using articles is the **definiteness** of a noun: *The university* refers to a clearly specified university (e.g. *The university should cover these expenses*); *a university* refers to any university (e.g. *A university is a safe haven for people of all kinds*); and *university* without an article refers to the institution in the most general sense (e.g. *I would like to study at university one day*). Exceptions are, of course, possible, and certain phrases do not require the article despite the fact that the university is clearly identified (e.g. *I'm leaving at eight in the morning to go to university*). Article usage becomes particularly complex when a word is semantically ambiguous, such as *people* in the three examples: *a people* is possible in any variety, but it usually refers to a specific group of people who share a cultural or ethnic background.

An example from ICE-Singapore is given in (6.21), with *the university* being the NP of interest.

(6.21) We don't need to go to the university to acquire you know a degree in mathematics simple arithmetic will get you the answer (ICE-SIN S2A-002)

Background of the study

In 2004, when Sand released her paper on article usage in different varieties of English, systematic studies using the ICE components were still a bit of a novelty. Furthermore, large-scale comparisons of varieties were rare. Thus, she took the opportunity to compare contact and 'non-contact' varieties of English as well as Learner English. A particularly interesting aspect covered by her study is the investigation of 'New Englishisms' (Simo Bobda 2000). New Englishisms or angloversals are features presumed to be shared across all or a majority of (second-language) varieties of English, with the potential reasons behind their emergence ranging from general vernacular tendencies to effects of Second Language Acquisition (SLA).

Aim of the study and research questions

Sand does not explicitly spell out the aims of her study, but they become apparent in the introductory part to her article: she wants to contribute to comparative corpus work on World Englishes and add a piece to the puzzle of which features are shared amongst different varieties of English. In particular, she is interested in the role of language contact: she wants to find out if the article usage in speakers' mother tongues affects the way that speakers use the articles in English. Thus, she wants to find empirical evidence for or against an increased or reduced article usage based on the system in the major contact language of a variety. If, for instance, a first

Interpreting variation and change in WEs | 145

language does not have direct articles, an underuse in the variety of English would be expected.

Method

Sand (2004) primarily employs ICE components for her study, but enriches the ICE-based dataset with additional corpus material. Since her interest is in comparing article usage in contact and non-contact as well as learner varieties, using quite different material emerges as a necessary by-product.

The contact varieties of interest in Sand's study are represented in ICE-Singapore, ICE-India, the Kenyan component of ICE-East Africa, ICE-Jamaica, and the *Northern Ireland Transcribed Corpus of Speech* (NITCS). We know that ICE-Ireland is available today and has been for several years, but in 2004, the date of the paper's publication, it was not yet ready to be used. ICE-Great Britain and ICE-New Zealand serve as the 'non-contact' varieties, although we will discuss this terminology below. Finally, Sand also analyses the German component of the *International Corpus of Learner English* (ICLE), which features 40,000 words. (For a closer discussion of learner corpora, we refer you to Chapter 7.)

⇒ Remember what you have learned so far about the varieties covered by Sand (2004). How are they different and how are they similar? Do you see any problems with Sand's classification of BrE and New Zealand English (NZE) as non-contact varieties?

◊ Sand's reasoning to consider these varieties as a contrast to contact varieties is obvious, since they are native languages in their countries. However, we know that, for instance, cities such as London are melting pots of many different cultures and languages: English is certainly in contact with many other languages there (and elsewhere, too).

Further comparisons are made possible by Sand's references to studies that investigated article usage in corpora from the Brown family of corpora.

Findings

Sand (2004: 287) first reports the findings for the definite article across all corpora and text types, using the section headings of ICE for navigation. Table 6.3 shows the normalised figures per 1,000 words in each analysed text type and variety. As an example, 45.6 tokens of the direct article can be found on average in the private conversations in ICE-Jamaica., marked by S1A. For a full list of the included text types, we refer you to Chapter 4.3; a quick reference for convenience follows: S1A = private dialogues; S1B =

146 Interpreting variation and change in WEs

public dialogues; S2A+B = monologues; W1A = non-professional writing; W2A = academic writing; W2B = non-academic writing; W2C = reportage; W2D = instructional writing; W2E = persuasive writing; W2F = creative writing.

⇒ Based on the results shown in Table 6.3, which conclusions can we draw about the distribution of the definite article in spoken and written language in general and in the included varieties in particular?

◊ The definite article is generally more frequent in written language, although it is less frequent in fiction (W2F) than in the other included types of writing. The differences between contact and non-contact as well as learner varieties do not seem extreme, although there are some clear outliers (for instance, 88.1 tokens in the W2C, E section of ICE-India). In general, academic writing features higher frequencies of the direct article compared to other text types.

Sand cannot identify a strong influence of the article system in the contact language on the variety of English, with the small exception of the informal spoken conversations: ICE-Nigeria and NICTS feature higher frequencies of the direct article there, and they represent the only two contact varieties with a direct article system.

In order to delve deeper into differences between contact varieties and BrE and NZE, Sand considers examples on a qualitative level. She finds, for instance, that "[t]he definite article is found recurrently with collective nouns with a generic meaning, such as society, people, men, women, boys or girls" (2004: 290) as well as to refer to institutions, such as *church* or *college*. Two examples from the ICE corpora are shown in (6.22) and (6.23):

Table 6.3 Definite articles across all text types and corpora normalised per 1,000 words

	S1A	S1B	S2A, B	W1A	W2A, B, D,	W2C, E	W2F
ICE-GB	27.2	50.6	57.5	73.9	74.0	72.0	54.5
ICE-NZ	33.8	56.3	68.6	86.6	76.8	68.4	65.5
ICE-JAM	45.6	56.0	52.7	78.0	74.1	79.2	51.5
ICE-EA(K)	35.1	60.0	64.9	67.6	67.8	71.9	53.3
ICE-IND	31.3	69.9	78.7	62.8	76.5	88.1	63.5
ICE-SIN	30.9	53.1	61.3	79.7	67.0	63.0	52.3
NITCS	47.3	–	–	–	–	–	–
ICLE-GERM	–	–	–	60.7	–	–	–

(adapted from Sand 2004: 287; reprinted by permission from Wiley)

(6.22) The girls tend to fare better in these subjects. (ICE-SIN W1A-007)

(6.23) So you must be wondering why people must go to the church (ICE-EA (K) conversations)

Evaluation and follow-up research

A major conclusion that Sand draws is that "the substrate hypothesis with regard to article use cannot be substantiated through quantitative analysis" (2004: 294). Hypotheses about expected article usage based on contact languages do not hold for the ICE data except for the spontaneous conversations. Differences that can be attributed to text type seem much more important; they even "override any variety-specific preferences" (2004: 295).

In terms of methodology, Sand's study is a good early representative of a trend that has become more fashionable in the late 2000s and the 2010s. Rather than zooming in on a feature in one variety, studies now often compare different varieties and even varieties belonging to ENL, ESL, and EFL. This entails using several corpora and building on a solid methodological foundation. For instance, while ICE and learner corpora can be compared, it should always be pointed out in which contexts the corpora were created and in which ways they are similar or different.

⇒ Sand (2004) considers the definite and the indefinite articles, but which category is missing – and what could be a reason for that omission?

◊ The third option that is available to speakers is zero, that is, the omission of the article. Identifying instances of what is not there in a corpus is still a big challenge, which can sometimes be tackled by using a parsed corpus. Reading a corpus in its entirety can also be a good alternative, but the manual work involved in that task is enormous and certainly close to impossible for the dataset that Sand (2004) uses. A further aspect that could be added in her study is a comparison of how certain nouns or kinds of nouns are treated across the corpora: It would be interesting to know if the same noun that takes an article in one case is used without one in another NP – and why. However, these are rather detailed considerations that may well open up avenues for further research.

Two more recent studies concerned with article usage in World Englishes are Sharma (2005) and Filppula and Klemola (2017). Unlike Sand (2004), Filppula and Klemola select a narrower focus and only investigate article usage with names of social institutions (e.g. *church* and *university*) and quantifying expressions (e.g. *both of* and *half of*).

148 Interpreting variation and change in WEs

Replication task

One way of replicating Sand's study would be to look for indefinite and definite articles in the ICE corpora that have been released since 2004. Using a regular expression would be crucial here in order to only find tokens relevant to your study. You can also look into specific examples in GloWbE to see whether the qualitative differences in direct article usage between World Englishes suggested by Sand (2004) hold up, which would be an easier task. Consider, in particular, the following examples from Sand's study:

- collective nouns: *society*; *people*; *men*; *women*; *boys*; *girls*
- nouns referring to institutions: *church*; *university*; *college*; *school*; *jail*

In a next step, you could quantify these results by calculating the normalised frequencies on the basis of the size of the different GloWbE components (see Chapter 4.4).

6.4 Researching sentence structure

We have already touched upon basics of English sentence structure in Chapter 2.4. Syntax is a topic as fascinating as it is vast, which means we can only offer you some appetisers and encourage you to explore further on your own. Unfortunately, studying syntactic patterns in corpora also takes a bit more effort: You would need at least a POS-tagged corpus, since syntactically parsed corpora are still thin on the ground.

We can look at sentence structure from different perspectives. First of all, there are four basic sentence types: the plain statement or **declarative**, the question or **interrogative**, the command or **imperative**, and finally the **exclamative** such as 'What a difference a day makes!' Sentences can also be joined by **conjunctions** to form larger units. **Compound** sentences are independent of each other and joined by coordinating conjunctions such as *and, or*. **Complex** sentences consist of a main clause and a subordinate clause.

⇒ Determine the sentence type of each of the following examples (6.24) to (6.28) and add whether the sentence is simple, compound, or complex:

(6.24) and how many times have you seen the the accused mister chow (ICE-NZ:S1B-069#9:1:C)

(6.25) my friend leave this place or don't do this thing (ICE-NIG con01)

(6.26) oh what a great feeling of freedom that is. (ICE-PHI:W1B-013#133:3)

(6.27) Kandy has been the focal point in the advancement of agriculture in the country, and a ramble in any direction from the hill capital will present a landscape portraying the vestiges of a bygone agricultural era. (ICE-SL: W2B-002#56:1)

Interpreting variation and change in WEs   149

(6.28) The authors of a joint work are co-owners of the copyright in the work, unless there is an agreement to the contrary. (ICE-USA:W2D-004#19:1)

These sentences follow the basic English word order of subject-verb-object (SVO). You might protest straight away and point at example sentence (6.24), which is nowhere close to SVO. When linguists refer to *basic* word order, they have the word order in declaratives in mind. Many (but not all) languages have a different word order for interrogatives.

In English, the position of subjects, verbs, and objects in a sentence is quite fixed; only adverbials have more freedom of movement. With this in mind, consider the examples (6.29) to (6.32) from World Englishes:

(6.29) East African English: My daughter *she* is attending the University of Nairobi (PWH: 120)
(6.30) Indian English: Because *Hindi* they have declared as National Language (PWH: 121)
(6.31) Malaysian English: What time he come? (PWH: 127)
(6.32) Indian English: Do you know what *will be the rate*? (PWH: 127)

Example (6.29) is a straightforward declarative, but with one additional element – a repetition of the subject 'my daughter' by the pronoun 'she'. PWH call this 'pronoun-copying' (1984: 119), a strategy common in all Englishes, but more frequent in New Englishes. The additional pronoun also goes by the label 'resumptive pronoun', and a technical term for the whole construction is **Left Dislocation** or LD. **Right Dislocation** or RD also occurs, as in this example (6.33):

(6.33) you know it's a wankers' table that <,> (ICE-GB: S1A-052#078:2:A)

Sample sentence (6.30) departs from the basic word order. The object 'Hindi' is moved to the beginning of the sentence in a position even before the subject. Such **fronting** occurs across Englishes, but in Inner Circle varieties it has a special meaning. The fronted constituent carries special emphasis and would also be stressed in spoken language. Fronting, or **topicalization** (Leuckert 2019), typically creates a contrast to something else, as in:

(6.34) Big white Wyandotte ducks
No uh *Aylesbury ducks* I should say (ICE-GB:S1A-028 #304–305:1:A)

The next two examples deal with variation in the form of interrogatives. English questions are generally formed by letting the subject and the auxiliary verb change their position. The technical term is **subject-auxiliary inversion** or simply **interrogative inversion**. Exceptions do occur, but again these are related to special emphasis, as in the exasperated question 'You did WHAT?' If a sentence has no auxiliary, then a form of 'do' has to do the job of moving in front of the subject. In example sentence (6.31), the question is formed without an additional form of 'do'. Example

150   Interpreting variation and change in WEs

sentence (6.32) is even more intriguing. Here we have a complex sentence consisting of the main clause 'Do you know' and the subordinate clause 'what will be the rate'. Taken together, the construction is an indirect question, and those generally do not invert. Some varieties such as IndE and Irish English (IrE) are reported to lack inversion, as we will see shortly. But before we continue, we need two more technical terms concerning interrogatives. Consider these two questions, (6.35) and (6.36):

(6.35) And uh did you find out what was going on (ICE-CAN S1B-062 #134:1:A)

(6.36) Sweetie where did you get those lamps from (ICE-CAN S1A-074 #77:1:B)

The first question is a **polar interrogative** that can be answered by *yes* or *no* and begins with an auxiliary. The second question, a **constituent interrogative**, is introduced by a question word and requires a more elaborate answer.

Example study: interrogative inversion (Hilbert 2008)

Background of the study

The starting point of Hilbert's study is the common observation that the forms of interrogative constructions may differ in non-standard varieties of English. She applies the label 'non-standard varieties' to Inner Circle dialects such as African American Vernacular English (AAVE) as well as Outer Circle Englishes. Her main focus is on IndE and SinE, representing contact varieties of English.

Aim of the study and research questions

One aim of the study is to find out whether the claim about IndE made by the Indian linguist Rakesh Bhatt is empirically correct. He says:

> in vernacular IndE inversion is restricted to embedded questions; it does not apply in matrix questions. The question formation strategy in vernacular IndE is the mirror image of that of StIndE [Standard Indian English], where inversion is restricted to matrix contexts.
>
> (Bhatt 2004: 1020)

Hilbert also wants to go beyond IndE and the relatively straightforward matter of proving or disproving a single observation about its structure. Her ultimate aim is not only to take stock of interrogative inversion. Rather, she is looking for "the factors determining their occurrence or non-occurrence in order to actually *explain* their development" (Hilbert 2008: 262). Her main emphasis is on IndE, but SinE is included as well because it "is generally described to display very similar properties as Indian English" (2008: 270).

Method

The study is based on the spoken section of ICE-India and ICE-Singapore. Hilbert's search method limits the results somewhat, as we can infer from this description:

> The discussion will be largely restricted to constituent interrogatives as they are unambiguously retrievable from the corpus by means of the interrogative pronouns. The analysis of polar interrogatives in Indian English is based only on the mark-up in ICE-India, which has question marks in part of the spoken section of the corpus, a mark-up which is not used in the other ICE corpora. Main clause constituent interrogatives are selected independently of this mark-up.
>
> (2008: 270)

Later on in her investigation, she also adds data from ICE-Great Britain for comparison.

Findings

Tables 6.4 and 6.5 present her figures for interrogative inversion/absence of inversion in main clauses and in indirect questions.

These figures clearly prove Bhatt wrong: lack of inversion in main clauses is not the majority option in IndE nor is inversion in indirect questions pervasive.

Table 6.4 Inversion in main clause interrogatives in ICE-India (Hilbert 2008: 273; reprinted by permission from John Benjamins)

	Polar interrogatives		Constituent interrogatives	
	tokens	%	tokens	%
+ inv	474	63	540	81
- inv	261	37	67	11

Table 6.5 Inversion in indirect questions with constituent interrogatives in ICE-India and ICE-Singapore, relative frequencies (in %) (Hilbert 2008: 276; reprinted by permission from John Benjamins)

	ICE-India	ICE-Singapore
+ inv	18	14
- inv	82	86

152 Interpreting variation and change in WEs

Moreover, a question lacking inversion is not automatically non-standard, as this example shows:

(6.37) How come you're asking this idiot question like that (ICE-IND:S1A-049#201:1:B)

Uninverted questions such as a surprised *You've been there?*, are also possible across Englishes. Hilbert does not examine possible non-standard constructions – uninverted main clause interrogatives and inverted indirect questions – any further. In the following, she focuses solely on the standard-like cases for both types of interrogative and proceeds to look at the verb type. She first turns to her results for constituent interrogatives (those introduced by a question word). Her two bar charts visualise her figures quite clearly, even though she does not provide the exact percentages or the absolute frequencies. Still, the bar charts for ICE-India and ICE-Singapore show an interesting correlation between verb type and presence or absence of inversion. Questions with 'be' as full verb overwhelmingly show inversion (around 90%), questions with a modal verb have an inversion rate of around 80%. Finally, questions with a full lexical verb, which require a form of 'do' for inversion, are least likely to invert, with a rate of around 60% to 70%. The figures for polar interrogatives from ICE-India are quite similar.

Hilbert now proceeds with an analysis of verb types in indirect questions or 'embedded constituent interrogatives'. Recall Table 6.5 above, which gives us an indication of the relative frequencies of this construction, but unfortunately no absolute figures. Still, it is interesting to note that "[i]nversion almost exclusively occurs with forms of *be* in both varieties" (Hilbert 2008: 275). She then concludes:

> The presence of inversion in Indian English and Singapore English is thus based on the availability of frequent and fixed chunks, rather than the application of a productive rule. Inversion in embedded interrogatives is not a case of overgeneralisation of the main clause word order to embedded clauses, but rather again of the availability of fixed chunks that are used to introduce an embedded interrogative clause.
>
> (2008: 276)

The remainder of her paper explores the idea that the patterns found in IndE and SinE match those found in SLA. Hilbert draws on many studies of how learners acquire the rules of question formation, and she also finds parallels when it comes to 'chunks' or formulaic language. In the case of interrogative inversion, such 'chunks' would be combinations of *how, what, why, who, where, when*, and a form of *be*. Learners typically make their lives easier by memorising readymade chunks rather than a complex rule. Hilbert thus concludes that such learner strategies have also shaped second-language (L2) Englishes,

Interpreting variation and change in WEs   153

"learner development can become fossilised in the context of group second language acquisition" (2008: 284).

Evaluation and follow-up research

Hilbert published a follow-up study in 2011 on a slightly different dataset. The spoken data for ICE-India and ICE-Singapore were restricted to the direct conversation files (Hilbert 2011: 130), and data for IrE were added. Inversion in indirect questions is known to occur in IrE and is generally explained with language contact with Irish Gaelic. Hilbert said in her earlier paper that "a closer analysis of the form in which embedded inversion occurs is necessary in order to solve such uncertainties" (2008: 286). If IrE patterns with IndE and SinE in the frequencies and distribution of verb types in interrogative constructions, then a contact explanation would be less convincing.

The paper reprints the bar charts with the relative frequencies of verb types in inverted and non-inverted constituent interrogatives (Hilbert 2011: 130–131). Now we are faced with a potentially misleading inaccuracy: According to the author, data for the first paper came from "the spoken sections" of the ICE corpora (Hilbert 2008: 270). Recall from Chapter 4.3 that the spoken part of every ICE corpus comprises different spoken registers and amounts to around 600,000 words. The ICE conversation files are a subset of these, of around 100,000 words. For a study to be fully replicable, make sure to always be precise about your database, your method of retrieval, and your actual figures!

Hilbert's data on IrE do not come from ICE-Ireland, which was not available at the time of writing. She also does not provide information on her data source, the *Hamburg Corpus of Irish English* (HCIE) (Hilbert 2011: 125), and again no absolute frequencies. She considers only indirect questions in IrE, since the variety does not feature lack of inversion in main clauses. She provides no counts for the frequency of inverted as against uninverted indirect questions in IrE. The two tables, Tables 6.6 and 6.7, list the relative frequencies of verb types in inverted indirect questions.

Table 6.6 Verb types in inverted embedded constituent interrogatives (Hilbert 2011: 133; reprinted by permission from John Benjamins)

+ inv	IrE	IndE	SinE
be	94%	98%	89%
modal	0%	0%	7%
full verb	6%	2%	3%

154 Interpreting variation and change in WEs

Table 6.7 Verb types in inverted embedded polar interrogatives (Hilbert 2011: 134; reprinted by permission from John Benjamins)

+ inv	IrE	IndE	SinE
be	22%	100%	90%
modal	28%	0%	0%
full verb	50%	0%	10%

Remember that the earlier study only included data for polar interrogatives from ICE-India, which were retrieved by searching for the question mark (Hilbert 2008: 270). This later paper does not mention data retrieval, so we might assume that the problem of finding relevant constructions has been solved in the meantime, perhaps by simply reading all conversation files and manually marking the relevant constructions.

All in all, IrE patterns with IndE and SgE when it comes to the preferred verbs in constructions such as (6.38):

(6.38) Let me know how is all the old Neighbours (Hilbert 2011: 133).

But with polar interrogatives, illustrated by the next example (6.39), IrE stands out, as Table 6.7 shows.

(6.39) You ask me is Hamilton home from New Zealand. (Hilbert 2011: 134)

Hilbert concludes from her investigations that the different verb choices in IrE as compared to IndE and SinE point to different motivations for the phenomenon. Strategies of SLA may best explain the patterns in the two Asian varieties, while substrate influence may be the underlying factor for the subset of IrE interrogatives that pattern differently.

Replication task

If you want to tackle embedded inversion, then the paper "Investigating Irish English with ICE-Ireland" by Gerold Schneider (2013) is just for you. Schneider lists several morphosyntactic features of IrE and then shows us how to actually find them in a corpus with the help of regular expressions (see Chapter 3.4).

Schneider first describes the properties of embedded inversion in IrE (2013: 154). He notes that the construction is typically introduced by verbs such as, *ask, know, wonder, see,* and some others. And indeed, the two example sentences quoted above from Hilbert's study do contain *know* and *ask*. You can replicate Schneider's results (and test Hilbert's) by opening

Interpreting variation and change in WEs   155

AntConc, loading the spoken files from ICE-Ireland (or any other corpus you are interested in), and searching for the following regular expression:

- \bask\w*\w+ (was|is|are|will|would) (Schneider 2013: 155)

This query retrieves all forms of the lemma *ask*, followed by one intervening word and then by any form of *be*. Not all hits are relevant, but Schneider finds 11 'true positives' in this way. Try this query for the other verbs as well!

Schneider points out that most relevant tokens across ICE corpora with *know* are negated. The regular expression to track them down goes like this:

- n['?o]t know\w*\w+ (was|is|s|are|will|ll|would)\b (Schneider 2013: 155)

Schneider found that IrE patterns more with other Outer Circle than with Inner Circle varieties in the results for this particular query. ICE-Hong-Kong and ICE-Philippines have the highest number of tokens, followed by ICE-Singapore and ICE-Ireland with the same number (Schneider 2013: 156). Now it is your turn to continue the investigation!

6.5 Researching the lexicon

We saw in Chapter 2.3 that the first stages of contact between English-speaking settlers and indigenous populations typically went along with the **borrowing** of lexical items for plants, animals, or natural phenomena in general. We would therefore expect all varieties of English to have their own unique set of words, reflecting local experience. Global Englishes, on the other hand, share a 'common

Figure 6.1 Madam & Eve (from https://twitter.com/madamevecartoon/status/426232112824328192; reprinted by permission from the creators)

156 Interpreting variation and change in WEs

core', as the linguist Gerald Nelson has demonstrated in a study from 2006 based on six ICE corpora. The South African cartoon strip from the series 'Madam & Eve' (Figure 6.1) illustrates what is special and what is shared across varieties. The Mielie lady sells corncobs, which are called *milies* or *mealies*, a borrowing from Dutch into South African English. Then she takes a *selfie break* – an expression that did not even exist at the time when the first ICE corpora were compiled, but might now be part of the common core of Englishes around the world!

Studying the lexicon of World Englishes is a fascinating endeavour, since creative forces are always at work when the vocabulary is expanded. We can see this kind of creativity in our everyday lives. Advertising, youth language, and branding are just some areas in which new words are constantly created.

Example study: word-formation (Biermeier 2014)

The first question that you might have with regard to the vocabulary might be the following: How do new words enter a language or a variety of a language? Of course, words and even structures may be borrowed from another language. This is a very important strategy for the lexicon of World Englishes, in particular in their early developmental stages: As we mentioned above, colonisers explored other countries and needed words for the local flora and fauna and cultural phenomena – which the indigenous community usually already had. However, new words may also be created using one of the many word-formation techniques available to us. We can (re-)combine words, add or remove parts of a word, and even create entirely new words on the spot. Some of these processes are more 'common' than others and can be applied to more words; we call them productive and refer to their **productivity**.

⇒ Consider the examples given in (6.40): Which word-formation patterns resulted in the creation of these words? Which of the processes are (highly) productive and which are not? Finally, can you spot an example that is semantically ambiguous?

(6.40) a. *reconsider*; *unknown*; *debone*
      b. *flu*; *lab*; *gas*
      c. *blackbird*; *greenhouse*; *English teacher*
      d. *friendliness*; *neighbourhood*; *thoughtful*

◊ The examples in a. are instances of prefixation (=a prefix is added to a word); those in b. represent clipping (=parts of a word are removed, e.g. *in-* and *-enza* from *influenza*); the words in c. result from compounding (=two words are joined to create a new word); and, finally, the words in d. involve suffixation (=a suffix is added to a word). With the exception of clipping, all of these word-formation processes are highly productive in English. A clearly ambiguous example is *English teacher* in c. Depending on whether the primary stress in this example falls on *English* or *teacher*, the teacher is a teacher of English or a teacher from England.

In World Englishes, but not only there, studying how new words are formed, and in which contexts they are used is a highly interesting endeavour. Word-formation in varieties of English can give insights into culture and creativity, which is why we focus on an example study by Biermeier (2014) here.

Background of the study

Word-formation did not receive a great deal of attention in World Englishes until the 2000s, which Biermeier takes as his primary incentive to carry out his own study on this topic. After all, "the number of speakers and writers in countries where English is non-native has steadily grown in recent years" (2014: 312): We want to find out how and to what extent word-formation processes are similar or different between second-language varieties, but also between native and second-language varieties of English.

Although it is not a focus of Biermeier's article, linguistic creativity in English literary writing is another highly interesting development to consider. Poetry, prose, and any other kind of literature and text production in a wider sense promises intriguing insights into how English gradually becomes accepted in communities. In producing creative texts, writers frequently make use of word-formation processes and introduce or popularise local phenomena.

Aim of the study and research questions

For Biermeier, charting the territory and developing a sense of word-formation patterns across World Englishes is the primary objective. In particular, he is interested in compounding and suffixation. The research aim he explicitly states is "to show that the new varieties under inspection use these techniques of making words widely and creatively" (2014: 312). For this section of the chapter, we limit ourselves to compounds in Biermeier's analysis.

Method

Biermeier (2014) compares compounding and suffixation in twelve varieties of English as they are represented in ICE (see Table 6.8). The study covers varieties from both the Inner and the Outer Circle.

⇒ One of Biermeier's aims is to assess which lexemes are 'new'. Which strategy can we apply to assess if a word can reasonably be called a neologism? How would you deal with this problem?

◊ It is probably impossible to say for certain that a word or an expression has never been used before, since we do not have recordings of all language ever produced. Still, some methods can be used to be relatively sure about its

158 Interpreting variation and change in WEs

Table 6.8 Varieties covered in Biermeier's (2014) study on prefixation and compounding in World Englishes

Variety	Corpus
Inner Circle/L1 varieties of English	
American English	ICE-US (written component)
British English	ICE-Great Britain
Canadian English	ICE-Canada
New Zealand English	ICE-New Zealand
Outer Circle/L2 varieties of English	
Ghanaian English	ICE-Ghana
Hong Kong English	ICE-Hong Kong
Indian English	ICE-India
Kenyan English	ICE-East Africa
Nigerian English	ICE-Nigeria
Philippine English	ICE-Philippines
Singapore English	ICE-Singapore
Tanzanian English	ICE-East Africa

status. Biermeier follows a common path by looking for the respective word in dictionaries and big corpora. The dictionaries he uses are *Collins English Dictionary* [CED], *Merriam-Webster's Collegiate Dictionary*, *Oxford English Dictionary* [OED], *Oxford Dictionary of English* [ODE], and *Random House Webster's Unabridged Dictionary*. We would also recommend to try to ensure that a word truly is a neologism by double-checking in various dictionaries and corpora!

Findings

Biermeier (2014) is a follow-up study to a larger analysis carried out in an earlier work (Biermeier 2008). Thus, the analysis in the article is limited to 180 compounds, divided into

*   100 compound nouns,
*   40 compound verbs,
*   and 40 compound adjectives.

Quantitatively, Biermeier does not identify major differences between the varieties; he comments that "[s]peakers and writers of L2 varieties use the same compounding techniques with more or less similar frequencies" (2014: 315). The most interesting findings in the study on compounds concern creativity, with some unusual compounds found in more than one variety.

⇒ Some examples of compounds identified in the study are *petrol kiosk*; *to queue-vote*; *comfort room*; and *to dog proof*. Can you guess their meaning?

◊ *Petrol kiosk* is perhaps the clearest example in terms of its meaning – it refers to a petrol station and occurs in SinE. *To queue-vote*, found in Kenyan English, means to "wait in a queue for your turn to vote" (Biermeier 2014: 316).

Evaluation and follow-up research

Biermeier's work in this article and beyond has become important research on word-formation in World Englishes. Criticism that could be directed specifically at the article we discuss here is the lack of a stronger theoretical background. In order to get a better idea of the theory behind the article, it is necessary to consult Biermeier (2008) as well as other additional literature.

On a surface level, it also seems critical to restrict the number of compounds under analysis to items in a prefabricated list. Since Biermeier points out his choice and addresses it clearly, it can hardly be criticised: Not limiting the number of possible compounds would indeed lead to an analysis that would no longer be appropriate for the scope of an article. Perhaps, it would actually be impossible to go into detail with all compounds found in a corpus. Thus, if you are interested in doing research on compounds yourself, you should find a way to limit the scope of the study – this is another scenario in which ambition and pragmatism need to be balanced.

A positive aspect is the very detailed qualitative and quantitative analysis of the dataset. Biermeier provides many fascinating examples from the varieties and gives a good idea of some frequency differences between the corpora. For more recent work on word-formation processes, we suggest you consider Horch (2017 and 2019). These publications might be particularly interesting to you, since Horch makes a case for complementing corpus studies with experimental data. This obviously entails more work but may also lead to more robust results.

Replication task

Similar to other studies we discussed in this chapter, Biermeier (2014) only focuses on a set of varieties. You can use the appendix provided by Biermeier (2008) in order to look for compounds in additional varieties. It should also be quite interesting to consider Learner Englishes: do corpora of Learner English also contain many instances of creative compounding – and are the frequencies comparable to first- and second-language varieties or are there differences?

6.6 Researching pragmatics

You know from the end of Chapter 2.4 that pragmatics is not about structural aspects of language, but about communication and our intentions in doing so. In pragmatics, we do not analyse isolated sentences but utterances in context and try to uncover what the speaker meant or wanted to achieve by saying something. Language is a highly sophisticated tool for social organisation that all humans have in common. However, how we organise our living together is quite culture-specific, so we would expect culture-specific differences in peoples' communicative behaviour to be reflected in their use of English. In some cultures, speakers habitually address each other by their first names, in others speakers add a respectful 'ma'am' or 'sir', and in still others children are told not to address their parents directly by their names.

Terms of address belong to the field of linguistic **politeness**. Politeness in general is concerned with respecting each person's **face**, "the public self-image that every member wants to claim for himself [or herself]" (Brown & Levinson 1987: 61). The notion of 'face' has two sides to it. **Positive face** refers to your desire to belong, to be part of a group. **Negative face** is connected to your desire for autonomy and independence. Imagine you share a flat with others, and you are horrified by the state of your communal kitchen. If you shout 'clean up this mess now!' you are threatening your flatmates' negative face directly. By saying 'would you mind doing a bit of cleaning?' you are more indirect and give your flatmates more options, thus making your request more polite. You can also choose a positive politeness strategy. By saying 'hey, let's get this mess cleaned up' you emphasise everybody's belonging to a group.

It has probably already dawned on you that a corpus-linguistic approach to linguistic politeness will be limited at best. We can easily search for terms of address in our corpora or get the frequencies for 'thank you', but right now we have no easy way of searching for more or less direct requests, or more generally for strategies of positive or negative politeness. ICE-Ireland stands out as the only member of the ICE family that is pragmatically annotated for **speech acts**.

Example study: intensifiers (Aijmer 2018)

Sometimes, an adjective on its own is not quite enough to convey the meaning we intend to convey – in those situations, we have the opportunity to choose from a variety of words to 'emphasise' or 'intensify' the meaning of the adjective. This section illustrates the functions of such words, so-called **intensifiers**, in World Englishes. Read the following sentences in (6.41) and focus on the function of the words *very*, *so*, and *really*:

(6.41) a. They are very competent.
  b. This is so important!
  c. Investigating World Englishes is really interesting.
    (made-up examples)

Interpreting variation and change in WEs 161

⇒ What function do *very*, *so*, and *really* have in these sentences? Which kinds of words do they occur with?

◊ These words are often referred to as 'intensifiers'. They are adverbs that do not provide lexical content but instead strengthen the meaning of a statement. They 'intensify' the meaning of adjectives, with the adjectives in the examples being *competent, important,* and *interesting.*

For an example study, we are going to consider Aijmer's (2018) article on "Intensification with *very*, *really*, and *so* in selected varieties of English". One example each from different ICE corpora that Aijmer considered is given in (6.42) to (6.44). The intensifier and the adjective it modifies are in italics.

(6.42) cos he looks married and like oh *so so cheeky*. (ICE-SIN:S1A-031:55:1:A)
(6.43) but this book is *really top notch* (ICE-NZ:S1A-100#164:1:M)
(6.44) That was *very awful* was when when he when he uhm when the guys grabbed the girls (ICE-SIN:S1A-030#16:1:A)

Background of the study

Aijmer's study is interested in links between pragmatics, lexis, and World Englishes research in a wider context. While the focus of her article is on a set of lexical features in varieties of English, intensifiers inherently have a pragmatic dimension. As Aijmer points out, the (relatively 'new') field of variational pragmatics (Barron & Schneider 2009) fostered the idea that variation can also be studied systematically in the area of pragmatics and discourse (2018: 107). Her motivation to study intensifiers in American English (AmE), BrE, NZE, and SinE is twofold: First, studies on intensification in varieties beyond the Inner Circle are relatively scarce. Second, the studies that have been carried out indicate that there is cross-cultural and cross-varietal variation in intensifier usage.

⇒ Think about what you know already about the intensifiers *really*, *so*, and *very*. Do you associate one or more of these with particular varieties or age groups? Which one(s) would you expect to be more frequent in BrE and AmE?

Aim of the study and research questions

As we might expect, intensifiers are relatively common in spoken language. We often use them to lend further weight to an adjective and, in addition, many of them represent easy-to-remember words. However, it is also rather expected that different intensifiers are preferred in different varieties. Another aspect to consider is that not all intensifiers only 'strengthen' the meaning; we can also

162 Interpreting variation and change in WEs

use them to weaken an adjective's meaning. In an attempt to address these and some additional aspects, Aijmer poses the following four research questions in her article:

Are the intensifiers used with the same frequency and distribution in the varieties compared?
What is the meaning of the adjectives modified by one of the intensifiers?
What types of evaluation (good or bad, strong or weak) do they express?
How can we explain the differences between the patterns in terms of the variety of English and the social and linguistic norms the speakers adhere to? (Aijmer 2018: 107)

Thus, the analysis combines qualitative and quantitative perspectives and already points towards a meaningful contextualisation of the results in the last research question. Instead of only talking about more or less abstract quantitative aspects related to intensifier usage, Aijmer seeks to find a connection between the purely linguistic and the social.

Method

Aijmer (2018) investigates intensifier usage in AmE, BrE, NZE, and SinE. As her data, she uses the data in the private dialogues sections in the corresponding ICE corpora. Since there is no spoken component of ICE-US yet, Aijmer falls back on a section from the *Santa Barbara Corpus of American English* (SBCAE). The relevant intensifiers *very*, *really*, and *so* "were extracted from the four corpora and investigated quantitatively and qualitatively" (Aijmer 2018: 109). In the context of the study, Aijmer considers the frequency of these intensifiers as well as the (semantic) context in which they are used. The word count analysed in her study is shown in Table 6.9.

Initially, a corpus search for *very*, *really*, and *so* seems straightforward. We can type these words into a concordance tool and look for all instances; perhaps some fine-tuning by means of a regular expression can be added. This would be relevant, for instance, to exclude words that feature *so* at the

Table 6.9 Corpora, word count, and corresponding circle of the included varieties in Aijmer (2018) (Aijmer 2018: 109; reprinted by permission from Brill Rodopi)

Corpus	Word count	Circle
ICE-GB	200,000 words	Inner Circle
SBCAE	249,000 words	Inner Circle
ICE-NZ	200,000 words	Inner Circle
ICE-SIN	200,000 words	Outer Circle

beginning (e.g. *something*) or the end (e.g. *also*). Aijmer notes that some manual labour was involved for *really*. Examples in which *really* was not immediately followed by an adjective, for instance, were excluded (Aijmer's example is *it's really a good film*, see 2018: 111). This is another good example highlighting the fact that methodological choices are important and should be spelled out in the article to ensure that the reader is aware of them. In addition to the quantitative analysis, Aijmer also categorises the tokens semantically.

Findings

The first findings presented in Aijmer's study concern the frequency of the three intensifiers, illustrated in Table 6.10.

⇒ Recall your own thoughts about the expected frequencies of the intensifiers. What does Table 6.10 tell us about the distribution of the three intensifiers across the four investigated varieties? Which differences are particularly noticeable and, perhaps, unexpected? Pay attention to the overall frequencies of the intensifiers too!

◊ Maybe the most surprising result is that *really* occurs less frequently than both *very* and *so* in AmE. As Aijmer notes, this result "seems to go against the tendencies mentioned in earlier studies" (2018: 112). This might be attributed to the age of the SBCAE, since more recent research suggests that *really* is the dominant intensifier in AmE. Yet another surprise concerns AmE, since the overall amount of intensification with the three intensifiers is rather low. However, as Aijmer herself notes, this might be due to speakers preferring other options – either other intensifiers or completely different means. SinE features the highest frequency of intensifiers, with *very* occurring particularly often.

Aijmer explains the high frequency of intensifiers in SinE with its advanced developmental stage in Schneider's Dynamic Model. *Very* emerged as Singaporeans' 'favourite' intensifier, which is a choice that had time to settle and become nativised.

Table 6.10 Frequencies of *very*, *really*, and *so* per one million words in AmE, BrE, NZE, and SinE (adapted from Aijmer 2018: 112)

	very	*really*	*so*
SBCAE (AmE)	654	602	835
ICE-GB (BrE)	2595	855	520
ICE-NZ (NZE)	535	1560	310
ICE-Sin (SinE)	3745	360	1430

In addition to considering the general frequencies, Aijmer discusses semantic aspects as well as noteworthy developments. One of these developments is the usage of *real* as an intensifier. We know that speakers sometimes omit the *-ly* ending (see Chapter 4) and instead opt to use an adverb in the same form as its corresponding adjective. This would give us examples such as *real silly* or *real expensive*.

⇒ Which variety out of the four that Aijmer (2018) investigates would you expect to have the highest frequency of *real* used as an intensifier?

◊ AmE features by far the highest frequency of *real* used as an intensifier (433 pmw), with NZE coming in second (194 pmw). Aijmer found few tokens in BrE (27 pmw) and SinE (33 pmw). She lists *real good*, *real cute*, and *real nice* as the most frequent examples in AmE. Some interesting examples showed in NZE, such as *real bizarre* and *real psycho* (2018: 130).

Evaluation and follow-up research

Aijmer's study is an excellent example of how pragmatics, lexis, and World Englishes can be joined. She is very clear about her methodology and offers examples and overviews that can easily be understood. The use of the SBCAE in order to complement the ICE corpora is common practice today.

The results of Aijmer's study are very recent, which is why no direct follow-up study has been published. However, we recommend you read Kirk's (2018) work on *well* and Wagner's (2017) study on amplifiers. Both choose rather different approaches, as Wagner considers GloWbE and Kirk focuses on ICE. Furthermore, Wagner's study places more emphasis on a particular aspect: The co-occurrence of an intensifier with an adjective as a bigram, that is, combinations of intensifiers and adjectives as 'fixed' or, at least, frequently co-occurring units.

Replication task

Analyse the frequencies of *really*, *very*, and *so* in further ICE corpora. How do the results compare to Aijmer's study? In addition, add further intensifiers into the mix: many adverbs are used as intensifiers and can be analysed rather easily by searching for them in ICE or another corpus. However, you should be careful in your selection of tokens, since some examples may not fit the bill. In particular, intensifiers that can occur as members of other word classes or in different positions should be treated with care.

6.7 Summary

This chapter had two main goals: we wanted to showcase the corpus-based work of the World Englishes community, and we further wanted to enable you

Interpreting variation and change in WEs 165

to take it from there and set up your own studies with the theoretical and practical expertise you have accumulated so far. This double purpose also drove our selection of sample studies: we foregrounded those which are more accessible to beginners. Once you have developed a taste for corpus linguistics in connection with Word Englishes, there is a world of research out there for you to explore, with more extensive coding, more elaborate scripts, and way more complex statistics – but also even more rewarding.

The studies we discussed are on the track of variation and change in World Englishes, variation among each other, and their collective difference to their historical input variety. Schneider (2004) on particle verbs and Sand (2004) on article use were early examples of making the most of the ICE corpora available at the time. After the publication of Schneider's Dynamic Model in 2007, many studies combined this comparative perspective with a specific research agenda. Researchers tried to find a correlation between a variety's stage in the Dynamic Model and its preference for innovative features. One common line of reasoning is that Postcolonial English will become more and more 'liberated' from the norms of BrE in the course of its development. That is, the more innovative features a PCE has, the more advanced it is in Schneider's model, and vice versa. While this certainly seems like an intuitively obvious hypothesis, we should keep in mind that the varieties that have completed Schneider's cycle – for example AmE – are not so drastically different from their historical input variety after all.

Other studies such as Hilbert's (2008) on interrogative inversion are interested in the origin of a specific construction. Such origins can be language contact, or universals of SLA, as we saw in Chapter 5. Both are difficult to pin down precisely, and multicausal explanations for a specific development are always possible. The complexity of how to explain a feature's distribution across World Englishes also became evident in Aijmer's (2018) study on intensifiers. Explaining why specific intensifiers are used much more frequently in SinE than in AmE is no easy feat but, similar to other studies, the Dynamic Model proved helpful. Finally, Biermeier's (2014) study highlights one aspect in particular that World Englishes share: the tendency to use language creatively and effectively; to find expressions suited to the needs of the community.

If anything, we hope this chapter helped to show you some pieces of the amazing scope of World Englishes – and, by extension, the many ways that corpus linguistics can help us explore them.

References

Aijmer, Karin (2018). "Intensification with *very, really* and *so* in selected varieties of English." In Hoffmann, Sebastian, Andrea Sand, Sabine Arndt-Lappe, & Lisa Marie Dillmann (eds.), *Corpora and Lexis*. Leiden: Brill Rodopi, 106–139. doi: 10.1163/9789004361133_006.

Barron, Anne & Klaus P. Schneider (2009). "Variational pragmatics: Studying the impact of social factors on language use in interaction." *Intercultural Pragmatics* 6(4): 425–442. doi: 10.1515/IPRG.2009.023.

Bhatt, Rakesh M. (2004). "Indian English: Syntax." In Kortmann, Bernd, Kate Burridge, Rajend Mesthrie, Edgar W. Schneider, & Clive Upton (eds.), *A Handbook of Varieties of English. Volume 2: Morphology and Syntax.* Berlin: de Gruyter, 1017–1130. doi: 10.1515/9783110175325.2.1016.

Biermeier, Thomas (2008). *Word-Formation in New Englishes: A Corpus-Based Analysis.* Berlin: LIT.

Biermeier, Thomas (2014). "Compounding and suffixation in World Englishes." In Buschfeld, Sarah, Thomas Hoffmann, Magnus Huber, & Alexander Kautzsch (eds.), *The Evolution of Englishes: The Dynamic Model and Beyond.* Amsterdam: John Benjamins, 312–330. doi: 10.1075/veaw.g49.18bie.

Brown, Penelope & Stephen C. Levinson (1987). *Politeness. Some Universals in Language Usage.* Cambridge: Cambridge University Press.

Filppula, Markku & Juhani Klemola (2017). "The definite article in World Englishes." In Filppula, Markku, Juhani Klemola, Anna Mauranen, & Svetlana Vetchinnikova (eds.), *Changing English: Global and Local Perspectives.* Berlin: de Gruyter, 155–168. doi: 10.1515/9783110429657-009.

Hilbert, Michaela (2008). "Interrogative inversion in non-standard varieties of English." In Siemund, Peter & Noemi Kintana (eds.), *Language Contact and Contact Languages.* Amsterdam: John Benjamins, 262–289. doi: 10.1075/hsm.7.15hil.

Hilbert, Michaela (2011). "Interrogative inversion as a learner phenomenon in English contact varieties: A case of angloversals?" In Mukherjee, Joybrato & Marianne Hundt (eds.), *Exploring Second-Language Varieties of English and Learner Englishes: Bridging a Paradigm Gap.* Amsterdam: John Benjamins, 125–143. doi: 10.1075/scl.44.07hil.

Horch, Stephanie (2017). *Conversion in Asian Englishes: A Usage-Based Account of the Emergence of New Local Norms.* Ph.D. Dissertation, Albert-Ludwigs-Universität Freiburg. URL: https://freidok.uni-freiburg.de/data/12910. (Last access: 4 July 2019).

Horch, Stephanie (2019). "Complementing corpus analysis with web-based experimentation in research on World Englishes." *English World-Wide* 40(1): 24–52. doi: 10.1075/eww.00021.hor.

Kirk, John M. (2018). "The pragmatics of *well* as a discourse marker in broadcast discussions." In Hoffmann, Sebastian, Andrea Sand, Sabine Arndt-Lappe, & Lisa Marie Dillmann (eds.), *Corpora and Lexis.* Leiden: Brill Rodopi, 140–172. doi: 10.1163/9789004361133_007.

Koch, Christopher, Claudia Lange, & Sven Leuckert (2018). "This hair style called as "duck tail"': The 'intrusive *as*'-construction in South Asian varieties of English and Learner Englishes." In Deshors, Sandra C., Sandra Götz, & Samantha Laporte (eds.), *Rethinking Linguistic Creativity in Non-Native Englishes.* Amsterdam: John Benjamins, 21–46. doi: 10.1075/bct.98.02koc.

Leuckert, Sven (2019). *Topicalization in Asian Englishes. Forms, Functions, and Frequencies of a Fronting Construction.* London: Routledge.

Mukherjee, Joybrato & Sebastian Hoffmann (2006). "Describing verb-complementation profiles of New Englishes: A pilot study of Indian English." *English World-Wide* 27(2): 147–173. doi: 10.1075/eww.27.2.03muk.

Nelson, Gerald (2006). "The core and periphery of World Englishes: A corpus-based exploration." *World Englishes* 25(1): 115–129. doi: 10.1111/j.0083-2919.2006.00450.x.

Platt, John, Heidi Weber, & Mian Lian Ho (1984). *The New Englishes*. London: Routledge & Kegan Paul.

Sand, Andrea (2004). "Shared morpho-syntactic features in contact varieties of English: Article use." *World Englishes* 23(2): 281–298. doi: 10.1111/j.0883-2919.2004.00352.x.

Schneider, Edgar W. (2003). "The dynamics of New Englishes: From identity construction to dialect birth." *Language* 79(2): 233–281.

Schneider, Edgar W. (2004). "How to trace structural nativization: Particle verbs in World Englishes." *World Englishes* 23(2): 227–249. doi: 10.1111/j.0883-2919.2004.00348.x.

Schneider, Edgar W. (2007). *Postcolonial English: Varieties around the World*. Cambridge: Cambridge University Press.

Schneider, Gerold (2013). "Investigating Irish English with ICE-Ireland." *Cahiers de l'ILSL* 38: 139–162. doi: 10.5167/uzh-87751.

Sharma, Devyani (2005). "Language transfer and discourse universals in Indian English article use." *Studies in Second Language Acquisition* 27(4): 535–566. doi: 10.1017/S0272263105050242.

Simo Bobda, Augustin (2000). "Research on New Englishes: A critical review of some findings with a focus on Cameroon." *Arbeiten aus Anglistik und Amerikanistik* 25(1): 53–70.

Wagner, Susanne (2017). "*Totally new* and *pretty awesome*: Amplifier–adjective bigrams in GloWbE." *Lingua* 200: 63–83. doi: 10.1016/j.lingua.2017.08.004.

Chapter 7

World Englishes, Learner Englishes, and English as a Lingua Franca

Key terms:

Key concepts and terms:
code-switching; Lingua Franca and English as a Lingua Franca (ELF); innovation; learner; Learner Englishes; redundancy; Second Language Acquisition (SLA)

Learner corpus design:
Common European Framework of Reference for Languages (CEFR); error annotation; learner-related variables; task-related variables

Learner corpora:
International Corpus of Learner English (ICLE); *International Corpus Network of Asian Learners of English* (ICNALE); *Louvain International Database of Spoken English Interlanguage* (LINDSEI)

Corpora of English as a Lingua Franca:
Asian Corpus of English (ACE); *Corpus of Video-Mediated English as a Lingua Franca Conversations* (ViMELF); *Vienna-Oxford International Corpus of English* (VOICE)

7.1 Introduction: World Englishes, Learner Englishes, and ELF

Who is a learner – and who is not?

Think back to your own experiences as a learner of the English language. It may have been taught to you as a 'foreign language', a 'second language', or even your 'first language', but chances are that you were considered a '**learner**' of the language for a period of time. This period may have occurred earlier or later in your life and your whole learning career is certainly unique (as it is for

WEs, Learner Englishes, and ELF 169

everyone else), but we all share that we have to learn a language in some way before we can use it passively or actively. A problem is that, depending on who you talk to, notions such as 'learner' and 'native speaker' come with a certain amount of ideological baggage. As we discussed in Chapter 5, World Englishes have long been dismissed as 'incorrect', 'improper', or 'imperfectly learned' versions of English. Forms of **English as a Lingua Franca** (ELF), the English used between speakers who do not share another language, have regularly been described as 'defective' English. Finally, **Learner Englishes** have long been considered a matter exclusively relevant to pedagogy and teaching, with the focus being on the eradication of learner errors. What these (largely negative) perspectives share is that they draw a line between a kind of English that is acceptable and one that is not, with native speakers often coming out on top. Despite sharing a history of being neglected in linguistic research, World Englishes and Learner Englishes have been treated separately for a long time.

The 'paradigm gap'

Traditionally, Learner Englishes were the focus of **Second Language Acquisition** (SLA), while World Englishes have mostly been discussed in terms of issues such as language contact and variation. Sridhar and Sridhar (1986) famously referred to the distinct treatment of Learner Englishes and WEs as a 'paradigm gap': "the Second Language Acquisition (SLA) paradigm deals almost exclusively with Learner Englishes without accounting for the acquisition of World Englishes, whereas that of World Englishes pays very little attention to learner varieties" (Laporte 2012: 264). In recent years, interest in bridging this paradigm gap has seen a revival, with several publications looking for connections between the two fields; we list some examples in the 'Recommended reading' section below if you are interested. An important aspect in joining the two fields of study has been the notion that both postcolonial and non-postcolonial Englishes share certain developmental paths. Furthermore, processes typical of SLA can fruitfully be applied to World Englishes as well (see Percillier 2016), which we will briefly show later in this chapter.

What this chapter has to offer

Following in the footsteps of the publications mentioned above, we considered it fitting to include a chapter on the vast field of Learner Englishes in this book. Many of the opportunities and challenges are similar between these varieties and World Englishes, but there are also unique aspects to consider when working with learner and ELF corpora. Thus, we provide you with some background on the following key aspects in this chapter:

- What are typical components of a learner corpus?
- What are some important learner and ELF corpora?
- What kind of study can be carried out on Learner Englishes and ELF?

7.2 Learner corpus design and learner corpora

Learner corpus design

We introduced the typical components of corpus design in Chapter 3 and provided examples of World Englishes corpora in Chapter 4. Learner and ELF corpora represent the last kinds of corpora we will introduce in this book. While they share many traits with World Englishes corpora, they often include additional elements and are compiled a bit differently due to differing objectives. At their core, learner corpora are collections of written and/or spoken texts produced by learners.

⇒ Think about learner language and its representation in corpora. Which aspects might be relevant in the analysis of learner language but not necessarily for World Englishes? In addition, which corpus design features (in terms of metadata and annotation) would you include specifically for learner corpora?

◇ Modern learner corpora often add some kind of annotation for mistakes and errors ('**error annotation**'), since they are, among other things, used to identify typical problems that language learners have. We should point out again that the line between error or mistake and innovation can be thin; we discussed this in Chapter 5. Other important information that is frequently gathered in learner corpus design concerns proficiency in the language and, if language production tasks are involved, what the criteria for the tasks were.

An aspect to consider as well is that, for learner corpora even more so than for World Englishes corpora, obtaining natural data is very challenging. For a long time, the problem has been that "the data used was rather artificial, i.e. resulting from highly controlled language tasks, and therefore not necessarily a reflection of what learners do in more natural communication contexts" (Granger et al. 2015: 1). Ultimately, the question has to be raised to what extent English is (or any other language a person is learning) used outside of a classroom context.

⇒ Identify when and where you use English (or any other language that is not your mother tongue) in your everyday life. How much of your exposure to the language is passive and when do you get to use it actively? If you are a native speaker of English: What would be your expectations with regard to these questions for a person from, for instance, Germany or Brazil? Finally, which problems can you think of that would arise when trying to build a corpus using this information?

◇ In many Western countries, exposure to English has become common. It is regularly used in product naming and advertising and a substantial amount of people now watch movies and TV shows in English. While the individual experience may vary quite drastically, tendencies can be observed. Active usage of English might be less frequent and, in the present day, can be

WEs, Learner Englishes, and ELF 171

expected to be most frequent on the internet, at school, and in international encounters (either on- or offline). In corpus building, using learner language produced in some of these contexts is problematic, since it lacks the systematicity that would make the data comparable. Furthermore, how much English a person produces certainly depends on where and how they live.

The pedagogical focus in the context of Learner Englishes as well as the various problems in obtaining learner data mean that often specially created tasks have been used for learner corpora. Thus, metadata for learner corpora typically include **learner-related variables** and **task-related variables**. We want to know who the learners are and we want to get context for the circumstances under which the corpus texts have been produced. Some examples of typically included variables are depicted in Table 7.1.

It is evident from Table 7.1 that some information is important for both World Englishes and learner corpora, such as age, gender, region, and mother tongue. Other languages are usually also included for both, while proficiency level is only sometimes included for World Englishes corpora. In order to illustrate learner corpus design with actual corpora, we discuss three of these below.

–Takeaway Note–

The criteria for the compilation of learner corpora differ from World Englishes corpora in some respects. Most importantly, the majority of learner corpora is based on specific tasks (such as essay writing or discussions of assigned topics), which means that task-related variables are typically included in the metadata. Information on the mother tongue and other languages a learner is proficient in is crucial.

Table 7.1 Learner-related and task-related variables in learner corpus design (see Granger 2008: 264)

Learner-related variables	Task-related variables
Age	Medium
Gender	Genre
Region	Task type
Mother tongue	Task conditions
Proficiency in L2	Field
Learning context of L2	
Other languages spoken	

172   WEs, Learner Englishes, and ELF

Learner corpora, example 1: ICLE and ICLEv2

Perhaps the best-known learner corpus of English is the *International Corpus of Learner English* (ICLE), of which two versions exist. The first version was released in 2002; the second, abbreviated as ICLEv2, was published in 2009. ICLE contains argumentative essays of 500 to 1000 words written by learners of English from various countries, such as Bulgaria, Germany, Russia, and Sweden. Texts written by native speakers are also included to allow for comparisons. At 3.7 million words, ICLEv2 is larger than the first ICLE. In total, 16 nationalities are featured, once again including several regions. Mother tongues spoken by learners in ICLEv2 include, amongst others, Chinese, Italian, Spanish, and Tswana. Both ICLE and ICLEv2 provide metadata on learner and task variables gathered via a learner profile. The information included in this profile is shown in Table 7.2. For the task variables, possible options are given below the variable.

Essays included in ICLE are written on a variety of topics, with some suggested topics by the corpus team being 'Crime does not pay' and 'The role of censorship in Western society'. ICLE and ICLEv2 can be ordered via the *Centre for English Corpus Linguistics* or CECL (https://uclouvain.be/en/research-institutes/ilc/cecl) hosted by the Université catholique de Louvain, which is also

Table 7.2 Learner and task variables included in ICLE and ICLEv2 (adapted from https://cdn.uclouvain.be/public/Exports%20reddot/cecl/documents/LEARNER_PROFILE.txt)

Learner variables	Task variables
Surname, first name(s)	Essay title
Age	Approximate length required (fewer or more than 500 words)
Male/Female	Conditions (timed/untimed)
Nationality	Examination (yes/no)
Native Language	Reference tools (yes/no)
Father's mother tongue; mother's mother tongue	If yes: What reference tools?
Language(s) spoken at home	• Bilingual dictionary
Medium of instruction in primary and secondary school	• English monolingual dictionary • Grammar • Other(s)
Current studies, current year of study, institution, medium of instruction	
Years of English at school; years of English at university	
Year, length, and location of stay in an English speaking-country (if any)	
Other foreign languages in decreasing order of proficiency	

WEs, Learner Englishes, and ELF 173

where you can find further information about the two corpora. Since the corpora will not be affordable to most junior scholars, it is worth checking if your institute already has a version of the corpus and, if that is not the case, considering the purchase of an institutional licence.

Learner corpora, example 2: LINDSEI

The next learner corpus we would like to introduce is the *Louvain International Database of Spoken English Interlanguage* (LINDSEI). The key difference between the ICLE corpora and LINDSEI is that, as the name of the latter suggests, it features spoken rather than written language. As of 2019, 11 components are available in LINDSEI, with each component consisting of 50 interviews with learners of English from a specific region. Each component features 100,000 words of spoken learner language. The interviews are based on discussions of a set topic, free discussion, and picture description. Similar to the *International Corpus of English* (ICE) and many other corpora, a corpus with native English has been compiled in order to allow for comparisons. This corpus is referred to as LOCNEC, the *Louvain Corpus of Native English Conversation*.

Each interview is complemented by 23 variables relating to the interviewee and the interviewer, including first language (L1), age, gender, relation to each other, and many others. Like ICLE and ICLEv2, LINDSEI needs to be purchased via the CECL at the link given above.

Learner corpora, example 3: ICNALE

The last learner corpus we would like to introduce in this chapter is the *International Corpus Network of Asian Learners of English* (ICNALE). Unlike the previously introduced corpora, ICNALE specifically focuses on Asian learners of English. ICNALE features spoken and written components, but the former are still in development. As of June 2019, Spoken Dialogue Baby 0.3 can be accessed; a full release of the spoken component is scheduled for 2020. The structure of the corpus and the current size of the components is illustrated in Table 7.3.

Based on their results in widely accepted proficiency tests such as the *Test of English as a Foreign Language* (TOEFL), learners in ICNALE are assigned to the following ranks of the **Common European Framework of Reference for Languages (CEFR)**: A2, B1.1 (B1 low), B1.2 (B1 high), and B2+.

⇒ Read up on the precise requirements for each level assigned by the CEFR, for instance at the homepage of the Council of Europe (www.coe.int/en/web/common-european-framework-reference-languages/table-1-cefr-3.3-common-ref erence-levels-global-scale). What does it mean when a speaker is classified as, for instance, having an A2, B1.2, or C.1 proficiency level?

174 WEs, Learner Englishes, and ELF

Table 7.3 Structure of ICNALE (adapted from http://language.sakura.ne.jp/icnale/index.html#6)

Modules	Number of samples	Number of tokens	Contents
Spoken Monologue 2.0	4,400	ca. 500,000	60-seconds monologues about two ICNALE common topics.
Spoken Dialogue Baby 0.3	285	ca. 1,050,000	30–40-minutes oral interviews including picture descriptions and role plays, and 3–5-minutes follow-up first-language (L1) reflections. Interview tasks are related to two ICNALE common topics.
Written Essays 2.3	5,600	ca. 1,300.000	200–300-words essays about two ICNALE common topics
Edited Essays 2.0	640	ca.150,000	Fully edited versions of learner essays about two ICNALE common topics. Rubric-based essay evaluation data is also included.
Additional modules			
Written Essays UAE 0.1	200	ca. 47,000	200–300-words essays about two ICNALE common topics written by college students in the United Arab Emirates.

◊ The proficiency levels describe 'Basic Users' (A1-A2), 'Independent Users' (B1-B2), and 'Proficient Users' (C1-C2). Individual applications to learning/teaching scenarios apply and are even recommended by the Council of Europe. For more details, you can consult the website given above. It might also be interesting for you to look into the specific requirements given in descriptions of common proficiency tests, such as TOEFL for the case of English.

Metadata are collected in addition to attitudinal information on the participants in the following three major areas (adapted from http://language.sakura.ne.jp/icnale/index.html#2):

(A) Basic Attributes (e.g. gender; age; years of studying English)
(B) Motivation (e.g. grades; learning is fun; understanding English)
(C) L2 Learning Backgrounds (usage contexts of English for all active and passive skills)

The countries and regions included in ICNALE are visualised in Figure 7.1, with Hong Kong and Singapore highlighted in black and all other featured countries coloured in dark grey.

WEs, Learner Englishes, and ELF 175

Figure 7.1 Countries and regions included in ICNALE (map created with mapchart.net; CC Attribution-SA 4.0 International Licence)

The main advantage of this corpus over the ones listed above is that it is freely available and only requires a password that can be requested by filling out the form linked at http://language.sakura.ne.jp/icnale/download.html. The content of one of the text files in the corpus is given in (7.1). The name of the file indicates that it is a spoken text from a Thai learner, with PTJ2 referring to the fact that it is the second monologue about part-time jobs. The number 27 refers to the file and A2 tells us the speaker's proficiency level according to the CEFR.

(7.1) I like part-time. I don't like part-time. Sorry, I don't like part-time, but I think when you're doing part-time, you don't time for everything – for – don't [***] time for study, don't time for reading, don't time for – a – search, internet search or – for – for – for study, so [***] for study, I don't study. When – when you – when you do part-time, you're stupid [***]. You do [***]. You do . (S_THA_PTJ2_027_A2_0.txt)

–Takeaway Note–

Three important learner corpora are ICLE, LINDSEI, and ICNALE. While they differ in terms of regions covered and variables included, some of their components can be compared very well. Out of the three, only ICNALE is freely available and can be accessed after obtaining a password from the corpus creator.

7.3 Comparing World Englishes, Learner Englishes, and ENL

The previous sections introduced you to learner corpora, but what are they good for – in particular in relation to World Englishes? Let us consider an example: A house can *blow up*, you may *crack up* after hearing a joke, and you may have been asked to *eat up* more than once in your life. Phrasal Verbs (PVs) featuring *up* are the focus of an example study by Gilquin (2015). PVs consist of a verb followed by one or more adverbs and/or preposition, with further examples being *to make up for* and *to pull something down*. Often, these additional words are referred to as 'particles'. In her article, Gilquin provides four case studies to illustrate how 'New Englishes' (NEs; varieties such as Indian and Singapore English), Learner Englishes (LEs), and English as a Native Language (ENL) can fruitfully be compared. We give a description of her case study on PVs with *up* in the following paragraphs and provide an incentive for a follow-up study.

Coming up with a rationale

One of the reasons to conduct corpus-linguistic research on PVs is to find evidence or counter-evidence to the claim that they are "one of the most notoriously challenging aspects of English language instruction" (Gardner & Davies 2007: 339). If they are indeed particularly challenging, learners or even second-language speakers of English probably use them less frequently due to their complexity. In corpus-linguistic terms, this means that a quantitative comparison of different variety types could potentially be revealing.

⇒ Before we move further in the description of Gilquin's study, ask yourself: Why are PVs considered such a challenge in language learning? Also, in which contexts are they mostly used (in general)?

◊ There are many possible reasons making PVs difficult to teach and learn. First, the meaning of PVs is often not obvious from the combination of words: *to break up* means to end a relationship, but this meaning needs to be memorised and does not become evident just by looking at the verb. Second, there is an abundance of PVs in English, and the fact that some share the same particle does not mean that the meaning is in any way related – see, for instance, PVs such as *blow up*, *look up*, and *show up*. As far as the expected usage context

WEs, Learner Englishes, and ELF 177

is concerned, PVs are more typical of informal spoken language than of formal written language.

Adding up the numbers

Now that we have an idea of why an analysis of PVs might be useful, let us consider the data as well as the results of Gilquin's study. In order to compare the three types of Englishes, Gilquin (2015) uses data from corpora we already introduced in Chapters 4 and 7: ICE for Hong Kong, India, Kenya, the Philippines, Singapore, and Tanzania representing World (or 'New') Englishes; ICLEv2 and LINDSEI representing Learner Englishes; and ICE-Great Britain representing ENL. The genres she included as well as the size of each corpus is given in Table 7.4.

A frequency comparison across all corpora and variety types, visualised in Figure 7.2, shows that PVs with *up* are used more frequently in ENL compared to both NEs and LEs, suggesting some similarity between the latter two variety types. The bars indicate the frequency of PVs with *up* per 100,000 words.

⇒ Consider the information provided in Table 7.4 again. Which aspect should we also consider when disentangling the overall frequency comparison – and why?

◊ The bars in Figure 7.2 are interesting but provide us only with the frequency across all of the corpus components. We noted above that PVs are more typical of spoken language, which means that frequency differences between the spoken and the written corpus segments would be expected. Thus, a more detailed depiction of frequencies in the spoken and written texts should help us get a better idea of the distribution of PVs.

Indeed, Gilquin (2015) shows that such differences exist in the corpora. Figure 7.3 clarifies that, for ENL and NEs at least, PVs with *up* predominantly occur in spoken language.

Table 7.4 Corpora used in Gilquin's (2015) study of phrasal verbs with *up* (adapted from Gilquin 2015: 104; reprinted by permission from John Benjamins)

New Englishes			Learner Englishes			ENL		
Corpus	Genre	Size	Corpus	Genre	Size	Corpus	Genre	Size
ICE (HK, IND, KEN, PHI, SIN, TAN)	Acad. writing	544,612	ICLEv2 (all)	Arg./lit. essays	3,163,142	ICE-GB	Acad. writing	87,128
	Direct conv.	1,035,122	LINDSEI (all)	Informal interviews	792,141		Direct conv.	183,366

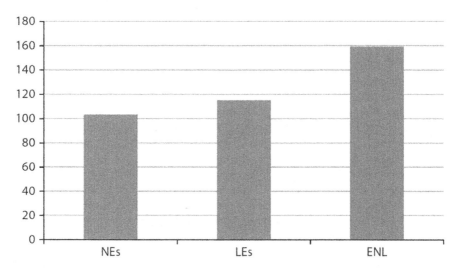

Figure 7.2 Frequency comparison of PVs with *up* between NEs, LEs, and ENL (Gilquin 2015: 105; reprinted by permission from John Benjamins)

The most interesting aspect about the frequency bars is clearly the distribution of PVs in LEs: Why are LEs the only variety type in which PVs dominate in written language?

⇒ Hypothesise about the possible reasons for the higher frequencies of PVs with *up* in written learner texts. Use your knowledge about the acquisition of NEs (from Chapters 2 and 5) and the usage contexts of ENL compared to LEs as hints.

◊ Gilquin (2015: 106) refers to two key aspects explaining this difference: First, LEs are typically used less frequently in everyday contexts, but we associate PVs with 'naturalistic' language. Although there are obviously differences between learning environments, it seems unlikely that PVs play a large role until a relatively high proficiency level is reached. Even then, PVs may not be the preferred choice in a rather formal classroom setting. Second, "[f]oreign learners of English […] have been shown to mix registers by using spoken-like features in writing […] and written-like features in speech" (ibid.). This is confirmed for PVs with *up* in the results shown above.

The previous summary has focused on quantitative aspects only, but Gilquin also considers some interesting individual examples and highlights two tendencies shared between NEs and LEs: **redundancy** and **innovation**. We introduced

WEs, Learner Englishes, and ELF   179

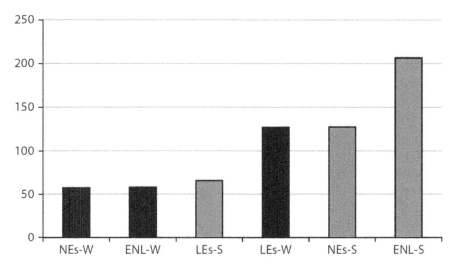

Figure 7.3 Frequency comparison of PVs with *up* in spoken and written NEs, LEs, and ENL (Gilquin 2015: 106; reprinted by permission from John Benjamins)

both terms in Chapter 5, but will give a brief repetition here: Learners of English sometimes use redundant structures or expressions, which means that they add a word whose meaning is implicit in another word or repeat a construction. This strategy, known in SLA as 'redundancy' (Schneider 2012) and 'explicitness' (Rohdenburg 1996), helps learners to avoid being misunderstood; it means they are 'on the safe side'. Gilquin (2015) found examples of such redundancy with *up* in both NEs (7.2) and LEs (7.3).

(7.2) Certain problems can **surface up** and need to be expected. (ICE-TAN: W2A-037)
(7.3) Although the time passes they cannot share the things and the tension **rises up**. (ICLE-TU:CUK-0121.1)

In both cases, the meaning conveyed by *up* is already present in the verb, which is why the addition of *up* is redundant.

Apart from adding the particle *up* in order to create redundancy, speakers sometimes also use it in an innovative way. In fact, Gilquin (2015) shows that all three variety types occasionally create new PVs that feature *up*; examples from NEs (7.4), LEs (7.5), and ENL (7.6) are shown below.

(7.4) I've been trying my best to keep it clean then he comes and he **meddle up** all over again (ICE-SIN:S1A-054)

(7.5) because of the instructions to **fashion** your jeans **up** by stone-washing and colouring them (ICLE-GE:AUG-0048.3)

(7.6) our cars worth over a grand if I'd **sprayed** it **up** and put it on the market (BNCBaby:KD3)

⇒ Can you guess the meaning of each innovation in the three examples?

◇ The first, *meddle up*, is described by Gilquin as a potential combination of *mess up* and *meddle with*, "referring to the act of ruining or spoiling something by touching it when you are not supposed to" (2015: 107). The example *fashion up* suggests that the jeans are 'dressed up' in the sense of making them more fashionable. *Spray up*, finally, refers to increasing the value of the car by spraying it with a new colour.

Bringing up important points

The qualitative and quantitative analysis of PVs with *up* has shown that – as expected – LEs underuse them compared to ENL. Interestingly, the same can be said of NEs, which means that a first similarity between the two variety types can be identified. In terms of register, LEs use PVs more frequently in written language and are the only variety type to do so in Gilquin's dataset. Finally, redundancy occurs in both NEs and LEs but not in ENL, while innovative uses can be found in all corpora in the study. All in all, this case study illustrates the value of a comparison between NEs, LEs, and ENL.

Following up on Gilquin (2015)

Although we gain a lot of insight from Gilquin (2015), expanding upon previous studies and confirming, modifying, or even rejecting results is an important part of doing academic work. Since more complex exercises are typically given at the end of chapters, we refer you to exercise 7.1 below. For now, it should suffice to say that a follow-up study could go in many different directions.

–Takeaway Note–

Learner Englishes can be studied very effectively using corpora. For scholars of World Englishes, comparing aspects such as innovation and effects of SLA has recently been a focus. Many studies, Gilquin (2015) being one of them, have shown that different kinds of varieties, such as Learner, World, and Native Englishes, can be compared meaningfully.

7.4 Corpus linguistics and English as a Lingua Franca (ELF)

What is ELF?

The previous sections introduced you to Learner Englishes. English as a Lingua Franca also covers World and Learner Englishes, but considers a specific context: Very often, speakers from different backgrounds need and want to communicate with each other. In a time when conversing with people from around the globe online has become an everyday occurrence, the question of selecting a shared language comes up frequently. As another case in point, consider your own trips abroad: Which language do you use to talk to people in another country? Which language would two people from, for instance, China and Germany use in order to discuss business? Although English is far from the only possible option, it is often the chosen language. We refer to the language used in such a situation as a '**Lingua Franca**', which is a term derived from a medieval link language spoken around the Mediterranean Sea. Barbara Seidlhofer, one of the leading scholars in research on **English as a Lingua Franca** (ELF), defines it as "any use of English among speakers of different first languages for whom English is the communicative medium of choice, and often the only option" (2011: 7).

Why study ELF?

Studying ELF presents us with a variety of methodological opportunities and challenges. One of the most exciting questions relates to mutual intelligibility in ELF encounters. Linguistic features that might be dismissed as mistakes or even errors from a prescriptive point of view, such as the omission of an article, might actually be beneficial in an ELF situation, because more or less superfluous elements are omitted from the conversation. Thus, it is interesting to observe the many possible scenarios. ELF encounters do not necessarily only involve learners of English, since English might also be the Lingua Franca in a conversation between a native speaker from, for instance, Australia, and a tourist from Poland. This individual nature of ELF encounters is also where some of the challenges are located, since it is questionable to which extent such encounters are and can be alike. As part of this investigation, Jenkins (2000) asked which (phonological) features are necessary for a successful ELF encounter and labelled this set of features the 'Lingua Franca Core'. Another question pertains to the acceptability and visibility of ELF, which has, for a long time, simply been neglected as a form of 'defective' English.

ELF and World Englishes

With regard to the connection of ELF and World Englishes, scholars have taken different perspectives. In an interview from 2016, Jenkins commented that she was "not qualified to talk about World Englishes, as this is a very different field from that of ELF" (TEFL Equity Advocates and Academy 2016), but *The Oxford Handbook of World Englishes* published in 2018 features a chapter on ELF in academia (Mauranen 2018). Whatever one's stance may be, it is evident that the ever-increasing importance and popularity of English and ELF encounters promise insights into language development, globalisation, and linguistic strategies fostering mutual intelligibility. Thus, this sub-chapter aims at introducing corpus-linguistic approaches to ELF as well as questions concerning ELF that could be answered using a corpus.

7.5 ELF corpora

ELF corpora serve to illustrate ELF conversations between people from different national or linguistic backgrounds. In this sub-chapter, we introduce three ELF corpora to you: the *Vienna-Oxford International Corpus of English* (VOICE), the *Asian Corpus of English* (ACE), and the *Corpus of Video-Mediated English as a Lingua Franca Conversations* (ViMELF).

ELF corpora, example 1: VOICE

The *Vienna-Oxford International Corpus of English* (VOICE) is a corpus containing 1 million words produced by speakers with a total of 50 different first languages. As a spoken language corpus, it presents unscripted face-to-face interactions by a total of 1250 speakers. The text types featured in the corpus, listed at www.univie.ac.at/voice/page/corpus_description, range from relatively formal to rather informal settings:

- interviews
- press conferences
- service encounters
- seminar discussions
- working group discussions
- workshop discussions
- meetings
- panels
- question-answer-sessions
- conversations

Accessing VOICE is very simple: You can either use the online version of the corpus at http://voice.univie.ac.at/, which requires registration, or download the XML version at www.univie.ac.at/voice/page/download_voice_xml, for which you have to enter your e-mail address. Both the online and the XML version come with or without POS-tagging. Figure 7.4 is a screenshot of the online interface with POS-tagging.

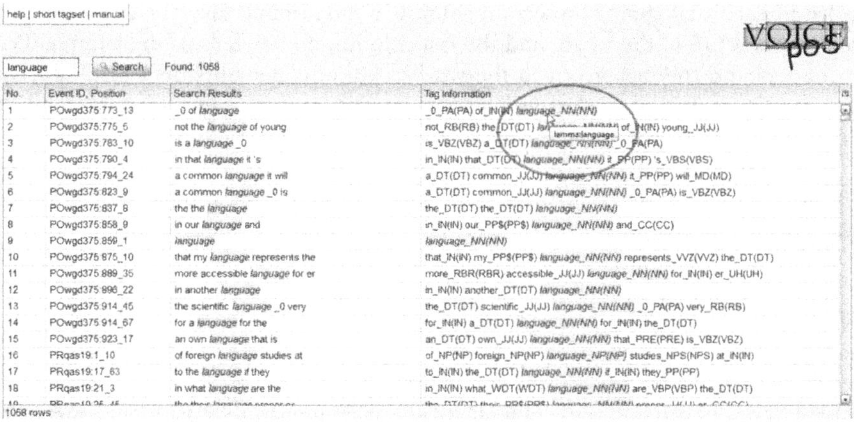

WEs, Learner Englishes, and ELF 183

Figure 7.4 VOICE Online with POS-tagging (www.univie.ac.at/voice/images/help/10_lem ma_popup.jpg)

The full mark-up conventions applied to VOICE can be accessed via the VOICE website. An example conversation between is given in (7.7); the first two lines from the POS-tagged version of the same file are given in (7.8).

(7.7) POcon549:1 S8: would it be very impolite if i asked someone to photocopy
POcon549:2 S10: no not at all
POcon549:3 S8: a a the air ticket for me
POcon549:4 S10: no not at all if you give it to me I'll ask if (POcon549)

(7.8) POcon549_1:1 would MD(MD) will
POcon549_1:2 it PP(PP) it
POcon549_1:3 be VB(VB) be
POcon549_1:4 very RB(RB) very
POcon549_1:5 impolite JJ(JJ) impolite
POcon549_1:6 if IN(IN) if
POcon549_1:7 i PP(PP) i
POcon549_1:8 asked VVD(VVD) ask
POcon549_1:9 someone NN(NN) someone
POcon549_1:10 to TO(TO) to
POcon549_1:11 photocopy VV(VV) photocopy
POcon549_1:12 _0 PA(PA)
POcon549_2:1 no RE(RE) no
POcon549_2:2 not RB(RB) not
POcon549_2:3 at RB(RB) at
POcon549_2:4 all RB(RB) all (POcon549)

⇒ The first column in (7.8) indicates the file name, the line of dialogue, and the word in each dialogue. The second column is the original text, the third column tells us the POS of the word, and the last column, finally, tells us the lemma. Try to understand the tags given to the words: Are any elements unclear? Look up any tags you do not understand in the tagging and lemmatisation manual at www.univie.ac.at/voice/page/documents/VOICE_tagging_manual.pdf.

◊ The tags are all given in the file; the only outstanding example here is probably _0, which refers to a very short pause of up to 0.5 seconds.

One of the biggest advantages of VOICE is that, in addition to being supplied in different versions suiting different needs, audio files accompanying some of the transcriptions are available. Similar to the corpus itself, these can be accessed in VOICE Online after registration. A potential drawback of VOICE, but also one of ELF corpora in general, is the potentially idiosyncratic nature of ELF encounters.

⇒ In order to illustrate what we mean by that, consider the structure of VOICE and the kind of interactions featured in it. Which effect may the differences in proficiency, communicative setting, and language background in the individual encounters have?

◊ Different language backgrounds, different proficiency levels, and different communicative settings mean that the actual comparability between two ELF interactions can be relatively low. This problem might arguably affect any interaction featured in corpora, but is something to consider in particular for ELF studies.

ELF corpora, example 2: ACE

The next ELF corpus we briefly introduce to you is the *Asian Corpus of English* (ACE), which has been modelled after VOICE. This means that the two corpora are similar in several ways but, unlike VOICE, ACE covers ELF encounters in an Asian context. More precisely, conversations included in the corpus are held by speakers from the ASEAN+3 countries, depicted in Figure 7.5. ASEAN is short for the *Association of Southeast Asian Nations*, which includes Brunei, Cambodia, Indonesia, Laos, Malaysia, Myanmar, the Philippines, Singapore, Thailand, and Vietnam. The '+3' in the name refers to China, Japan, and South Korea in cooperation with the ASEAN member states.

⇒ Consider the countries included in ACE. Can you identify a major difference in terms of the role English plays in the countries?

◊ In the Philippines and Singapore as Outer Circle countries, English comes from a colonial background. In others, English is a foreign language without many (or

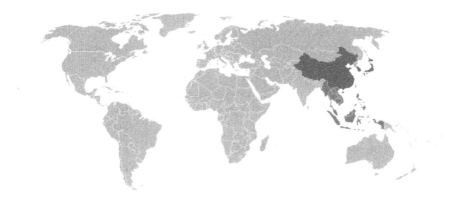

Figure 7.5 ASEAN+3 countries in the *Asian Corpus of English* (ACE) (https://de.wikipedia.org/wiki/ASEAN_Plus_Three#/media/Datei:ASEAN_Plus_Three_members.png; CC BY-SA 3.0 Licence)

any) intranational functions. This results in a certain heterogeneity in how effortlessly English is used by some inhabitants of the countries included in the corpus. As Andy Kirkpatrick, the creator of ACE, puts it: "ASEAN[+3] ELF is not a single variety" (Kirkpatrick 2008: 28).

ACE, which contains a million words, is structured according to the following distribution of situations in which conversations were recorded:

- Education 25%
- Leisure 10%
- Professional business 20%
- Professional organisation 35%
- Professional research/science 10%.

Speakers in the corpus are supposed to be proficient in English; the person collecting the data should ideally be a silent observer. An example from ACE is given in (7.9).

(7.9) S1: because erm i always very excited you know what's up h h (MS_LE_con_6)

⇒ The example illustrates a phenomenon that is quite common in ELF conversations and has been discussed under different assumptions. First, describe the phenomenon from a neutral, descriptive perspective. Then, evaluate it: Why do you think it occurs in the example? What could be a potential explanation for its repeated occurrence in other ELF encounters?

186   WEs, Learner Englishes, and ELF

◇ The speaker in the example omits the verb, which could be a form of *be* or *get* in this case. Omission, in particular of function verbs, is quite common in ELF conversations. Different explanations for this tendency are possible, since omission could either be the result of speakers wanting to omit superfluous information or of imperfectly learned English.

Similar to VOICE, ACE can be accessed online, with unannotated and POS-tagged versions available at http://corpus.eduhk.hk/ace_tagged/.

ELF corpora, example 3: ViMELF

A corpus that differs in certain ways from VOICE and ACE is *Corpus of Video-Mediated English as a Lingua Franca Conversations* (ViMELF), which represents a multimodal ELF resource. In simplest terms, 'multimodal' here means that the texts are available in more than one format: although the corpus is relatively small at 154,472 words in the annotated version, the material is rich in that videos are available for 14 of the 20 conversations and audio is available for the remaining 6 conversations. In total, the corpus contains 20 conversations amounting to ca. 12.5 hours, with all conversations lasting longer than 30 minutes to ensure that effects such as those of the Observer's Paradox (see Chapter 3.3) are reduced to a minimum. The corpus is available in numerous versions, ranging from docx to txt and POS-annotated files.

⇒ It is worth highlighting the multimodal nature of this corpus: In your opinion, which advantages could the availability of video material have for the linguistic analysis of interactions?

◇ Having access to videos means that you are able to see and hear how the conversations proceed. This can be advantageous, for instance, to get a better idea of how an interlocutor reacts to an utterance or if there is a specific tone to the conversation. Furthermore, and very importantly, you can see where speakers pause, how they intonate their utterances, which words might pose a problem for them, etc. Getting an idea of whether the people involved in the conversation like each other can also be helpful, since they are more likely to speak naturally if there is sympathy between them.

In order to give the interactants, who did not know each other beforehand, something to talk about, a selection of topics has been prepared by the corpus compilers:

- 'So, what are you studying' – Course of studies and job prospects
- 'And what do you do all day?' – Life as a university student
- 'The role and future of English' – Lingua Franca & global attitudes
- 'Should learning be virtual?' – Mobile learning, online courses: pros & cons

WEs, Learner Englishes, and ELF   187

- 'How do you celebrate?' – Cultures and traditions
- 'Let's talk about food' – Eating habits and preferences: What do you like to eat?
- 'What's on?' – Popular Culture: Talk about your favourite TV show

Conventions used in transcribing the corpus are available at www.umwelt-campus.de/fileadmin/Umwelt-Campus/SK-Weiterbildung/Dateien/Condensed_overview_CASE_transcription_conventions_0318.pdf. If you would be interested in working with ViMELF, you can access the data by contacting the corpus compilers via the e-mail address provided at www.umwelt-campus.de/campus/organisation/fachberei chuwur/sprache-kommunikation/caseproject/access-vimelf/.

–Takeaway Note–

English as a Lingua Franca (ELF) is a highly intriguing and active research area with interesting connections to World Englishes. ELF corpora can be used to study how speakers from sometimes very different backgrounds interact and which linguistic strategies they employ to have a successful conversation. VOICE and ACE are two essential ELF corpora and ViMELF represents an innovative data resource with multimodal elements.

In the next section, we show you an example study using ViMELF as a corpus and, in the process, highlight certain aspects that are important when analysing ELF data.

7.6 Multilingual conversations: code-switching in ELF

Imagine the following situation: You, as a bi- or multilingual person with a mother tongue other than English, stand in line at an airport in a foreign country, waiting to board a plane. Perhaps you are a little stressed and, as it is your turn to show your passport, you realise that it is still in your backpack. In the heat of the moment, you forget the English word for *passport*, but you want to let the staff know that you need to look for it – what do you do? Different strategies apply. There is a good chance that the staff will tell you what to do anyway, which would not require much of a response. However, you may also start a sentence explaining your situation in English and simply replace the English expression with a word you know in another language – after all, airport staff are usually able to speak two or more languages.

As speakers of several languages, we have multiple languages at our disposal. It is not always necessary or useful to access all linguistic strategies we know but, in ELF situations in particular, so-called '**code-switching**' plays a very important role: When speakers code-switch, they use words or expressions from a different language other than the one that dominates the conversation. This phenomenon is in focus in Brunner & Diemer's (2018) study on code-switching in ELF conversations held via Skype. The following paragraphs give you a brief overview of the study and highlight aspects of ELF conversations. In addition, you get an idea of how ELF texts can be analysed meaningfully.

Setting and rationale of the study

Brunner & Diemer (2018) are interested in Skype conversations between speakers from different linguistic backgrounds. As a component of their study, they want to know in which instances speakers resort to another language: Is it just because they do not know a specific word in English or is there more behind it? Part of their analysis is revisiting the motivations and functions of code-switching, since the term has been under scrutiny for a long time. We cannot go into all the details here, but you can refer to the study itself if you are interested in some of the problems that come with the notion of code-switching.

Marking and analysing instances of CS

In their corpus analysis, Brunner & Diemer indicated which language a speaker switched into as well as how long the switch took (cf. 2018: 65–66). Marking instances of code-switching in the corpus allowed the authors to retrieve all these instances easily for further analysis, since the tags can be typed into concordance software. In addition to counting the tokens, they were also analysed with regard to their function. This is the most interesting aspect, since we are interested in why speakers code-switch into another language in the conversation. On a surface level, this is not an unproblematic strategy: After all, the interlocutor may not understand an expression in a different language.

Findings in Brunner & Diemer's (2018) study

Overall, Brunner & Diemer found 107 instances of code-switching in their data. As would be expected, speakers in the corpus tend to switch mostly to their first language. However, this is not always the case: In some instances, speakers switch to the language of another participant. Code-switching is used in many of the conversations in the corpus, but not in all of them. In terms of the elements that are code-switched into, speakers in Brunner & Diemer's study mostly switched to single words (53.27%) and short phrases (30.84%). The least frequent kind is phrases longer than five words (15.89%).

An interesting and, as Brunner & Diemer point out, unexpected finding is that the first instance of code-switching seems to "signal […] 'permission' to use CS as

WEs, Learner Englishes, and ELF **189**

a legitimate conversation strategy" (2018: 68): After the first participant used code-switching, more such cases frequently follow in the conversation.

Interpreting the findings

Brunner & Diemer suggest that code-switching is primarily used for interpersonal and discursive reasons as well as for addressee specification (2018: 72). Interpersonal motivations and functions include the emphasis of group membership and identity and the creation of rapport, while discursive motivations and functions refer to closing gaps, metalinguistic commentary, and including so-called *mots justes*. A *mot juste* is used to "convey concepts that are untranslatable and possibly unknown to the interlocutor" (Brunner & Diemer 2018: 79). As an example, let us focus on the function of underlining group membership and identity, which is the primary function assigned to the case found in (7.10).

(7.10) ST14: (1.4) uhm we've got some celebrations?
>do you- < do you know what,
... *Noches de San Juan* ((Spanish (1.2))) is?
SB73: (1.2) uh *Noche de San Juan* ((Spanish (2.0))),
ST14: ... mhm? {nods}
SB73: ... I don't think so no?
ST14: (1.2) well the shortest night of the year.

⇒ Note that the speaker with the label ST14 is from Spain; both speakers use the expression *Noches de San Juan* (or *Noche de San Juan*). Why did Brunner & Diemer classify this as a case of underlining group membership and identity and why could it also qualify as a *mot juste* according to the definition given above?

◊ *Noches de San Juan* refers to festivities in Spain and can technically be translated into English, although there is no common translation for it. The speaker wants to share knowledge about these festivities with their interlocutor and does so by mentioning and explaining what it is, marking themselves as an expert of their specific culture in the process. The expression can also be classified as a *mot juste* since there is no equivalent in English. In these cases, the example was assigned to both motivations/functions in Brunner & Diemer's study.

–Takeaway Note–

Code-switching is an important strategy employed in ELF conversations and World Englishes alike. Having the opportunity to access a broad linguistic repertoire for successful communication or to underline one's identity is an essential advantage of being bi- or multilingual. For linguistic research, including words and expressions in languages other than English (or

> whichever language is currently studied) in the analysis is important and can give insight into what interlocutors consider important in their interactions.

7.7 Summary

This chapter introduced you to Learner Englishes and English as a Lingua Franca by

- linking them to World Englishes and English as a Native Language;
- presenting important learner and ELF corpora; and
- discussing case studies in the two fields.

Both Learner Englishes and ELF are very active research areas, which is why many articles and books on these kinds of Englishes are published at the moment. Corpus-linguistic methods are a very important component in studying both kinds of Englishes, since they allow us to systematically analyse recurrent patterns and common linguistic features. Most importantly, perhaps, this chapter served to help tear down some walls. Both Learner Englishes and ELF have carried a certain stigma for a long time and are still not seen as 'worthy' of serious linguistic study by some. We believe, as do many others, that they are, and that we can learn a lot about English and its many forms and functions by conducting comparative studies of World Englishes, Learner Englishes, and ELF.

7.8 Exercises

Exercise 7.1

An idea for a follow-up study to Gilquin (2015) that also brings in the ELF component would be to compare the frequency and usage patterns of phrasal verbs with *up* in VOICE to Gilquin's data. In order to conduct the study, you need VOICE and AntConc or other concordance software.

(a) As mentioned above, VOICE is available both with and without POS-tagging. You may choose either of the two versions. Find all PVs with *up* in VOICE by conducting a search using a (simple) regular expression. You may refer to www.linguisticsweb.org/doku.php?id=linguisticsweb: tutorials:linguistics_tutorials:basics:regex:regex-antconc if this step is too difficult. Pay attention to false positives!

(b) Calculate the normalised frequency per 100,000 words for the feature. How do PVs with *up* in VOICE compare to Gilquin's (2015) data?

WEs, Learner Englishes, and ELF 191

(c) Which verbs occur most and which ones the least frequently with *up* in VOICE? Can you confirm Gilquin's (2015) findings with regard to redundancy and innovation for VOICE?

Exercise 7.2

Error annotation can be a very useful addition to a learner corpus, since it can be used, for instance, to identify recurring problems in language learning for individual speakers or speaker communities. The following Table 7.5 contains errors that might occur in a learner corpus containing interlanguage produced by learners of English. For each error, formulate a 'target hypothesis', that is, the form that would be expected in Standard English. In addition, assign the linguistic levels/features given below to each error. In some examples, more than one error can be identified.

Linguistic level/feature: auxiliary; orthography; subject-verb agreement; tense/aspect; lexis

7.9 Recommended reading

Learner Englishes

Perhaps the most comprehensive list of titles about learner corpora or studies including learner corpora can be found at the CECL (https://uclouvain.be/en/research-institutes/ilc/cecl/learner-corpus-bibliography.html), which is an excellent resource for any study on Learner Englishes. The contributions to Mukherjee and Hundt (2011) as well as Nesselhauf (2009), Laporte (2012), and Gilquin (2015) give insight into the relation between World Englishes, Learner Englishes, and English as a Native Language.

Granger et al. (2015) is a collection of essential articles on learner corpora and learner corpus research. Although the volume is less suitable for absolute

Table 7.5 Error annotation task

Error	Target Hypothesis	Linguistic Level/Feature
The birds are singing every day.		
What know we about the universe?		
Englisch is a difficult language to learn for many people.		
He smashed the door very hardly.		
The student come and go as she pleases.		

beginners, it can and should be consulted if you are interested in delving deeper into the world of Learner Englishes and how to study them.

ELF

Seidlhofer (2011) is an ideal resource to get an understanding of what ELF is and how it can be approached. As soon as the basics are covered, you can read contributions to the *Journal of English as a Lingua Franca*, which provides insight into current research in the field. With a total of 47 contributions, Jenkins et al. (2018) is a tome featuring an abundance of interesting chapters on ELF. Since it features a section on 'Conceptualising and positioning ELF', it can be used as an introductory resource, but most of the contributions to the book consider more specific aspects related to ELF. Among these, the spread of ELF in various areas, linguistic features of ELF, the use of ELF in different domains, and ELF in academia dominate the book.

List of Corpora

ACE (2014). "The Asian corpus of English." Director: Andy Kirkpatrick; Researchers: Wang Lixun, John Patkin, & Sophiann Subhan. URL: http://corpus.ied.edu.hk/ace/. (Last access: 21 June 2019).

Brunner, Marie-Louise, Caroline Collet, Stefan Diemer, & Selina Schmidt (2018). *ViMELF -Corpus of Video-Mediated English as a Lingua Franca Conversations*. Birkenfeld: Trier University of Applied Sciences. Version 1.0. The CASE project. URL: http://umweltcampus.de/case. (Last access: 21 June 2019).

Gilquin, Gaëtanelle, Sylvie de Cock, & Sylviane Granger (eds.) (2010). *Louvain International Database of Spoken English Interlanguage (LINDSEI)*. Handbook and CD-ROM. Louvain-la-Neuve: Presses universitaires de Louvain.

Granger, Sylviane, Estelle Dagneaux, Fanny Meunier, & Magali Paquot (eds.) (2009). *International Corpus of Learner English*. Version 2 (Handbook + CD-ROM). Louvain-la-Neuve: Presses universitaires de Louvain.

Ishikawa, Shin'ichiro (2013). "The ICNALE and sophisticated contrastive interlanguage analysis of Asian learners of English." In Shin'ichiro Ishikawa (ed.), *Learner Corpus Studies in Asia and the World 1*. Kobe, Japan: Kobe University, 91–118.

VOICE (2013). "The Vienna-Oxford international corpus of English." (version 2.0 online). Director: Barbara Seidlhofer; Researchers: Angelika Breiteneder, Theresa Klimpfinger, Stefan Majewski, Ruth Osimk-Teasdale, Marie-Luise Pitzl, & Michael Radeka. URL: http://voice.univie.ac.at. (Last access: 21 June 2019).

References

Brunner, Marie-Louise & Stefan Diemer (2018). "'You are struggling forwards, and you don't know, and then you . you do code-switching ...' – code-switching in ELF skype conversations." *Journal of English as a Lingua Franca* 7(1): 59–88. doi: 10.1515/jelf-2018-0003.

Gardner, Dee & Mark Davies (2007). "Pointing out frequent phrasal verbs: A corpus-based analysis." *TESOL Quarterly* 41: 339–359. doi: 10.1002/j.1545-7249.2007.tb00062.x.

Gilquin, Gaëtanelle (2015). "At the interface of contact linguistics and second language acquisition research: New Englishes and Learner Englishes compared." *English World-Wide* 36(1): 91–124. doi: 10.1075/eww.36.1.05gil.

Granger, Sylviane (2008). "Learner corpora." In Lüdeling, Anke & Merja Kytö (eds.), *Corpus Linguistics: An International Handbook*. Berlin: de Gruyter, 259–275.

Granger, Sylviane, Gaëtanelle Gilquin, & Fanny Meunier (eds.) (2015). *The Cambridge Handbook of Learner Corpus Research*. Cambridge: Cambridge University Press.

Jenkins, Jennifer (2000). *The Phonology of English as an International Language: New Models, New Norms, New Goals*. Oxford: Oxford University Press.

Jenkins, Jennifer, Will Baker, & Martin Dewey (eds.) (2018). *The Routledge Handbook of English as a Lingua Franca*. London: Routledge.

Kirkpatrick, Andy (2008). "English as the official working language of the Association of Southeast Asian Nations (ASEAN): Features and strategies." *English Today* 24(2): 27-34. doi: 10.1017/S0266078408000175.

Laporte, Samantha (2012). "Mind the gap! Bridge between World Englishes and Learner Englishes in the making." *English Text Construction* 5(2): 264–291. doi: 10.1075/etc.5.2.05lap.

Mauranen, Anna (2018). "Second-order language contact: English as an academic Lingua Franca." In Filppula, Markku, Juhani Klemola, & Devyani Sharma (eds.), *The Oxford Handbook of World Englishes*. Oxford: Oxford University Press, 735–753. doi: 10.1093/oxfordhb/9780199777716.013.010.

Mukherjee, Joybrato & Marianne Hundt (eds.) (2011). *Exploring Second-Language Varieties of English and Learner Englishes: Bridging a Paradigm Gap*. Amsterdam: John Benjamins.

Nesselhauf, Nadja (2009). "Co-selection phenomena across New Englishes: Parallels (and differences) to foreign learner varieties." *English World-Wide* 30(1): 1–26. doi: 10.1075/eww.30.1.02nes.

Percillier, Michael (2016). *World Englishes and Second Language Acquisition: Insights from Southeast Asian Englishes*. Amsterdam: John Benjamins.

Rohdenburg, Günter (1996). "Cognitive complexity and increased grammatical explicitness in English." *Cognitive Linguistics* 7(2): 149–182. doi: 10.1515/cogl.1996.7.2.149.

Schneider, Edgar W. (2012). "Exploring the interface between World Englishes and second language acquisition – and implications for English as a Lingua Franca." *Journal of English as a Lingua Franca* 1(1): 57–91. doi: 10.1515/jelf-2012-0004.

Seidlhofer, Barbara (2011). *Understanding English as a Lingua Franca*. Oxford: Oxford University Press.

Sridhar, Kamal K. & Shikaripur N. Sridhar (1986). "Bridging the paradigm gap: Second language acquisition theory and indigenized varieties of English." *World Englishes* 5(1): 3–14. doi: 10.1111/j.1467-971X.1986.tb00636.x.

TEFL Equity Advocates and Academy. (2016). "English as a Lingua Franca – Interview with Jennifer Jenkins." URL: http://teflequityadvocates.com/2016/02/03/english-as-a-lingua-franca-interview-with-jennifer-jenkins/. (Last access: 16 January 2019).

Chapter 8

The state of the art and the way ahead

The final chapter brings together and evaluates the different perspectives put forward in this book. However, rather than solely providing a summary of the many things we discussed and showed you throughout the book, this chapter both indicates the state of the art and the way ahead. The outcome of research over the last decades is definitely impressive, with ever more corpora generating ever more research opportunities, but it has to be kept in mind that corpus-linguistic methods have their limits when it comes to tracking down and accounting for variation in World Englishes. Taking all of these aspects into account, this chapter comments on new Englishes, new corpora, new models, new tools, and opportunities for adding more statistics to your research. Then, some important limitations of corpus-linguistic methods are pointed out. The chapter closes with a brief summary of key aspects of the book and a broader outlook on the importance of corpus linguistics for World Englishes.

8.1 New Englishes

Where do you hear or read English on a regular basis? What are typical situations in which you would have a conversation or write a text in English? Expected answers for many people around the globe would probably be: on the internet and when they are abroad. Mair succinctly points out two possible directions for further corpus-based research on World Englishes, as "innovation should be encouraged in two directions. The first concerns mining the World-Wide Web for relevant data, whereas the second is a plea to take seriously the multilingual settings in which most World Englishes are used" (2017: 118). Indeed, these are two contexts that currently receive a lot of scholarly attention.

Globalisation and grassroots Englishes

Globalisation is an important force in the spread and development of English, since it requires a shared language not only in business and various other contexts, but also in tourism. When most people travel to another country where their mother tongue is not spoken, chances are that they would prefer to speak in

English. In tourist contexts, such as hotels or restaurants, people on their travels also tend to expect that the people offering their services are able to communicate with them in English. Certain circumstances prevent many locals to learn English in a formal context, however. This led Schneider (2016) to focus on what he calls 'grassroots Englishes' in tourism: the need to acquire some proficiency in English is evident to many service providers, but the context in which they acquire it varies drastically and is often not necessarily formalised. Studying such grassroots Englishes is an important avenue for further research, since they provide us with important information about the situations in which English is acquired and used.

World Englishes and the web

Another important field for research on World Englishes is Computer-Mediated Communication (CMC) and the internet. As we pointed out in Chapter 4, the incredible amount of data on the internet provides linguists with immense research possibilities. Despite some criticism directed at large-scale corpora such as GloWbE, they illustrate that the World Wide Web is an important resource for corpus linguistics and World Englishes. Exciting work on World Englishes online can also be found in the work by various scholars (e.g. Mair & Heyd 2014; Heyd 2016) on the Nigerian forum *Nairaland* (www.nairaland.com/): Users on the forum use many 'typically spoken' expressions in a digital context, which means that the forum can be used as a proxy for innovations in Nigerian Englishes. Similar avenues can be followed for other varieties as well, since the internet is growing every single day. We should also consider the possibility that entirely new Englishes develop on the internet with their own mixture of features.

Summary

New Englishes keep developing and being used across the globe and across the internet. Furthermore, World Englishes and their status in countries often change: Singapore English, for instance, is now a variety that has native speakers; some families raise their children with Singapore English as their mother tongue or one of their mother tongues. Corpus-linguistic methods allow us to investigate such new contexts and keep track of important changes. Corpora are not and never will be the only means to study new varieties of English, but they are an incredibly important resource that we can use for this purpose.

8.2 New corpora

One of the most obvious opportunities for progress in corpus linguistics for World Englishes is the creation of new corpora. The world is rich with varieties of English and they all deserve to be studied. Of course, the creation of new corpora emerges as a direct consequence of the emergence of new varieties of English. While far from the only way to study World Englishes, corpora remain one of the key resources for that purpose. Creating a new corpus is a lot of hard work (and sometimes a huge financial investment), but a well-structured and well-constructed corpus can be a significant research tool for years to come. Furthermore, the development of World Englishes is not likely to stop any time soon. This means that there is a lot of value in revisiting varieties for which corpora already exist, since updates allow us to compare how they have developed.

ICE age 2

A project in line with this trend is the coming of the next 'ICE Age', which refers to a new generation of ICE corpora. 'ICE-Age 2', as noted by Kirk & Nelson (2018: 701), can have two meanings: It can refer to second-generation corpora of the same variety or to corpora that are now being compiled, where '2' refers to new technologies or levels, as in 'web 2.0'. Many ICE corpora have been compiled in the 1990s and are thus relatively old. Updated versions will allow us to compare changes in varieties and give a fresh view on a variety's linguistic features. The second interpretation of the term means that digital components could be added: Blog writing in a variety, online news, and several other components from the internet could be added. This change would reflect the new reality of how and when Englishes are used. If you are indeed interested in working with ICE, we highly recommend you regularly check the ICE website and read new publications on the corpus – exciting changes lie ahead!

Historical corpora of World Englishes

Another recent development that is closely linked to ICE is the creation of historical corpora of World Englishes. So far, we mostly have access to historical corpora of British and American English, with the *Helsinki Corpus* (British English) and the *Corpus of Historical American English* (COHA) as cases in point. It might come as a surprise to you, but there is plenty of material in postcolonial countries to build corpora of, at least, written material; in some cases, spoken material is also available. These spoken texts may be audio recordings (which means that we cannot go very far into the past) or written recordings of spoken language, such as trial proceedings. An example of a historical corpus of an African variety of English is *The Historical Corpus of English in Ghana* (HiCE Ghana), compiled by Thorsten Brato (see Brato 2019).

Summary

So far, we only commented on two of many exciting new directions for the creation of new corpora. However, we should also mention the compilation of

The state of the art and the way ahead   197

news corpora, which can now be done very well by using the internet: Coding languages such as Python and other tools make it possible to download newspaper content from websites and build corpora. Newspaper language has its own register-specific features and can be a fantastic resource to study which innovations have made it to rather formal written language in a variety. Finally, there are new studies using corpora of Expanding Circle Englishes. We recommend you look into two impressive and rather accessible studies of English in the Netherlands (Edwards 2016) and English in South Korea (Rüdiger 2019). Both of these studies use newly created corpora to ask, among other things, to what extent the Englishes under consideration are truly 'foreign' languages in their country and which linguistic features we can find in them. Overall, similar to new Englishes, many fascinating developments occur in the field of new corpora and suggest a bright future for World Englishes research.

8.3 New models

Chapter 2 introduced you to important models of World Englishes. One of the most influential models, Schneider's Dynamic Model, was only intended to apply to Postcolonial Englishes – varieties of the Inner and Outer Circle. Yet the dynamics of the spread of English have taken a new turn with increasing globalisation over the last decades. Schneider originally acknowledged what is happening in the Expanding Circle as 'postcolonial attraction' and associated it with a fifth settlement type (besides those described in Chapter 2), where 'settlement' has to be taken metaphorically since acquiring English is no longer tied to a specific territory (Schneider 2012: 574). In a later paper, he changed the label to "Transnational Attraction – the appropriation of (components of) English(es) for whatever communicative purposes at hand, unbounded by distinctions of norms, nations or varieties" (Schneider 2014: 28). Meanwhile, the evidence from English usage in countries as diverse as Namibia and the Netherlands has prompted a reconsideration of Schneider's model.

EIF model

How does a variety of English develop when it has the status of a second language in a country as opposed to the status of a foreign language? Do varieties of English that come from a colonial history enter different developmental paths compared to varieties that do not have such a background? These questions are part of the reassessment of traditional World Englishes modelling and have been addressed by Buschfeld and Kautzsch (2017, 2020). They propose the 'Extra- and Intraterritorial Forces' model and argue that we can, in fact, identify similar developments in varieties with and without a (post-)colonial background. Various forces, such as globalisation and language policies, affect all varieties of English, which is why they suggest a joint approach in their analysis. The traditional distinctions between ESL and EFL and postcolonial vs.

'non-postcolonial' varieties are broken up by their approach. We cannot introduce you to all the details of their model here and instead refer you to their article. This model currently receives a lot of attention, with an edited collection featuring analyses on its applicability in the works (see Buschfeld & Kautzsch 2020). Corpus-linguistic methods are amongst the methods chosen to test how well it can be applied to varieties of English.

Summary

Apart from the EIF model, some proposals have been made to move beyond a country-based approach to how we assess a variety. This claim stems from the fact that aspects such as international mobility, globalisation, and the presence of, at times, many varieties in one country challenge the assumption 'one country equals one variety'. While the idea itself is not new, it certainly makes sense to rethink carefully how we can and should categorise varieties of English. Once again, corpora can play an important part in theorising: they help us understand which linguistic features are used in which World Englishes and how varieties across the globe develop. As we pointed out before, you should always have a critical eye: What kind of English are you working with? Who are the speakers in a corpus; where do they come from? Many aspects need to be considered and new models allow us to put on a new pair of glasses when we analyse World Englishes.

8.4 New tools

Technological advancements have exciting developments in store for both corpus compilers and corpus users. New software is being developed to, for instance, align transcripts of conversations with their audio files. For corpus users, emphasis is placed on making working with corpora easier. Powerful online tools such as *Sketch Engine* or *Lancsbox* allow users to carry out studies even without sophistication in working with a computer. An exciting development particularly for the World Englishes community is the creation of ICE-online, a digital interface for the analysis of the ICE corpora.

Many very useful tools for corpus linguists have been and are being developed by Laurence Anthony, who also coded the immensely useful tool *AntConc* (see Chapter 3). Software he created can be downloaded from www.lauren ceanthony.net/ – be sure to check his website from time to time, since new tools may further assist you in your research.

8.5 More statistics

This book only covered bits and pieces of descriptive statistics in Chapter 3.8. We deliberately tiptoed over the whole field of inferential statistics because we considered it too much for an introductory textbook like this. However, a lot

The state of the art and the way ahead   199

of current research uses sophisticated statistical modelling to handle their data. Chapter 3 closed with the hint that most statistically-inclined researchers work with *R*, and provided some references for textbooks which combine an introduction to statistics with an introduction to *R*. If you cannot see yourself learning a programming language such as *R*, but would still like to become more of a stats geek, we have two more recommendations for you. Vaclav Brezina's *Statistics in Corpus Linguistics: A Practical Guide* (2018) takes you along at a gentle pace and takes great care in explaining each step in a statistical analysis. The book also comes with a companion website which provides access to online tools for recreating all analyses presented in the book. Sebastian Rasinger's book from 2013, *Quantitative Research in Linguistics: An Introduction*, draws on a resource that a lot of people have pre-installed on their computers, namely *Microsoft Excel*. You will be surprised how much statistics you can do with a spreadsheet!

Quantitative approaches, using at times quite sophisticated statistical methods, are very popular at the moment – not only in World Englishes research but in linguistics in general. Even basic knowledge in this field will be useful, so it makes sense to invest some time in understanding why and how statistics can be applied to linguistic data. Many recent publications in journals compare linguistic features across several varieties of English and make good use of statistical methods.

8.6 Limitations

Now that you have come this far in this book, you are familiar with the achievements of corpus linguistics applied to World Englishes. You have come to know the remarkable degree of sophistication that went into theory- and tool-building over the last decades. However, being able to confidently work with methods, models, and corpora also implies being aware of their specific limitations, and we will discuss some of these in turn.

The importance of knowing your data

Some limitations arise from the available corpora themselves, from their size, their overall design or their date of compilation. Chapter 4 introduced you to corpora big and small, and we already discussed the advantages and disadvantages connected to small but balanced versus large (monitor) corpora. Always make sure to know your corpora! You have to be familiar with the design and the content of the corpora you work with if you want to achieve reliable results. An investigation into rare syntactic features requires a much larger corpus than, say, a study of the present perfect. If you are looking for discourse markers, a corpus of written language will not get you very far, and if you want to do a comparative study across varieties, make sure your corpora are compiled along similar lines, such as the ICE corpora.

200 The state of the art and the way ahead

Comparability and explanatory power of corpora

The ICE family of corpora also exemplifies two important points that might potentially limit the scope of our research. The ever-growing family of ICE corpora, just like a real family, spans different generations, with all ups and downs that this might entail. Older ICE corpora may not be annotated and transcribed as carefully as new ones are, which is certainly also due to the fact that computer technology has developed significantly since the 90s. Furthermore, if you want to compare two corpora, you should always look at the dates of their compilation. If one corpus is 20 years older than another, you will need to acknowledge and be careful of that in the interpretation of the data. The reason for this is the ever-changing nature of language – it is unlikely that a variety has not changed over the course of two decades.

Another very important aspect you need to consider is that, "unless the corpus represents the whole population, the absence of evidence is not the evidence of absence" (Brezina 2018: 19). What this means for you and linguists in general is that we cannot say for certain that speakers or writers of a variety do not use a certain feature solely based on a corpus. This is part of why the comparison of a corpus to a snapshot works so well: we get to see a part of the picture but never the full picture. Similar to the problem described above, the main aspect to take away here is that a careful approach to your data and how you interpret your findings is incredibly important.

New corpora, new issues: copyright and privacy

Even though corpus creation has become so much easier, there are still copyright issues. If you create your own corpus of, say, recently published science fiction stories and write a term paper about it, that is fine. But to make it publicly available you would need the permission to do so from the copyright holders. Such issues of copyright compel many research teams to keep their material on site. Therefore, if you want to access their corpus, you have to be physically present at their university or research institute.

Data mined from websites, in particular social media websites, also bring a problem. The legal situation tends to be unclear as service providers often do not clarify sufficiently if it is acceptable from a legal perspective to use data from their platform for research. Unfortunately, we cannot solve this problem here; it is usually recommendable to ensure as well as you can if using data from a certain source is fine with a publisher.

In general, we suggest you stay well-informed about recent developments on copyright and data protection. The general trend in the last decade has been to strengthen the rights of individuals, which can certainly be lauded. This means for us as linguists that we need to be sure that participants are fine with being included in a corpus of any sort, which can be achieved by having people sign a consent form.

8.7 Summary

This book serves as an introduction to corpus linguistics for World Englishes. We showed you what World Englishes and corpus-linguistic methods are and how you can apply the latter to study the former. In addition, we gave you a glimpse into the history and the theory of studying World Englishes. Furthermore, we provided you with several example studies and opportunities to test your acquired skills and knowledge.

As a major takeaway, we would like to stress once more that variation in Englishes used around the globe is something precious: it is an expression and an artefact of individuality, of different cultures, and of history. Corpora are windows into these expressions, which turns them into invaluable tools; they become promoters of diversity that should be cherished.

References

Brato, Thorsten (2019). "The Historical Corpus of English in Ghana (HiCE Ghana): Motivation, compilation, opportunities." In Esimaje, Alexandra U., Ulrike Gut, & Bassey E. Antia (eds.), *Corpus Linguistics and African Englishes*. Amsterdam: John Benjamins, 119–141. doi: 10.1075/scl.88.06bra.

Brezina, Vaclav (2018). *Statistics in Corpus Linguistics: A Practical Guide*. Cambridge: Cambridge University Press.

Buschfeld, Sarah & Alexander Kautzsch (2017). "Towards an integrated approach to postcolonial and non-postcolonial Englishes." *World Englishes* 36(1): 104–126. doi: 10.1111/weng.12203.

Buschfeld, Sarah & Alexander Kautzsch (eds.) (2020). *Modelling World Englishes: A Joint Approach towards Postcolonial and Non-Postcolonial Varieties*. Edinburgh: Edinburgh University Press.

Edwards, Alison (2016). *English in the Netherlands: Functions, Forms and Attitudes*. Amsterdam: John Benjamins.

Heyd, Theresa (2016). "Global varieties of English gone digital: Orthographic and semantic variation in digital Nigerian Pidgin." In Squires, Lauren (ed.), *English in Computer-Mediated Communication: Variation, Representation, and Meaning*. Berlin: de Gruyter, 101–122. doi: 10.1515/9783110490817-006.

Kirk, John & Gerald Nelson (2018). "The International Corpus of English project: A progress report." *World Englishes* 37(4): 697–716. doi: 10.1111/weng.12350.

Mair, Christian (2017). "World Englishes and corpora." In Filppula, Markku, Juhani Klemola, & Devyani Sharma (eds.), *The Oxford Handbook of World Englishes*. Oxford: Oxford University Press, 103–122. doi: 10.1093/oxfordhb/9780199777716.013.008.

Mair, Christian & Theresa Heyd (2014). "From vernacular to digital ethnolinguistic repertoire: The case of Nigerian Pidgin." In Lacoste, Véronique, Jakob Leimgruber, & Thiemo Breyer (eds.), *Indexing Authenticity: Sociolinguistic Perspectives*. Berlin: de Gruyter, 244–268. doi: 10.1515/9783110347012.244.

Rasinger, Sebastian M. (2013). *Quantitative Research in Linguistics: An Introduction*. London: Bloomsbury.

Rüdiger, Sofia (2019). *Morpho-Syntactic Patterns in Spoken Korean English*. Amsterdam: John Benjamins.

Schneider, Edgar W. (2012). "Contact-induced change in English worldwide." In Nevalainen, Terttu & Elizabeth Traugott (eds.), *The Oxford Handbook of the History of English*. Oxford: Oxford University Press, 572–581. doi: 10.1093/oxfordhb/9780199922765.013.0049.

Schneider, Edgar W. (2014). "New reflections on the evolutionary dynamics of World Englishes." *World Englishes* 33(1): 9–32. doi: 10.1111/weng.12069.

Schneider, Edgar W. (2016). "Grassroots Englishes in tourism interactions." *English Today* 32(3): 2–10. doi: 10.1017/S0266078416000183.

Appendix A: Answer key

Answers for Chapter 2

Exercise 2.1

Tick the box in Table A.1 if the term in the header of the column applies to the varieties of English in the left column. If you are unsure about the location and/or status of a variety, we recommend the *electronic World Atlas of Varieties of English* (eWAVE), accessible at http://ewave-atlas.org/, as a quick reference guide.

Answer: see table A.1

Answers for Chapter 3

Exercise 3.1

(a) Count the types and the tokens in the following sentences:

(3.6)
Many years have passed since the unification of Germany.

Answer: There are 9 types and 9 tokens. Each type only occurs once in the sentence.

(3.7)
A child may play with a bow, but it shouldn't play with a bow.

Answer: This sentence is a bit different from (3.6): There are 9 types but 14 tokens. There are three tokens of the type *a*, two tokens of the type *play*, two tokens of the type *with*, and two tokens of the type *bow*. However, see the next exercise for a comment on *bow*. Furthermore, contractions such as *shouldn't* are often transcribed with a space between the verb and *not* in a corpus in order to have both words count.

204   Appendix A

Table A.1 Classifying varieties of English (solutions)

Variety	New English	World English	Postcolonial English
Chinese English		×	
Jamaican Creole		×	×
Newfoundland English		×	×
Nigerian English	×	×	×
Sri Lankan English	×	×	×

(b) Which semantic phenomenon proves problematic in example (3.7)? What can we do to deal with such examples in a corpus analysis?

Answer: The words *bow* and *bow* in (3.7) are semantically ambiguous, which means that their exterior form is insufficient to decide which meaning they have – they both look and, most likely, also sound the same. The likeliest interpretation is that the first *bow* refers to an item used for decoration, while the second *bow* refers to a hunting tool or a musical item.

(c) Consider the famous sentence *Buffalo buffalo Buffalo buffalo buffalo buffalo Buffalo buffalo.* Can you disentangle its meaning? Read up on the sentence in order to understand its structure. Why is this sentence a challenge in a corpus analysis?

Answer: This sentence is an extreme example of syntactic and semantic ambiguity and has become famous for that reason. Figure A.1 shows a parsed version of the sentence, with the following abbreviations being used: S = Sentence; NP = Noun Phrase; PN = Proper Noun; N = (Common) Noun; V = Verb; RC = Relative Clause; VP = Verb Phrase.

The verb 'to buffalo' means 'to mislead', 'to bully', or 'to deceive' someone and is mostly used in American English. 'Buffalo' as a noun refers to the location in the state of New York or the animal. Thus, an interpretation of the sentence could be: 'Buffalo from Buffalo, who are being bullied by buffalo from Buffalo, bully buffalo from Buffalo'. As you might have guessed, such sentences are a nightmare in corpus parsing!

Exercise 3.3

Preparation

Consider the made-up data in Table A.2. The table shows the absolute frequency of adverbs formed with -*ly*, such as *happily*, and adverbs which would typically be formed with -*ly* but for which the speaker did not attach this

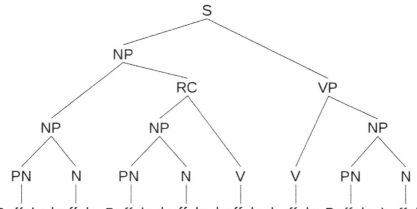

Figure A.1 Parsing of 'Buffalo buffalo Buffalo buffalo buffalo buffalo Buffalo buffalo' (from https://commons.wikimedia.org/wiki/File:Buffalo_sentence_1_parse_tree.svg; public domain)

Table A.2 Data for adverbs formed with and without -ly

	Adverbs formed with -ly	Adverbs with omitted -ly
Corpus 1 (C1)	27	195
Corpus 2 (C2)	68	112

ending. The data have been gathered for two corpora. Corpus 1 contains 9,568 words and Corpus 2 contains 8,349 words.

(a) Calculate the normalised frequencies per 10,000 words of adverbs formed with and without -*ly* in the two corpora.

Answer: The normalised frequencies per 10,000 words are 28.22 (C1) vs. 81.45 (C2) tokens for adverbs formed with -*ly* and 203.80 (C1) vs. 134.15 (C2) tokens for adverbs with omitted -*ly*. This means that there is a stronger tendency to retain the -*ly* ending in the second corpus.

(b) Calculate the statistical significance for the difference between the two corpora using the chi-squared test.

206   Appendix A

Answer: Similar to the example provided in Chapter 3, the result should be significant: The difference between the two datasets is most likely not due to chance; instead, the frequencies reflect variation between the corpora.

Answers for Chapter 4

Exercise 4.2

Find at least two nouns that would be considered non-count nouns in standard varieties of English (such as *furniture* in the example above).

Answer: Many examples are possible here; some options would be: *advice*, *information*, *knowledge*, *luggage*, and *software*.

a) Search for occurrences of the non-count nouns with a plural marker in GloWbE. Do the results suggested by *furnitures* (as being most frequent in East and Southeast Asian Englishes) hold up?

Answer: For the items listed above, the normalised frequencies suggest that the trend holds up. Some of the examples occur almost exclusively in Southeast Asian varieties. However, East and South Asia also feature noteworthy frequencies. The two countries with the highest normalised frequencies for each item are given below.

- *Advices* (Malaysia, Hong Kong)
- *Informations* (Bangladesh, Philippines)
- *Knowledges* (Sri Lanka, Malaysia)
- *Luggages* (Singapore, Malaysia)
- *Softwares* (Bangladesh, India)

Please note that using absolute frequencies here is sufficient to get a first impression, but for a solid analysis another more objective measure would have to be calculated. In GloWbE, this can be achieved by selecting 'per mil' or 'per mil+', with the latter providing both the absolute frequencies and the normalised frequencies per million words. Another aspect to consider is that the at times doubtful origins of the websites in GloWbE mean that we need to be careful in our assumptions. It is possible that tokens in, for instance, the US section have been written by South Asians, and vice versa. Finally, the topics of the articles certainly play a role as well – if there is a high number of Indian blogs on computer software in the corpus, a word such as *softwares* is more likely to occur there. You can look up literature on non-count nouns in World Englishes and will find articles that use GloWbE and other corpora as their data.

Appendix A   207

Table A.3 Error annotation task with solutions

Error	Target Hypothesis	Linguistic Level/Feature
The birds are singing every day.	The birds **sing** every day.	Tense
What know we about the universe?	What **do we know** about the universe?	Auxiliary
Englisch is a difficult language to learn for many people.	**English** is a difficult language to learn for many people./For many people, **English** is a difficult language to learn.	Orthography
He smashed the door very hardly.	He smashed the door very **hard**.	Lexis
The student come and go as she pleases.	The student **comes** and **goes** as she pleases.	Subject-verb Agreement

Answers for Chapter 7

Exercise 7.2

Error annotation can be a very useful addition to a learner corpus, since it can be used, for instance, to identify recurring problems in language learning for individual speakers or speaker communities. Table A.3 contains errors that might occur in a learner corpus containing interlanguage produced by learners of English. For each error, formulate a 'target hypothesis', that is, the form that would be expected in Standard English. In addition, assign the linguistic levels/features given below to each error. In some examples, more than one error can be identified.

Answer: In Table A.3, we provide suggested target hypotheses as well as the corresponding linguistic levels/features. Please note that, sometimes, there is room for interpretation: In the third sentence, for instance, the suggested hypothesis also depends on stylistic aspects, since it may be more idiomatic to begin the sentence with 'For many people'.

Appendix B: Varieties of English and corpora

Table B.1 gives an overview of national varieties of English, their representation in corpora, and their documentation in the *electronic World Atlas of Varieties of English* (eWAVE). The information about the date of corpus compilation and the release date for the *International Corpus of English* (ICE) corpora comes from the individual corpus manuals. All information is correct at the time of going to press; updates about new corpus releases can be found on the ICE project website (www.ice-corpora.uzh.ch/en.html). Other sources of information about new corpus projects include the *LinguistList* (https://linguistlist.org) and the *Corpus Resource Database* (CoRD) (www.helsinki.fi/varieng/CoRD/corpora/).

Table B.1 Availability of corpora for different World Englishes

Variety	ICE: (a) data collection (b) release date (c) speaker metadata	Included in eWAVE	Included in GloWbE	Other corpora
Australia	–	AusE: yes Aus. Vernacular E.: yes	yes	
Bahamas	–	yes	no	
Bangladesh	–	no	yes	SAVE
Cameroon	–	yes	no	
Canada	(a) 1990s (b) 2009(c) yes	Newfoundland E.: yes	yes	
East Africa (Kenya & Tanzania)	(a) 1991-96 (b) 1999(c) yes	Kenya: yes Tanzania: yes	yes	
ELF/Learner Englishes	–	no	no	ACE+VOICE,ICLE, ICNALE,LINDSEI

Variety	ICE: (a) data collection (b) release date (c) speaker metadata	Included in eWAVE	Included in GloWbE	Other corpora
Fiji	–	yes	no	
Ghana	(a) 2000s (written)	yes	yes	
Hong Kong	(a) 1990s (b) 2006 (c) no	yes	yes	
India	(a) 1992-96 (b) 1998 (c) yes	yes	yes	Kolhapur Corpus, SAVE
Ireland	(a) 1990s-2003 (b) 2007 (c) yes	yes	yes	
Jamaica	(a) 1994-2005 (b) 2009 (c) no	yes	yes	
Malaysia	–	yes	yes	
New Zealand	(a) 1990s (b) 1999 (c) no	yes	yes	
Nigeria	(a) from 2007 (b) 2014 (c) yes	yes	yes	
Pakistan	–	yes	yes	SAVE
Philippines	(a) 1991-2002 (b) 2004 (c) yes	yes	yes	
Singapore	(a) 1990s (b) 2002 (c) no	Colloquial SingE: yes	yes	
South Africa	–	White SAfE: yes Black SAfE: yes SAf Indian E.: yes	yes	
Sri Lanka	(a) 2000s (b) 2012 (written), 2019 (spoken)(c) yes	yes	yes	SAVE
Uganda	–	yes	no	
United Kingdom	(a) 1990s (b) 1998 (c) yes		yes	LOB, F-LOB; BNC, BNC 2014
USA	(a) 1990s (b) 2000s (written)(c) no	Colloquial AmE: yes	yes	Brown, Frown; Santa Barbara Corpus of Spoken American English (SBCAE)

Appendix C: Suggestions for course uses

Syllabus

Class:
Instructor:
Class Requirements:

Overview

The syllabus in Table C.1 suggests how *Corpus Linguistics for World Englishes* can be used as a core text for a 15 week semester in the German higher education system. We also offer some recommendations on how to use additional resources including the internet as well as some teaching methods below. The syllabus can be easily modified to fit different needs, for example, the syllabus can easily be shortened in order to fit educational systems in which semesters are shorter. Further eResources available for downloading can be found online on the book's accompanying website: www.routledge.com/9781138593459).

Week 1: introduction and organisation

Description: In the first session, the goals and structure of the class are introduced. Important organisational matters, such as exams and distribution of the texts, are discussed.

Approach: In order to make students immediately curious about the course's content, general questions can be discussed after the most important organisational issues have been introduced. For example: how many people actually speak English, what is the difference between English and Englishes, how are we able to study differences in dialects, and so forth. A personal component can be added by asking the students how they perceive their own and other dialects spoken in their country.

Appendix C   211

Table C.1 Syllabus using *Corpus Linguistics for World Englishes*

#	Date	Topic	Chapter
1	Week 1	**Introduction and Organisation**	/
2	Week 2	**Corpus Linguistics for World Englishes**	Chapter 1
3	Week 3	**Introducing World Englishes**	Chapter 2
4	Week 4	**Introducing Corpus Linguistics**	Chapter 3
5	Week 5	**Applying Corpus Linguistics Part 1**	/
6	Week 6	**World Englishes Corpora**	Chapter 4
7	Week 7	**Studying Variation and Change**	Chapter 5
8	Week 8	**Case Studies 1**	Chapter 6
9	Week 9	**Case Studies 2**	Chapter 6
10	Week 10	**Case Studies 3**	Chapter 6
11	Week 11	**Learner Corpora**	Chapter 7
12	Week 12	**Applying Corpus Linguistics Part 2**	/
13	Week 13	**Problems and Perspectives**	Chapter 8
14	Week 14	**Course Wrap-Up/Revision**	/
15	Week 15	**Course Wrap-Up/Final Exam**	/

Week 2: corpus linguistics for World Englishes

Description: After the introductory first week, the second session serves as the introduction to the more specific field of corpus linguistics for World Englishes. Emphasis can be placed on identifying what students already know about World Englishes and how they would approach the study of varieties of English. Different methodological approaches can be introduced in order to show that corpus linguistics is an important, but not the only way to study World Englishes.

Approach: Students could be asked to read the first chapter of this book and to prepare some answers to discussion questions. These could then be discussed either at the beginning or the end of the session. Another activity would be to create a little quiz (e.g. using www.kahoot.it) in order to assess what students already know about the topic of the class.

Note: The contents of Week 1 and 2 can be merged, depending on whether this is a class for 2nd or 3rd year/Master's students. This would allow for an additional practical session or an additional session of case studies later in the semester. Attention should be paid to avoiding repetition in the following weeks, which will serve as in-depth introductions.

212   Appendix C

Week 3: introducing World Englishes

Description: The third session serves as an in-depth introduction to World Englishes. Emphasis should be placed on important models of World Englishes, key terms and concepts, and the importance of English around the globe. Students should also be made to understand why studying World Englishes is important.

Approach: We suggest showing maps and video clips and playing audio files to demonstrate variation in World Englishes. YouTube is an excellent resource for video material, with many short clips of people speaking World Englishes. In an initial task, students could be asked to guess where speakers are from (e.g. using audio files from the *International Dialects of English* archive at https://www.dialectsarchive.com/).

Week 4: introducing corpus linguistics

Description: The fourth session is an introduction to corpus linguistics. Like the previous week, important terms and concepts continue to be introduced. Importance should be placed on what a corpus is, which criteria are important in the creation and analysis of corpora, and what students and researchers can use them for.

Approach: This session can work either with or without a practical component, although a typical 90 minute session is going to be too short to implement meaningful practical tasks. However, showing a computer screen with some of the basic corpus-linguistic tasks – such as opening *AntConc* and searching for a word in a corpus – can make the topic interesting for students.

Note: This session can be realised with or without students' computers. In our suggested syllabus, this session would be based on a mixture of lecturing and discussion, with week 5 providing hands-on application.

Week 5: applying corpus linguistics part I

Description: The fifth session gives the students their first opportunity to do practical tasks. The idea for this session is to apply some of the knowledge introduced in the previous sessions by working on exercises and actually using software on the computer.

Approach: Exercises from the various chapters are the foundation of this session. Basic tasks such as opening *AntConc* should come first, then opening files and folders with it, after which some of the tool's functionalities can be introduced. Depending on students' prior knowledge, initial small-scale studies, such as searching for an expression in a corpus, can be carried out. A typical problem in such practical sessions is that some students lag behind or give up quickly. This can perhaps be avoided by proceeding slowly or letting students look for different expressions in corpora and

Appendix C   213

having them report on their findings individually. Getting 'a feeling' for working with tools such as *AntConc* and taking away the fear of something rather technical is a great achievement and certainly necessary for the class to be a success.

Week 6: World Englishes corpora

Description: By the sixth session students should know the essentials of corpus linguistics in terms of the basic terms and concepts. In this week some of the most important World Englishes corpora are introduced. Two major outcomes should ideally be reached at the end of this session: students will get a better idea of the history of this very important linguistic discipline and will also learn about major data resources for World Englishes research.

Approach: Instead of simply listing corpora, it might be worthwhile to conceptualise this session as a discussion, which focuses on small vs. big data, the balancing of corpora, and the advantages and disadvantages of various corpora. This is also an ideal session to focus on various methodological issues – such as the Observer's Paradox or mistakes in annotation – by considering actual corpus examples, some of which can be taken directly from chapter 4. Examples from the corpora, some of which can be quite funny, can serve to make the session more entertaining to students.

Week 7: studying variation and change

Description: The seventh session sets up case studies by delving deeper into concepts related to language change and how varieties of English develop into what they are. Understanding World Englishes necessitates understanding the basics of sociolinguistics, language change, and language variation, which is why a more theoretical session before the case studies should be beneficial for the remainder of the class.

Approach: There are various angles to approach this session, but example studies such as Labov's study on (r) in New York City are typically quite interesting to students. Furthermore, explaining these concepts using examples means that various terms and concepts can be introduced practically, even though the focus of the session is theoretical. Many ideas related to this session also lend themselves to discussions – for instance, one may ask the students where they would draw the line between 'error' and 'innovation' or which group of people can be responsible for language change (to explain 'change from below' and 'change from above').

Week 8-10: case studies

Description: In order to provide a closer look at some studies of World Englishes using corpus linguistics, these sessions consider various case studies.

214 Appendix C

A selection of case studies from chapter 6 and chapter 7 could provide the basis for discussion as well as for presentations by the students.

Approach: There is a lot of flexibility in how these sessions can be designed. A good approach might be to begin each session with a couple of 'lightning talks' in which different students present another aspect of a case study: The first student introduces the rationale and motivation; the second student explains the methodology; the third student presents the results; the fourth student discusses the implications, etc. This procedure requires careful preparation but can be quite fruitful. In a next step, shortcomings and possibilities for follow-up studies could be discussed. Finally, if time permits, a brief investigation using another corpus could be added to get an idea if the results hold up in a different dataset.

Week 11: learner corpora

Description: The eleventh session is optional and could either be replaced by another case study or be expanded by adding a designated week for a case study on Learner Englishes. Since the World Englishes paradigm and Second Language Acquisition have moved closer again in recent years, considering comparative studies (such as the one presented in chapter 7) could be quite insightful for students. This might be more suitable for more advanced students, since it adds another layer of complexity.

Approach: The focus of this session could be either on learner corpus design, examples of learner corpora, studies on Learner Englishes, or some combination. Students could be asked to discuss their own exposure to a language they are learners of and relate this to corpus building (in the sense of variables that are important). The most useful outcome of this session would be for students to understand how World Englishes and Learner Englishes are related and how corpus-linguistic methods can be employed to conduct meaningful comparisons of the two variety types. Therefore, a more theoretical session based on a set of questions might be the best choice.

Week 12: applying corpus linguistics part 2

Description: The twelfth session is a placeholder. If the full 15 sessions can be realised, more applications of what has been learned before would be possible. It can also be used to catch up if previous sessions took up more time than expected.

Week 13: problems and perspectives

Description: A class can only ever do so much to get students acquainted with a topic, which is why chapter 8 can be used as a basis to discuss limitations as well as an outlook on the future of corpus linguistics. In particular, it should be

Appendix C   215

worthwhile to ask what we can and what we cannot learn about World Englishes using corpora. The potential of technical advances and the bright future of corpus linguistics should also receive attention.

Approach: Students can be asked to gather in small groups to each discuss one of the following: 'New Englishes', 'New Models', and 'New Tools' in relation to corpus linguistics. They can be asked to come up with problems and limitations related to each aspect but also to stress the potential of each one. In general, this session lends itself more to a discussion-based class.

Week 14: course wrap-up/revision

Description: The fourteenth session either serves as a revision class or, if a final exam is scheduled in the last session, as the course wrap-up. Since holidays and conferences often shorten the actual running time of a semester, this can also be planned as another buffer session.

Week 15: course wrap-up/final exam

Description: The fifteenth session is either a final course wrap-up or the final written exam, depending on the forms of examination selected for this class. This could be any of the following from *Ideas for Class Examinations*:

* Presentations: Students could be asked to give presentations in the sessions devoted to the case studies. In particular, they could introduce a study and show the methodology and results of their own follow-up research. This would mean that they have to present both a theoretical and an empirical component and discuss potential shortcomings of the original as well as their own study. Of course, short presentations on aspects from the various chapters would also be possible.
* Creation of a Wiki/Glossary: Some learning platforms at German and other universities feature Wiki-like functionalities, but they can also be created relatively easily if that is not the case. Every student could be asked to contribute a certain amount of words or terms to the Wiki so that, by the end, a complex glossary of terms has been created. This can be used to prepare for the final exam or as a reference guide for term papers, final theses, and so forth. Students could also be asked to review the contributions written by their peers.
* Create-Your-Own-Corpus Project: Students could be asked to build their own (small) corpus using, for instance, material from the internet. They would then be asked to hand in a description detailing their choice of data, the variety or varieties featured in their corpus, how they compiled the corpus, etc. This project would be more suitable for advanced students, but could also serve as a precursor to a final thesis based on the corpus.

- <u>Theoretical or Empirical Corpus Study</u>: For term papers and written assignments, having students carry out their own corpus-based or corpus-driven study is the most obvious and a very suitable choice for this class. In addition, it could be interesting to ask students to select a corpus and identify its advantages and disadvantages.

Index

Note: Page numbers in **bold** refer to tables; those in *italic* to figures.

accent 21, 54, 111; *see also* dialect; variety
actuation 128
American English 1–2, 14–16, 76, 112–13, 117
analogy 124
analytic *see* language
annotation *see* corpus
AntConc 42; collocations in 64; hiding tags in *52*, 55; interface *45*; n-grams and clusters in 47; opening files in 44; regular expressions in 64–66; word lists in 46
Asian Corpus of English 184, *185*, 186–87
aspect 137; *see also* verbs
Atlas of Pidgin and Creole Language Structures Online 125, 127
Australian English 19–20

balancing *see* representativeness
BeautifulSoup 101
big data and small data 75–76, 98
bigram *see* n-gram
bilingualism 15, 118–19, 127, 187; cline of 22, 31, 110–11, 119, 123
borrowing 13, 26, 32, 126–28, 132, 155–56
British English 9–13, 29, 97, 111
Brown family of corpora 76–81

calque 127
change from below 113, 120, 131
Chinese 172; Cantonese 19; Mandarin 9, 19
Chi-squared test 68
CLAWS Tagset 80
cline of bilingualism *see* bilingualism
clipping 156

Cockney 122
code-switching 127, 187–90
codification 13, 27, 130
colony: British 3, 9, 14, 18, 22, 24, 26, 115; exploitation 28, 121; German 17; plantation 29; settlement 29, 121; trade 28
Common European Framework of Reference for Languages 173, 175
compounding 156
concordance 55, *56*, 57
concordance software *see* AntConc; WordSmith Tools
conjunction 31, 34–35, 59, 130, 148
constituent structure 34
corpus: annotation of 51, 75–76; choosing a 74–76; creating your own 98–103; definition of 42–43; design features of 47–55; *see also* corpus linguistics
corpus linguistics: corpus-based and corpus-driven 43–44; deductive and inductive 43–44; definition of 1–2, 42; and software 44; *see also* corpus
Corpus of Contemporary American English 81, 97
Corpus of Historical American English 81, 196
Corpus of Video-Mediated English as a Lingua Franca Conversations 186–89
CQPweb 53, 61, 79–80
Creole 16, 20, 29

dative alternation 141–42
dialect 21; in Anglo-Saxon England 10–11; community 112; contact 29–30, 121, 126; Inner Circle 150; study of 46, 54; in the UK 25, 28, 111; *see also* accent; variety

218 Index

differentiation 28, **38**; *see also* Dynamic Model
dislocation, left- and right- 149
dispersion 63
Dynamic Model 25–28, **38**, 119, 137, 165, 197

Early Modern English 12–13, 37, 114
East India Company 14, 17–18
endonormative stabilisation 27, **38**; *see also* Dynamic Model
English as a Lingua Franca (ELF) 3, 169, 181–82, 187, 190, 192
error annotation 170, 191
exonormative stabilisation 26, **38**; *see also* Dynamic Model
Expanding Circle 22–23, 43, 197; *see also* Three Circles Model

face, positive and negative 160; *see also* pragmatics
false positives 64
feature pool 121, 126
foundation 26, **38**; *see also* Dynamic Model
Founder Principle 121; *see also* feature pool
frequency 31, 58, 63, **68**; absolute 59–60; interpreting 88–89; normalised 59–61; relative 59–60
fronting 149

gender paradox 113–14
generalisation 124, 131, 143
Ghanaian English **84**, 121, **158**, **209**
Global Web-based Corpus of English 95–97, 195
grammaticalisation 125

hapax legomenon 61, *62*
Hindi 9, 18, 35
historical input variety *see* variety
Hong Kong English **38**, 54–56, 89, **158**, **209**

index 111
Indian English 18, 21–22, **38**, **84**, 115–17, 149, **209**
Inner Circle 22–23, 25; *see also* Three Circles Model
innovation 32, 110, 116–21, *122*, 123–24, 128–31, 178–79
intensifiers 160–65
interference 22, 31, 116

interlanguage 116–17
International Corpus Network of Asian Learners of English 173, **174**, *175*
International Corpus of English: accessing the 85; advantages and disadvantages of the 93–95; annotation of the **51**, **86–87**, 87–91, **92**; components of **84**; structure and design of 82–84; *see also* metadata
International Corpus of Learner English 145, **172**, 173, 177–80
inversion: interrogative 149–54; lack of 115, 136
Irish English 118, 150, 154–55

Jamaican Creole 16

Kachru, Braj B. 21–24, 117
Keyword in Context (KWIC) 55
koinéisation 126

language change 58, 109–15, 121, 128
language contact 7, 10, 29, 116, 121, 126, 131, 144, 153, 165, 169
language: analytic and synthetic 12; of immediacy and of distance 48–49; pluricentric 20, 117; shift 118
learner: in contrast to native speaker 117–18; German 63; students of English as 116; *see also* Second-Language Acquisition
learner corpora 170, **171**
Learner Englishes 117, 123, 168–69, 171, 176, 180, 190
learner-related variables **171**
lemma *see* type
lexicon 30–32, 101, 128, 155–56, 161, 164
lexis *see* lexicon
linguistic variable 52, 76, 92, 113, 132
loanword *see* borrowing
Louvain International Database of Spoken English Interlanguage 173, 175

metadata: in Brown 80; in corpus creation 100, 102–03; corpus size and 74–75, 104; definition of 52–53; in GloWbE 96; in ICE 91–93; in learner corpora 171
Middle English 10, 12–13
modality *see* mood
monitor corpora 97, 199
mood 137; *see also* verbs
morpheme 30, 32, **33**, 34
morphology 32–33, 125

morphosyntax 33, 127
multilingualism: and code-switching
187–90; in India 18; and language
contact 31, 121, 127–28, 130; as the
norm 3, 22, 89; in postcolonial countries
19, 24–25, *118*; and World Englishes
92, 194
mutual intelligibility 21, 181–82

nativisation 26–27, **38**, 138, 140; *see also*
Dynamic Model
neologism 157–58
New Englishes 24, 29, 136, 149, 176–77
New Zealand English 20, 24
n-gram 47, 164
Nigerian English 16, 31, 125, 195
Nigerian Pidgin 125–26
Notepad++ 85, 91
noun: definiteness of 144; determiner 46,
59, 142; Noun Phrase 34, 142–43; pre-
and post-modifier 34, 142; quantifier
34, 142

Observer's Paradox 54, 94, 186
Old English 9–10, 13, 33
Outer Circle 22–24, 30, 43, 117–21, 137,
197; *see also* Three Circles Model

parsing 51, 93, 101
parts-of-speech tagging 53, 59, 80, 182–84
phoneme 30–32
phonotactics 31
phrase structure 34–35
Pidgin 20, 28–29
politeness *see* pragmatics
population 63, 67–68
Postcolonial Englishes 15, 20, 25, 29, **36**,
38, 119, 122–23, 126, 128, 165, 197
pragmatics 35, 160–61
prefixation 32, 127, 156, **158**
prestige, overt and covert 119–20
productivity 138, 140, 156
pronoun copying 149
propagation 128
p-value 68
Python 101, 197

qualitative and quantitative approaches 58,
68–69

R see statistics
reanalysis 125

Received Pronunciation 111
redundancy 124, 178–80
register 2, 49–50, 76, 110, 115, 153, 178
regular expression 64–66, 90, 103, 154–55
regularisation 123
replication, matter and pattern 126–27, 130
representativeness 2, 47–48, 61, 76, 100–01
rhoticity 30, 113, 122

sample 47, 67, 113
Schneider, Edgar W. 25–28, 137–42, 165,
195, 197
Second-Language Acquisition 22, 116,
123, 128, 131, 154, 165, 169, 178–79
sentence type 148
Singapore English 32, **38**, 59, **84**, 94,
126–27, 139–40, 195, 209
Singlish *see* Singapore English
Sketch Engine 78–80, 101, 198
South African English 24–25, 156
speech acts 160
speech community 25, 112–13, 119–21,
128, 131
spider 101
standardisation 13, 16, 20, 111,
119–20, 130
statistics 58, 66–69, 71, 198–99
stress-timed 30–31
style-shifting 112
subject complement 35
subject-auxiliary inversion *see* interrogative
inversion
substitution test 34
suffix 32–33, 80, 105, 125
suffixation 156–57
syllable-timed 30–31
syntax 34, 64, 80, 90, 148
synthetic *see* language

task-related variables **171**
tense 33, 137
text 2; collection of 42, 44; and corpus
creation 98–103; historical 9–10, 12;
spoken and written 44, 49; type 48–51,
61, 76
text type *see* text
Three Circles Model 22–23
token 59, 61
topicalization *see* fronting
transcription 43, 53, 75, 88, 94, 102,
184, 200
type 59

variation 1; according to use and to the user 110; and actuation and propagation 128; in the context of Postcolonial and World Englishes 131, 165; and errors 116; social and regional 110–11

variety 2, 21, **36**, **38**, 47; historical input 9, 15, 20, 25, 27, 29, 115, 119, 122, 131, 165; language shift 118; national 28, 115, 119, 120; standard 111; *see also* accent, dialect

verb: auxiliary 60, 137, 149–50; complementation patterns of 35, 141–42; ditransitive 141; intransitive 35, 56, 116, 141; particle 137–38, 141, 165; Verb Phrase 34, 136–37; stative 124, 137; transitive 35, 56, 141

vernacular 112–13

Vienna-Oxford International Corpus of English 182, *183*, 184, 187

web crawling 101–02

word list 2, 46, 52, 62

word-form *see* token

word-formation process *see* clipping, compounding, prefixation suffixation

WordSmith Tools 42, 44, *45*, 46–47, 55, *57*, 69

World Englishes 3, 21, 23, 29, 43, 71, 89, 109, 115, 128, 131, 137, 165, 169, 171, 176, 187, 190, 195